HUMANISTIC

PSYCHOTHERAPY

Sandy Taylor
Lockney, Tx.

HUMANISTIC
PSYCHOTHERAPY
The Rational-Emotive Approach

ALBERT ELLIS, Ph.D.
Edited by Edward Sagarin, Ph.D.

McGraw-Hill Book Company

New York • St. Louis • San Francisco • Düsseldorf

Mexico • Montreal • Panama • São Paulo • Toronto

Library of Congress Catalog Card Number: 72-94222

Reprinted by arrangement with The Julian Press, Inc.

First McGraw-Hill Paperback Edition, 1974

0-07-019237-5

  2 3 4 5 6 7 8 9 MU MU 7 9 8 7 6 5 4

CONTENTS

HUMANISTIC
PSYCHOTHERAPY

ACKNOWLEDGMENTS

Many of the essays in this volume appeared in a somewhat different version in various journals, and others are revisions of speeches delivered to professional organizations or of lectures at universities. Previous versions of these chapters have appeared or were delivered as shown below:

"Humanism and Psychotherapy" appeared in *The Humanist* 1972. "The Value of a Human Being" was delivered as a paper at the annual meeting of the American Ontoanalytic Association in San Francisco, May 10, 1970, and another version appeared in *Existential Psychiatry,* in press. "Rational-Emotive-Therapy and Other Therapies" is a revision of a chapter that appeared in *International Handbook of Direct Psychotherapies,* edited by R.M. Jurjevich (Coral Gables, Florida: University of Miami Press, 1972).

"The A-B-C's of Rational-Emotive Psychotherapy" is adapted from an article that appeared in *Readings in Introductory Psychology,* edited by William S. Sahakian (1973). "A Comprehensive

Approach to Psychotherapy'' is adapted from a paper originally presented at the annual convention of the American Psychological Association, Washington, D.C., September 1969. ''A Rational-Emotive Approach to Interpretation'' is an adaptation of an article originally published in *The Use of Interpretation in Treatment,* edited by Emmanuel Hammer (New York: Grune and Stratton, 1968), and of a paper delivered at the Symposium on Interpretation as a Tool in Psychotherapy, American Psychological Association, New York, September 5, 1966.

''A Rational-Emotive Approach to Leadership and Hostility'' is adapted from an article to be published in *Leadership Development: Theory and Practice,* Russell N. Cassell, editor (International Textbook Co., 1973). ''Reason and Emotion in the Individual Psychology of Adler'' is an adaptation of an article published in *The Journal of Individual Psychology,* May 1971. ''Self-Awareness and Personal Growth of the Psychotherapist'' is adapted from an article that originally appeared in *The Journal of Humanistic Psychology,* Fall 1966.

''Rationality and Irrationality in the Group Therapy Process'' was presented at the Conference on the Group Process, Adelphi University, Garden City, N.Y., on June 20, 1971. ''Theory Versus Outcome in Psychotherapy'' appeared in *Psychotherapy: Theory, Research, and Practice,* January 1964. ''A Cognitive Approach to Behavior Therapy'' is adapted from an article originally published in *The International Journal of Psychiatry,* December 1969.

''Phobia Treated with Rational-Emotive Psychotherapy'' appeared in *Voices: The Art and Science of Psychotherapy,* Fall 1967. ''Therapy with Psychotics and Borderline Psychotics'' is an adaptation of an article originally published in *Symposium on Therapeutic Methods with Schizophrenics* (Veterans Administration Hospital, Battle Creek, Mich., 1965).

The author and publisher are grateful to previous publishers for permission to adapt and reprint the material.

1

HUMANISM AND PSYCHOTHERAPY

Some years ago, at the first annual meeting of the Association for Humanistic Psychology, a subgroup of the assembled members came up with at least twenty different concepts of what they thought humanism was as applied to psychology, and these concepts differed radically in several significant respects. Moreover, as Charlotte Buhler pointed out in 1971, in her Presidential Address to the First International Invitational Conference on Humanistic Psychology, there are certain allegedly humanistic concepts which do not fit together because they contradict each other, and between which one has to choose. Thus, she indicated, one cannot simultaneously believe in the humanistic end goal of homeostasis and the end goal of a fulfilling self-realization.

To make matters still more complex, the term *humanism* itself has at least two major meanings that are overlapping but not necessarily the same. Psychologically, it seems to mean the study of the person, the individual as a whole (as opposed to the study of his discrete traits and performances), with the aim of helping him live a happier, more self-actualizing, and more creative existence. Ethically, it seems to mean the establishment of a set of rules for man to live by, characterized by an emphasis on human interests rather than on the interests of inanimate nature, of lower animals, or of some assumed natural order or god. The first of these meanings is emphasized by organizations such as the Association for Humanistic Psychology, and the second by groups such as the American Humanist Association.

It would appear that it is possible to present a definition of humanistic psychotherapy that includes both these concepts. Such a definition would keep humanistic psychology squarely within the scientific framework, and discourage it from wandering into anti-intellectual, unscientific, magical, and religious pathways where it is highly wont to wander these days. The essence of humanism, in both psychological and ethical areas, is that man is fully acknowledged to be human—that is, limited and fallible—and that in no way whatever is he superhuman or subhuman. One of his highly human, and utterly fallible, traits is that he has the ability to fantasize about, and to strongly believe in, all kinds of nonhuman entities and powers such as devils, demons, and hells, on the one hand, and angels, gods, and heavens, on the other hand. But as far as we know, no human beings *are* subhumans or superhumans; and it is most unlikely that there will ever be subhuman or superhuman persons.

One of the advantages—and ironies—of adding ethical humanism to psychological humanism is that the latter becomes truly scientific. For when Abraham Maslow originated the so-called "third force" in psychology and added humanism to behaviorism and psychoanalysis, he had no intention of becoming unscientific. But many of his followers have rushed pell-mell into astrology, magic, ESP, fortune-telling, and all kinds of nonscientific and antiscientific realms in their frantic need to "push back the boundaries of the human mind"; and in the process they have practically thrown "humanistic psychology" back into the dark ages and have dogmatically espoused all kinds of unverified and unverifiable claptrap.

Ethical humanism, however, goes hand in hand with the scientific method. For its fundamental postulate is that, until someone definitely proves otherwise, there is nothing beyond human existence; and that for a human being to substantiate, or scientifically validate, any hypothesis, this hypothesis must be backed by some form of data which are, in some final analysis, observable and reproducible. Any hypothesis which cannot be backed by evidence that ordinary humans can observe and replicate is deemed to be theological, supernatural, or magical, and cannot be considered in the field of general or psychological science.

Humanistic psychology, by this rule, becomes the study of the whole individual, by logico-empirical means that are distinctly human, for the purpose of helping him live a happier, more self-actualizing, and more creative existence. It completely accepts people with their human limitations; it particularly focuses upon and employs their experiences and their values; it emphasizes their ability to create and direct their own destinies; and it views them as holistic, goal-directed individuals who are important in their own right, just because they are alive, and who (together with their fellow humans) have the right to continue to exist and to enjoy and fulfill themselves. This concept of humanistic psychology, which includes both an ethical and a scientific orientation, has been espoused, at least implicitly and often explicitly, by many leading psychological theorists and practitioners, such as Charlotte Buhler, Wilhelm Dilthey, Viktor Frankl, Kurt Goldstein, Karen Horney, Abraham Maslow, Rollo May, Carl Rogers, and Ludwig von Bertalanffy.

Humanistic psychotherapy is an important offshoot of humanistic psychology; but it has often gone off in its own idiosyncratic realms and has been particularly preoccupied, in recent years, with experiential, nonverbal, and physical approaches to personality change. It has assumed that modern man has become too intellectualized, technologized, and unemotional, hence alienated and dehumanized; and it has therefore proposed itself as a corrective experiential force to make up for the lapses of classic behaviorism and orthodox psychoanalysis. In this respect, it has made notable contributions to psychotherapy and to the actualizing of human potential.

However, man does not live by emotional (and by highly emotionalized) bread alone. He is a remarkably complex, cognitive-emotive-behaving creature. Of his main traits, his high-level ability to think—and especially his ability to think about his thinking—is probably his most unique and most "human" quality. If, therefore, he is to work effectively against his strong individual and societal tendencies to "dehumanize" himself, he had better learn to employ vigorously some of the highest-level thinking and metathinking of which he is innately capable but which he easily neglects and avoids.

The cognitive therapies are in the vanguard of those methods effectively used, both preventively and also psychotherapeutically, to help man's "humanization." From its inception, I have been associated with one of the best-known cognitive schools—namely, rational-emotive therapy, or RET—a revolutionary humanistic approach to psychotherapy.

Unlike the orthodox psychoanalytic and the classical behavioristic psychologies, rational-emotive therapy squarely places man in the center of the universe and of his own emotional fate and gives him almost full responsibility for choosing to make or not make himself seriously disturbed. Although it weighs biological and early environmental factors quite importantly in the chain of events that lead to human disorganization and disorder, it insists that nonetheless the individual himself can, and usually does, significantly intervene between his environmental input and his emotionalized output, and that therefore he has an enormous amount of potential control over what he feels and what he does. Moreover, when he unwittingly and foolishly *makes himself* disturbed by devoutly believing in irrational and unvalidatable assumptions about himself and others, he can almost always *make himself* undisturbed again, and can do so often—if he utilizes rational-emotive procedures.

RET employs an A-B-C method of viewing human personality and its disturbance. When trying to help a person, the therapist usually begins with C—the upsetting emotional Consequence that he has recently experienced. Typically, he has been rejected by someone (this rejection can be called A, the Activating Experience) and then feels anxious, worthless, or depressed at C. He wrongly believes that A, his being rejected, has caused C, his feelings of anxiety, worthlessness, or depression; and he may even overtly voice this belief by saying something like, "She rejected me and *that* made me depressed."

The individual can be shown that A does not and really cannot cause C—that an Activating Event in the outside world cannot possibly create any feeling or emotional Consequence in his head and his gut. For if this were true, then virtually everyone who gets rejected would have to feel just as depressed as he does; and this is obviously not the case. C, then, is really caused by some intervening variable, or by B; and B is the individual's Belief System. Normally, where he is rejected at B he has two distinct Beliefs: one essentially rational, the other most irrational. His rational Belief (rB) generally is: "Isn't it unfortunate that she rejected me! I will suffer real losses or disadvantages by her rejection; and that is too bad. Now, how can I get her to accept me in the future; or, if I cannot, how can I get accepted by some other person who is somewhat equivalent to her and will probably bring me almost as much joy as I would receive if she had not rejected me." This Belief is rational because (1) it is designed to increase the individual's happiness and minimize his pain, and (2) it is related to observable, empirically validatable events. For it can easily be seen, by the individual himself and by others, that it *is* unfortunate that he was rejected by someone for whom he cares; that he *will* suffer real losses or disadvantages by her rejection; and that he probably *can* find another woman who will accept him and bring him almost as much joy as he would have received had he not been rejected by the first woman.

If this individual held rigorously to his rational Beliefs about being rejected and did not go an iota beyond them, he would usually experience pronounced feelings at point C (emotional Consequences), but they would *not* be those of anxiety, worthlessness, or depression. Instead, he would have feelings of disappointment, sorrow, regret, frustration, and annoyance. And his feelings would then be quite appropriate to the Activating Experience or Event, since they would motivate him to try to change his life so that he would in the future be accepted by a desirable female companion, and hence enjoy himself more.

Human beings, however, are biologically and sociologically prone to an illogical thinking process at point B, which can be termed "magical thinking." They have irrational Beliefs (iB's) in addition to their rational ones. Consequently, a patient (or client) will usually conclude: "Isn't it *awful* that she rejected me! I am *pretty worthless* because she has done so! *No* desirable woman will probably ever accept me! I *should* have done a better job of getting her to accept me; and *I deserve to be punished* for being so inept!" These Beliefs are highly irrational because: (1) they are almost certain to decrease the individual's happiness, maximize his pain, and prevent him from fulfilling his desires in the future; and (2) they are related to magical, empirically unvalidatable hypotheses for which there is not, nor probably ever can be, any factual evidence.

Thus, when the individual hypothesizes that it is *awful* (or *terrible* or *horrible*) that he has been rejected by the woman he desires, he contends (1) that it is exceptionally inconvenient for him to be rejected, and (2) that it is *more* than inconvenient. Although the first of these statements is verifiable, the second is not. It implies that he *should* not, *ought* not, *must* not be inconvenienced when he doesn't want to be; that there is a law of the universe that posits that his wishes *have to* be satisfied; and that he *cannot stand* living in a world where he is seriously deprived. But these are all absolutistic and autistic propositions that have no basis in reality, and that he has foolishly created in his head. *Awfulness* is really a devil that he invents—and with which he plagues himself. Inconvenience and disadvantage clearly exist; but awfulness and terribleness are made-up monsters and demons.

When the individual hypothesizes that he is worthless because a preferred woman has rejected him, he again resorts to an unvalidatable hypothesis—for the conclusion that he is *worthless* means (1) that his life has somewhat *less* worth or value now that he has lost the woman he wants, and (2) that it has and will forever after have *no* value. Although, again, the first of these propositions is connected with observable experiences or events, and hence is empirically validatable, the second proposition cannot really be proven or disproven, but is merely definitional. For how, except by definition, can it be shown that he, a very complex and ongoing human being, is and will always be of no value whatever because one preferred woman has rejected him? Even if he *never* wins a desirable female partner, he could normally do many other enjoyable things during his lifetime and could therefore have considerable value to himself.

When the individual hypothesizes that *no* desirable woman will probably ever accept him, because the one he now prefers has rejected him, he again is stating an unprovable assumption; for if he keeps trying, he almost always has a high probability of eventually winning the acceptance of a highly valued partner—as long as he does not so seriously affect and deflect himself by his foolish self-fulfilling prophecy that he *cannot possibly* win one.

When the individual concludes that "I *should* have done a better job of getting her to accept me and *I deserve to be punished* for being so inept!" he stoutly maintains several propositions that are magical and unverifiable: (1) He claims not only that *it would have been better* if he had done a better job of getting the woman to accept him, but that he *should* and *ought* to have done what would have been better. But how can he ever substantiate, with empirical evidence, this absolutistic *should* and *ought*? (2) He strongly implies that he is a worthless person for not inducing the preferred woman to accept him. But how could he ever become a totally bad *person* just because he has done a set of mistaken or inefficient *acts*? (3) He insists that because he has been inept in gaining the acceptance of this woman (*a*) he will be penalized or deprived by her loss and (*b*) he *deserves,* by some unalterable law of the universe, to be condemned, damned, and punished *forever*. Although the first of his contentions can be verified, the second one is a dogmatic, faith-backed hypothesis that can probably never be empirically substantiated.

In many ways, then, the individual's irrational Beliefs (iB's) are magical; and they are much more likely to lead to more harm than good. The more he devoutly and uncritically holds them, the more he will almost inevitably feel anxious, worthless, and depressed. These feelings, moreover, will usually sabotage, rather than help him solve, his original problem—namely, how to win the acceptance of the woman he prefers or of someone her equivalent.

The rational-emotive therapist talks with this disturbed individual,

7

showing him that A (his Activating Experiences or Events) does not normally cause C (his dysfunctional Consequences), but that he himself creates these poor Consequences by absolutistically and unscientifically convincing himself, at point B, of several highly irrational Beliefs. The therapist then leads the client on to point D—which consists of vigorously Disputing his irrational Beliefs. The disturbed person is to question and challenge these Beliefs by asking himself: (1) "Why is it *awful* that the woman I greatly prefer rejected me?" (2) "How am I *pretty worthless* because she has refused me?" (3) "Where is the evidence that *no* desirable woman will probably ever accept me?" (4) "Why *should* I have done a better job of getting her to accept me?" (5) "By what law do I *deserve to be punished or damned* for being so inept?"

If the therapist succeeds in inducing the individual who feels anxious, worthless, and depressed about being rejected to Dispute (at point D) his irrational Beliefs (iB's) about himself and the world, he then proceeds to E—new and better functioning Effects. First, he has a new cognitive Effect (cE), or a restatement, in more generalized form, of his original rational Beliefs (rB's). Thus, he will tend to conclude: (1) "It is not awful, but merely very inconvenient and disadvantageous for this preferred woman to reject me." (2) "Although, for the present, my life may be less enjoyable, or worth less, than it would have been had she accepted me, I am never a *worthless individual*—unless I foolishly define myself as one." (3) "There is of course no evidence that *no* desirable woman will probably ever accept me, and it is in fact highly likely that in the future one will." (4) "There are many reasons why *it would have been better* had I done a good job of getting her to accept me, but there is no reason why I *should* or *ought* to have done such a good job." (5) "There is no law that says I deserve to be punished or damned for being so inept, although if I continue to be inept at winning the allegiance of the woman I care most for, I will be penalized."

If the therapist encourages the individual to adopt these new philosophies of living, the latter will then get a new, and often very pronounced, behavioral Effect (bE): namely, he will tend, after a while, to stop creating such feelings again when similar Activating

Experiences (loss of approval by a desired woman) occur in his life. This, in simple outline, is the essence of rational-emotive therapy. In addition, it employs a large variety of evocative-emotive and behavioral-motorial methods of helping troubled individuals change their basic irrational values and philosophies and acquire more sensible, joy-producing and pain-minimizing ideas. Because it is exceptionally hard-headed, persuasive, educational, and active-directive, and because it straightforwardly attacks many of the sacred myths, superstitions, and religiosities that are so prevalent among human beings (and even among phychologists and other scientists), RET is often viewed as being antihumanistic. Thus, especially when it contends that people do not absolutely *need* love or success and that they have considerable ability to think about and to change their self-defeating emotions, RET is accused of being overintellectualized, mechanistic, and manipulative.

These accusations are not only mistaken, but they miss the important point that efficient therapies which stress the potentialities of cognitive control over dysfunctional emotional processes are in many respects the most humanistic means of personality change that have yet been invented. They are usually man centered, creativity oriented, and relevant to the maximum actualization of human potential. Although experientially oriented psychologists, such as Abraham Maslow, Frederick Perls, and Carl Rogers are outstanding humanists, so too are cognitively oriented therapists, such as Aaron T. Beck, Eric Berne, Charlotte Buhler, George Kelly, Arnold Lazarus, E. Lakin Phillips, and Julian Rotter.

Cognitive therapy in general and rational-emotive psychotherapy in particular are among the most humanistic of phychological treatment procedures for a number of reasons:

1. Cognitive therapies deal largely with beliefs, attitudes, and values rather than mainly with stimuli and responses, as do many of the other psychotherapies. Thus, psychoanalysis is largely hung up with the activating events of an individual's life, or the stimuli that impinged upon him during his early childhood. Classical behavior therapy is mainly preoccupied with his responses or symptoms. Experiential and encounter therapies are also focused on his responses

or experiences. But RET quickly zeros in on, and primarily stays with, his most uniquely human behaviors: namely, his cognitions and his beliefs. It recognizes, as Magda Arnold and Rudolf Arnheim have shown, that his perceptions, on the one hand, and his emotions, on the other, are both significantly influenced and even caused by his concepts and constructs; and that while lower animals may be importantly conditioned and deconditioned by externally applied reinforcement and extinction, man seems to be the only creature who can literally recondition or retrain himself by changing his basic ideas. RET, therefore, specifically deals with man as man, and not merely as a representative of the animal kingdom.

2. Cognitive therapies squarely put man in the center of the universe and give him a somewhat wider range of choice, of existential freedom, than do many other therapies. RET holds that man's behavior, although to some degree determined and limited by his biological nature and his history, is considerably less determined than the orthodox Freudians or behaviorists seem to think it is. It shows people how they can extend their choices of action and significantly change their personalities by (1) understanding precisely how they needlessly constrict themselves, (2) uprooting and modifying their rigidicizing philosophies of life, and (3) actively working against their self-defeating habituations until they break through their gratuitously restricting shell.

3. Cognitive therapies do not merely accept man the way he is, nor utilize his biosocial tendencies to be highly suggestible, prejudiced, and conforming to help him make more practical adjustments to social reality, but they also enhance the possibility of his transcending some of his biological and social limitations and making himself into a radically changed and different (though not superhuman) type of being. RET, in particular, teaches people to be less conditionable and suggestible, to think largely for themselves no matter what the majority of their fellows think and feel, and to minimize their dire needs for approval and success, which often force them to be nauseatingly conforming. Instead of relying only on ordinary kinds of reinforcement to effect personality change, RET also uses the reinforcements

of independent and creative thinking that are also an integral and important part of the human hedonistic calculus.

4. Cognitive therapies are deeply philosophic and reeducative and deal with the more elegant types of personality-restructuring solutions rather than with the less elegant types of sympton-removal solutions to human problems. Psychoanalysis, experiential, and behavior therapy may all help a troubled individual to forego a specific phobia, such as his fear of failing at love or at work. But it is almost impossible to get him to the point where he is not overly concerned with *any* form of failure unless the therapist engages in a depth-centered philosophic discourse about the general issues of failure, anxiety, and human worth. RET, for example, is one of the few psychotherapies in which the client can be clearly shown (1) that self-acceptance is a purely tautological and definitional concept, and may always be had for the asking by a person whose definitions are in good order; (2) that humans do not have to rate themselves *at all*, although they are generally better off if they accurately rate their traits and deeds; and (3) that virtually *all* human disturbance is the result of magical thinking (of believing in *shoulds, oughts,* and *musts*) and can therefore be directly and forthrightly eliminated by the individual's sticking rigorously to empirical reality. Not only, therefore, can the person who is troubled see quickly what his fundamental difficulties are in the course of a relatively few RET sessions, but he can also be taught a method of dealing with his problems increasingly well for the remainder of his life. This post-therapy effectiveness is notably prevalent in the cognitive approach.

5. The perceptual-cognitive-philosophic approach to therapy helps provide the individual with a neater, saner balance between his individualistic, self-seeking tendencies and his being a helpful and cooperative member of his social group than does virtually any other kind of approach that he is likely to learn during treatment. Where some forms of therapy, such as experiential or psychoanalytic methods, are likely to encourage him to indulge himself and somewhat antisocially hate others, and where others, such as relationship therapy, are likely to encourage him to be overly concerned with the

approval of those around him and to sacrifice himself for his social group, RET provides well-rounded, empirically based discussion of questions such as individualism versus conformity, which may enable him to arrive at a sensible mean between two unreasonable extremes. Since most major problems of living involve the individual's taking a two-sided, tolerant, somewhat compromising attitude toward himself, others, and the world, this kind of attitude is much more likely to be arrived at through intelligent, fact-centered psychophilosophical discussion with a well-trained and wise therapist than it is through immersion in more monolithic-oriented types of therapy.

6. The cognitive therapies make maximum use of a humanistic-scientific methodology that is based on relevance and pleasure seeking but that also is closely tied to scientific empiricism, objectivity, and controlled experimentation. RET starts frankly with a human-value system—namely, the assumption that pleasure, joy, creativity, and freedom are good or efficient for human living, and that pain, joylessness, uncreativeness, and bondage are bad or inefficient. It also assumes that what we call emotional disturbance is largely self-created and can therefore be self-dispelled. Since, however, it relies on induction from empirical evidence and on logical deduction from fact-based hypotheses (as every rational method of discourse essentially does), it ties its man-centered, hedonistic goals to the best available logico-empirical methods of achieving those goals. Instead, therefore, of being anti-intellectual and antitechnological, as are so many systems of psychotherapy and of philosophy today, it determinedly tries to *use* modern science and technology for clear-cut, humanistic purposes. RET shows the individual, for example, that he is *not* alienated by technology and science but that he alienates *himself* by irrationally sanctifying these human tools, and that he can unalienate or get in touch with himself and use such instruments to his own human advantage.

7. The cognitive therapies help the individual strike a sensible balance between short-range and long-range hedonism. Virtually all psychotherapies are essentially hedonistic, in that they encourage the individual to minimize needless pain (for example, anxiety and depression) and to maximize pleasure (for example, love and creative

work). Many therapies, however—especially those which are religious centered—stress and overstress self-discipline and long-range goals; and many other therapies—especially experiential and encounter-type methods—stress the short-term goals of here-and-now enjoyments. RET, being philosophic and nonextremist, emphasizes both the releasing pleasures of the here-and-now and the longer-range goals of future gain through present-day discipline. It holds that humans have the capacity to be contemporary *and* future-oriented hedonists; to work actively for personal and social change *and* to be relatively patient; to enjoy a wide range of appropriate emotional feelings (including, at times, deep-seated sadness and regret); *and* to control and change their inappropriate emotions (such as depression and rage).

8. The cognitive therapies employ a wide variety of educational and reeducational methods. RET teaches individuals how to understand themselves and others, how to react differently, and how to change their basic personality patterns through the therapist's giving the client full emphatic acceptance, a nonjudgmental environment, and practice in individual and group relating. It dramatically pushes him into risk-taking and adventurous activities, both inside and outside the therapy sessions. It forces him to express himself in more authentic, less defensive ways. It employs behavioristic desensitizing and operant conditioning procedures. But it also, along with these highly emotive and behavioral methods, didactically and directly teaches him the facts of life and the intricate pathways of his own self-defeatingness and childish demandingness through explanations, stories, persuasive arguments, scientific data, bibliotherapy procedures, audiovisual aids, philosophic discussions, and a host of other educational procedures which for many individuals are more efficient than the one-sidedly dramatic or one-sidedly behavioristic approaches used in many other therapies. Man, obviously, does not live by intellect alone, but he rarely lives very well without it. RET notably adds the rational-cognitive to many of the other time-tested, less didactic methods of psychotherapy.

9. The cognitive therapies are unusually effective for pain reduction and are therefore exceptionally humanistic. All psychotherapies,

naturally, are designed to reduce unnecessary emotional and physical suffering. But many of the most popular methods—especially classical psychoanalysis—take a minimum of two years and a maximum of five or more years before the client is appreciably helped to become less anguished. Rational-emotive therapy, because it stresses an active-directive, concentrated, multifaceted attack on the individual's basic irrational thinking and behaving, is frequently able to help him significantly in a matter of days or weeks. Moreover, as has been shown in clinical and research studies of RET and other forms of cognitive therapy, these methods are often able to achieve better results with problem-afflicted individuals than are less cognitive-oriented forms of therapy.

10. The cognitive therapies tend to be unusually accepting of human fallibility and to encourage maximum understanding of, and tolerance for, human frailty. Many psychotherapies wittingly or unwittingly encourage the individual to judge and condemn himself or others. Thus, psychoanalysis teaches him that his parents are to blame for his emotional problems, and implies that they are therefore reprehensible. Experiential, cathartic, and encounter therapies often show him that he is right in hating others and that he had better openly vent his spleen on them. They also encourage him, in many instances, to feel deeply hurt by others' rejections, and thereby to be self-damning. Religious-oriented and confession-type therapies tend to induce him to acknowledge his sins, to feel terribly guilty about them, to expiate them in various ways, and intrinsically to retain or even augment a self-flagellating philosophy of sin and atonement. RET is one of the few kinds of therapy that specifically and vigorously opposes all types of blaming, including the individual's negatively judging himself, others, or the universe. It persistently teaches the ashamed, hostile, and self-pitying individual that *no one* is to be blamed or damned for anything; that he can always unconditionally accept himself and others, no matter what are his or their deficiencies; and that no matter how rough or unfair the world is, it is a waste of time and energy for him to whine about and rant against it. It shows the person with problems, in other words, how he can humanistically refuse ever to loathe himself, other fallible people, or

the world at large; or how he can realistically accept humans as humans (instead of as superhumans or subhumans) and desist from deifying and devilifying himself and any of his fellows. In this particular sense, in its complete acceptance of man as being incredibly human and never anything but fallible and ungodlike, rational-emotive therapy is surely the epitome of humanistic psychology and psychotherapy.

Is RET a truly revolutionary approach to psychological treatment and to the prevention of emotional disturbance? In some ways, of course, it is not, since it basically stems from the teachings of stoicism, of logico-empiricism, of existentialism, and of humanism, all of which have been around for a good many years and are therefore no longer too revolutionary. But in some of its specific applications of these values and ideas to the field of psychotherapy, rational-emotive psychology is truly innovative and radical. For example:

1. It is an exceptionally clear-cut theory of personality disturbance—or human demandingness—that hypothesizes that people do not *get upset* but instead *upset themselves* by insisting that (*a*) they should be outstandingly loved and accomplished, (*b*) other people should be incredibly fair and giving, and (*c*) the world should be exceptionally easy and munificent. The rational-emotive therapist can, therefore, with practically no background information on the individual, usually zero in rather quickly on his fundamental disturbances, show him what he is doing to create them, and demonstrate how he can immediately begin to eradicate them if he wishes to work at doing so.

2. It is one of the few—perhaps the only—method of personality change that provides the person with severe emotional problems with the most elegant, deepest, and nonpalliative solutions of these problems; namely, his learning how to steadfastly refuse to berate himself, as a human, for *any* error; to accept himself, as a living creature, at *all* times; and to rate and measure *only* his traits and performances, and never his *self*. RET is the one regular mode of psychotherapy which truly solves the ego problem—by showing the individual how to stop esteeming or disesteeming himself for anything, and thereby eliminating pride or "ego."

3. It is one of the few systems of psychotherapy that will truly have no truck whatever with any kind of miraculous cause or cure, any kind of god or devil, or any kind of sacredness. Where many other systems deify feeling, experience, self-interest, social interest, self-disclosure, relationship, trust, reason, anti-intellectualism, and what have you, rational-emotive therapy deifies nothing, holds to no absolutes, and is quite comfortable with the world of probability, uncertainty, fallibility, and even disorder. It teaches people to *desire* and *prefer* many goals; but to *demand,* to *need*, and to *dictate* nothing. In this sense, and quite revolutionarily, it helps free humans of their own anxiety-creating, depression-invoking, and hostility-manufacturing grandiosity and demandingness. Not merely of the unfortunate symptomatic *results* of this demandingness, but of the essence of the demandingness itself.

Man is man; he will (in all likelihood) never be more than man. When and if he fully accepts that reality, together with the reality that there is no supernatural "force" in the universe that gives a damn about him or ever will, he will then be truly humanistic. Rational-emotive psychology is one of the main modern methods of helping him work toward that goal.

2

THE VALUE OF A HUMAN BEING:
A PSYCHOTHERAPEUTIC APPRAISAL

A basic tenet for rational living is that people not rate themselves in terms of any of their performances, but instead fully accept themselves in terms of their being, their existence. Otherwise, they tend to be severely self-deprecating and insecure, and as a consequence they function ineffectively.

Why should this be so? To value oneself in terms of any deeds or acts will work only as long as one is performing rather well. Even if such deeds or acts are excellent at the moment, it will probably be only a matter of time when they will become less praiseworthy. Among other things, the individual grows older with the passing years—and consequently does worse eventually at various feats at which he may do well in his youth. Besides, no one is perfect, and being fallible, all of us will sooner or later fail in many respects. Where will they be, then, who insist on rating themselves by performances?

Knowing, moreover, that the chances of ultimately failing at some prized goal are normally high, people tend to work overtime at worrying about the possibility of such failure; and in the process will frequently interfere with their chances of success. For worrying is distracting and time consuming and hardly enables one to cope with any kind of problem solving; on the contrary, it almost always sabotages.

The investment of personal value, or worth as a human being, in any performance, makes it very "dangerous" to attempt to do that thing. A man would be loath to risk the game at all, if he is prepared to define himself as a failure should his performance fail. He therefore tends to make up excuses and avoids trying; or if he pushes himself ahead and compels himself to make an effort, he does so while worrying, "Will I do well?" or "Is it going to be good enough?" Frequently he enjoys the action so little, and finds such difficulty in keeping at it, that he finally concludes with something like, "Hell! It's not really worth all this trouble. Who wants to do *that* sort of thing, anyway?" The result is often a withdrawal from the activity, a conviction that, in spite of a dearth of objective evidence to judge by, it is not really worth doing.

Thus, the artist who *wanted* to be a painter of fine murals would have a delightful goal to strive for, and would probably have a very fine time trying for it. But if he absolutely *had* to be a great muralist, and was convinced that he must be a marvelous painter, or else he is a person without worth, a nonperson, an inhuman, he would then soon find it too risky to paint—for who wants to prove what a worthless being he is? And rather than take that risk, the would-be artist will probably end up with excuses or rationalizations: "I don't have the time or money for painting," or "The lumbago in my arm is too painful for me to do any amount of painting," or "Nobody wants murals these days, anyway, so what's the use of trying to paint any?"

If a person must rate his self, his "personal worth," or "self-esteem," he had better do it in terms of some quite safe standard, such as his aliveness or his being. He can then, in accordance with this standard, quite justifiably conclude, "I am good, not because I do very well at anything, and not because certain people tend to approve of me, but just because I am alive, because I exist.'' For when he accepts his goodness as a human being in terms of being or aliveness, he obviously can accept himself under virtually all conditions that he may possibly face during a lifetime. By this standard, he would only fail to have goodness when dead.

Valuing oneself in relation to being or existence is the logical solution to the problem of self-worth. It is derived from the works of Paul Tillich, of Robert S. Hartman, and various other existentialist philosophers. Hartman has had a profound influence on the development of rational-emotive psychotherapy; for psychotherapy, as Perry London and various other practicing therapists have shown, is really largely concerned with morals and values, even when the therapist does not fully consciously recognize this fact. And the effective therapist would better have a good philosophy of life himself and be well prepared to discuss deeply philosophic questions with his clients if he wants to get very far with many of them.

Unfortunately, the more I used a modification of the Tillich-Hartman approach with my clients, and the more I tried to show them that they never really had to denigrate themselves as human beings no matter how poor their performances might be and no matter how little certain significant others cared for them, the more I began to encounter some very bright individuals who would not quite buy this line or who at least had serious philosophic objections to it. For these clients would object: ''You say that the individual is good just because he's alive, and that he needs no other requisites for self-worth. I can see how this may work. If someone really believes this idea, he cannot very well devalue himself in any serious way, even though he may fully admit that many of his actions are less than good or are even reprehensible. But how can you positively state that a person *is* good merely because he exists? How can you *prove* this hypothesis? He's alive, all right; you can definitely, empirically prove that. But what makes him good *because* he's alive? You might just as sensibly say, 'He's *bad* because he's alive.' For both these statements, that he's good or that he's bad because he exists, are definitions or tautologies, and neither of them is really provable.''

"Well," I could only agree, when I listened to the arguments of these clients, "they're right! How *can* I prove that the individual's aliveness equals his worthiness? I can, of course, disprove any client's assumption that because he exists and because he behaves poorly, he is indubitably worthless (that is, of no value to himself and deserving of being dead). For his assumption, too, is tautological, and there is no empirical data by which he can uphold it. But how can I prove to him that he really *is* intrinsically worthwhile?"

There really *is* no answer to the question, "What am I worth?" or "How do I prove that I am a good person?" since the question is rather meaningless and foolish in the first place. If I ask myself, "What do I do?" "What are my traits?" or "What is the value of this performance of mine?" such a question is meaningful, since it inquires about a trait, characteristic, or performance which (1) can be observed and (2) can to some degree be measured or rated. Thus, I play tennis, I possess a good backhand swing in this game, and my particular performance at tennis today was good, since I won all the matches I engaged in with competitors. But if I ask myself, "Who am I?" how am I going to answer this question *except* in the light of my traits, characteristics, and performances? How am I to give a meaningful answer to such a vague, undefinable, rather meaningless question?

I *am*, as David Bourland has noted, nothing very observable or measurable. For whenever we use any form of the verb *to be,* we tend to overgeneralize about ourselves. Thus, I really am not, although I may erroneously label myself as, "a tennis player." Instead, I am a person, an individual, who among many other things *sometimes plays tennis.* Nor am I a "good backhander at tennis." For I am an organism, a human who has several usual (and some unusual) tennis characteristics—including the one that I often hit the ball back at my opponent with a good backhand stroke *and* I often also do several other things while playing tennis, such as usually serve badly and retrieve the ball quickly, or hit it with a mean twist. Nor *am* I a great tennis player because my game today was particularly good. Rather, I am a man, a creature who today played very well, and who tomorrow may play very badly, the next day well again, and so on. If I *am* anything, then, I am very complex; and it is rather foolish and false to refer to me as simplistically *being* a tennis player, a psychologist, a writer, or almost anything else. I am, much more accurately, a *person who* does various kinds of things. So "Who am I?" is a silly question to ask about me. "What are my traits and how, at various times, do I perform them?" is much more sensible to ask.

Similarly, "What is my identity?" is a fairly meaningless question, despite the efforts of Erik Erikson to answer it. For the only conceivable answer to a question like this is, "I am a male," or "I am an American teenager," or "I am a writer of books on psychology." And all these are false overgeneralizations. I am really a human being, and I do innumerable things, some well and some badly. I cannot be legitimately characterized as a "leftwinger," a "rational-emotive therapist," a "musician," or by any similar overinclusive or underinclusive term. When I use these kinds of appellations to describe myself, I am using shorthand—and very inaccurate shorthand at that—which probably far more obscures than reveals what *I and my traits* truly are.

When I ask, moreover, "What is my identity?" what I really mean, when I am honest, is, "How do I shape up against you? Am I not a member of a group (such as the group of liberal middle-aged Americans) which is at least equal to, and preferably superior to, the group of which you are a member? Isn't my identity, as compared to yours, real, honest, true, and good? Don't I, because of my identity, deserve to live and prosper, while you (for all I care) can easily shrivel up and die?" The questions, "Who am I?" and "What is my identity?" could technically mean, as Erikson sometimes seems to imply, that I merely want to know what my traits are and what my real thing is, so that I may, with the use of this knowledge, enjoy myself during my seventy-five years or so of existence. But they truly, for the most part, are one of the main ways in which I play ego games—by which I devoutly hope to "prove" that I am great and you are not, that the world will justly honor me and damn you, and that I shall sooner or later get to heaven while you ignobly fry in hell.

That, in fact, is the basic reason for what we call self-esteem, feelings of worthwhileness, or ego strength: to show that I am good and you (that is, the entire rest of the world) are not; that because I am good, I deserve to go on living and to enjoy myself; and that because I am good and deserve to go on living and enjoy myself, I shall ultimately attain some kind of salvation. When I have a good ego, I don't merely want to live and enjoy—I want to undevilify and to deify myself.

"Well," you may observe, "that may all be true. But as the sages have noted for centuries, isn't it also necessary that things be so? Can a human really live satisfactorily *without* ego, self-esteem, pride, feelings of worth, or whatever you want to call it?"

Why can he not? "Certainly," I started to tell a client when I saw that it would not be easy to convince him that he was good just because he was alive, "I can't prove to you that you're really worthwhile, just as you can't prove to me that you're really not. For whatever standards or measures we seem to use in these arguments, we're being tautological. I say, 'You're good just because you exist,' and you rightly show me that that's merely my *definition* of goodness or worth. And you say, 'I'm worthless because I perform badly,' and I rightly show you that that's merely your *definition* of badness. We both get nowhere with such arguments, because they don't have, nor can they ever have, any empirical referent. But why do we even have to think about or label your worth or value at all? Why do we *need* such a concept?"

"Well, *don't* we? I just can't even think of a human being not rating himself at all—not liking or hating himself."

"Why not? Why does he *have* to invent *any* kind or type of self-evaluation?"

"So that he can efficiently live, I guess."

"Efficiently?" I ask. "Nonsense! The more he evaluates or rates himself, the less efficient he is likely to be. First of all, he spends much, or even most, of his time and energy doing this evaluating. Secondly, he never comes up with a very accurate or consistent answer. Thirdly, he ultimately—because he is immensely error-prone and demandingly perfectionistic—evaluates himself rather negatively and thereby seriously *interferes* with many of his own performances. How does all *that* help?''

"I see what you mean. But I still can't see how he could avoid evaluating himself completely.''

"Well, let me show you how he can,'' I confidently retort. Then I go on to show the client that all he really has to do is to keep entirely within the empirical realm and view his life in this manner:

1. He obviously exists or is alive—which can fairly easily be observably determined (and checked with others' observations).

2. He can either choose to remain alive or to let himself die—another empirically observable choice.

3. He can, if he chooses to remain alive, either strive for more pleasure than pain or for more pain than pleasure—a third empirically determinable choice.

4. He can decide in favor of living and of pleasure on the basis of the hypothesis, "*It* is good for me to live and to enjoy myself,'' or on the basis of the hypothesis, "*I* am good and therefore I deserve to live and enjoy myself.'' If he decides on the former basis, he avoids rating or evaluating himself, although he does rate or evaluate his performances (that is, living and enjoying). If he decides on the latter basis, he brings in ego and evaluates himself.

5. Without any self-evaluation and ego-rating, he can decide to continue to live and to have as much enjoyment in life as he can find. His major questions to himself then do not become, "Who am I?'' "What is my identity?'' or "What is my worth?'' They become, rather: "What are my traits?'' "What sort of things do I enjoy and not enjoy doing?'' "How can I improve some of my traits and find more things to experience—so that I will continue to live and to have a maximally satisfying existence?''

This is the main line that I now take with my clients. "Look,'' I tell them. "If you *must* rate or value yourself, or wallow around in what is ordinarily called ego and ego games—and I strongly advise you against it—you have a simple solution to the problem of worth. Just define yourself as good, in terms of your existence, your aliveness.

Dogmatically tell yourself, 'I am alive, and I am good because I am alive.' This simple formula, if you really believe it, will work, and will be virtually unassailable. For, believing it, you will never feel terribly anxious or self-deprecating as long as you are alive. And when you are dead, you still won't have much to worry about!

"But if you want a preferable solution to the problem of human worth—and I strongly suggest that you strive for this solution—then you'd better avoid rating yourself at all. You are not *good* and you are not *bad*—you are merely *you*. You possess many traits, most of which you may (and often would better) rate: your abilities to read, to talk, to write, to run, to jump, to drive, just to name a few. But you never have to jump, as if by magic, from rating these traits to rating *you*. You can, if you wish, give your various facets, your characteristics, your talents, a report card; but you'd better not give *you* a similar report card. Then, minus such a self-rating, and minus playing the ego game and the power struggle of vying for 'goodness' with other human beings, you can ask yourself 'What do I really want in life?' and can try to find those things and enjoy them."

No therapist will have an easy time inducing clients to give up rating themselves and to stick more rigorously, at most, to assessing, measuring, and evaluating their traits. Humans, unfortunately, seem to be almost universally born and reared to give themselves self-evaluations. They use, to be sure, different trait ratings for these self-rating standards. In the United States, for example, they rate themselves as "good" if they have lots of money, education, or artistic talent; while in many more primitive parts of the world they rate themselves as "good" if they have a considerable amount of physical strength, child-begetting ability, or perhaps head-hunting proclivity. But wherever they are, they are not prone merely to accept themselves, with whatever traits and talents they happen to have, and to look for enjoyments that *they* happen to like (rather than those other people think that they *should* like).

Is this self-rating tendency of human beings more or less inborn? I think so—for if people all over the world, no matter how they are raised, tend to deify themselves and denigrate others, or vice versa, and to depress themselves horribly when they do not succeed in whatever aspects of life their culture tells them that they *should*, there is some reason to suspect that they naturally and easily fall into a self-assessing and ultimately self-condemning pattern. Love, 'tis often said, makes the world go round. Yes: self-love, mainly, or the frantic striving on the part of the great majority of humans to achieve such love.

Although man has unique powers of observation and logic, and is consequently the one animal primarily born to be a scientist, he also has unique tendencies toward religiosity, magical thinking, anti-intellectualism, and nonempiricism. Rollo May thinks that man is innately predisposed toward what he calls the daimonic. But while May gives up and thinks that man had better make peace with his demon-creating tendencies and deeply imbedded roots in irrationality, I take a much more optimistic view. I contend that man *can* think more rationally, even though he rarely does; that he *is* able to give up superstition and magic; and that he can teach himself and fairly consistently stick with the logico-empirical method of confronting not only the external world but also himself and his own functioning. Further, if he really does this much of the time, he can stop his absurd ego games and self-rating, and can tolerantly accept both himself and others and look for a much saner goal in life: to enjoy the experience of living.

So I say, again, to my clients: "All right, face it: you have screwed up very badly much of your existence. You failed to do as well as you could have done in your work; you married the wrong girl and then endlessly goofed on making the most of a bad deal or getting out of it as quickly and gracefully as possible; and you have been far worse a father to your children than you probably could have been, and have consequently helped them cause themselves a lot of needless trouble. O.K. So you did all this with your deadly little hatchet and there's no point in trying to excuse your acts or say that they were right. They weren't right: they were stupid and wrong. *Now,* why are you blaming yourself and denying your worth for acting in these execrable ways?"

"Well, *should* I have done those wrong things, and thereby hurt myself and others?"

"Of course you *should*—because you *did*. *It would have been desirable,* of course, had you not acted in those ways; but because a thing is desirable never means that it *should* exist. Only some unalterable, godlike law of the universe could ever say that you should, you must, do what is desirable. And where is there such a law? Can you demonstrate that that kind of law ever has existed, or ever will?"

"No, I see what you mean. And if there's no invariable law of the universe that says that I *should* not have done what I did, then I guess you also mean that there's no supplementary law which says that I should be punished for breaking that law."

"Right! You are intrinsically penalized, of course, for many of your wrong acts. If you fail to do as well as you could have done at work, you lose out on some of the rewards of succeeding. If you stay with a wife who is incompatible, and you make conditions of living with her even worse than they had to be, you then lead something of a miserable married life. So acting poorly or inefficiently usually (though not always) has its intrinsic penalties. But when you think that you're a rotter and that you *should* be punished, you really mean that some magical, overlooking superbeing in the universe is spying on you, is noting your errors, and is determining to punish you for them. Well—is it likely that there really is such an overlooking superbeing who is so sadistically inclined that he's going to deliberately add *extra* punishment to your lot, when you have already seriously penalized yourself by your stupid behavior?"

"No, I guess it doesn't look like that. I guess I really do believe in some kind of devil when I think that I *deserve* to be punished when I have acted badly."

"You certainly do. And how about the hereafter business? Do you really believe that if you lead an error-prone, screwed-up life on this earth, you will be reincarnated somewhere else and made to suffer there for your earthian inadequacies?"

"Well, hardly! But my actions, admittedly, imply that on some level I do believe that kind of drivel. For I certainly often *feel* as if I'm going to be eternally damned when I don't do the right thing in this terrestrial existence."

"Yes. So you do keep damning yourself in various ways, and you do feel that you should be temporarily or eternally punished. The point is: you, as a human, are not rateable in any way, though your deeds may well be. Now, every time you do feel like a louse or a worm, you'd better fully admit that you are rating yourself negatively and then vigorously dispute this rating. You will not thereby necessarily solve the practical problems that beset you—such as the problems of how to work better, how to get along with your wife, or how to be a good father to your children—but you will solve your emotional problem. You will continually, unconditionally accept *yourself*, even though you will continue to dislike and refuse to accept a good deal of your behavior. You will keep rating your *traits*, but stop rating *you*."

"Can people really consistently do this?"

"Not perfectly, not always, not to the *n*th degree. But if they keep working at it, they can do it pretty well, and rarely have ego problems while otherwise remaining exceptionally human. In fact, to have an ego problem really means that you are striving to be *super*human and just will not fully accept your humanity, your fallibility. If you follow the rational-emotive procedure, which is one of the most humanistic methods of personal problem-solving ever invented, you will unconditionally accept yourself and others *as human*. This kind of tolerance is, I contend, the essence of emotional well-being. Why not try it and see for yourself?"

The rational-emotive approach to psychotherapy is not only unusually effective clinically, but is now backed by a considerable amount of experimental evidence which almost consistently supports its phenomenological tenets and indicates that human emotions and behavior are enormously influenced by cognitions. Besides being successfully practiced today by a number of clinicians who attest to its usefulness, it also has significant applications in education, in industry, and in other important aspects of human living. There is clinical, experimental, and other support for rational-emotive therapy.

All psychotherapy is, at bottom, a value system. The individual who is disturbed decides that he would rather be less anxious, depressed, hostile, or ineffective, and he thinks that he can be helped through talking with a therapist. On his part, the therapist agrees with the client that it is unnecessary for him to be so troubled and that he can somehow help him to feel and to behave better. Both the client and the therapist could agree, theoretically, that severe anxiety, depression, and hostility are beneficial—in which case the therapist could, as a social scientist, help the client to become more rather than less disturbed. But they both have similar prejudices or belief systems about what we tend to call emotional problems, and they agree to collaborate to minimize rather than to maximize such problems when the client feels that he is overafflicted with them.

It has been clinically observed that most of the time when the client is beset with anxiety, withdrawal, inhibition, and depression he values himself very poorly and thinks of himself as worthless, inadequate, or bad. As long as he has this picture of himself, or appraises his being in this manner, it seems almost impossible to help him very much with his basic emotional problems (although it may be possible palliatively to divert him from them in various ways). Consequently, the main goal of intensive, depth-centered psychotherapy usually becomes that of helping the client to stop devaluing himself and to gain what is usually called "self-confidence," "self-esteem," or "ego strength."

The rational-emotive approach to psychotherapy hypothesizes that there are two main approaches to helping the client gain self-acceptance, one inelegant and one elegant. The inelegant approach is to have him believe that he is "good" or "worthwhile" as a person, not because he does anything well or is approved by others, but simply because he exists. The more elegant approach is to show the individual that he does not have to rate, assess, or value himself at all; that he can merely accept the fact that he exists; that it is better for him to live and enjoy than for him to die or be in pain; and that he can take more delight in living by only measuring and valuing his traits, characteristics, and performances than by superfluously bothering to value his so-called *self*. Once the client is helped to be fully tolerant of all humans, including himself, and to stop giving them any global report cards, he has a philosophic solution to the problem of personal worth and can truly be self-accepting rather than self-evaluating. He will then consider himself neither a good nor a bad human being, but a person with fortunate and unfortunate traits. He will truly accept his humanity and stop demanding superhumanness from anyone.

3

RATIONAL-EMOTIVE THERAPY
AND OTHER THERAPIES

Rational-emotive therapy contrasts with psychoanalytic, behavior, and other therapies in theory, method, and effectiveness. Despite the concentration of psychoanalysis on early childhood experiences, classical Freudianism practically never arrives at the fundamental cause of an individual's basic emotional disturbances; and when it accidentally does so, it provides him with little information to help him change or eliminate this cause and thereby to become truly unanxious and unhostile and maximally self-actualizing. Although it claims to treat the individual's underlying disturbance rather than merely his symptoms, psychoanalysis actually does the opposite, sometimes enabling him to ameliorate his symptomatology but rarely to understand and forcefully attack his deep-seated, disturbance-creating tendencies. Worse yet, by inducing the client to focus upon great masses of irrelevant information about himself, by encouraging his prolonged dependency on the analyst, and by teaching him a number of highly questionable assumptions about the whys and wherefores of his behavior, psychoanalysis leads him to divert himself from doing exactly what he can do to help himself; namely, to work at scientifically questioning and challenging his irrational philosophic premises about himself and the world, and at training himself to behave differently from the indulgent, undisciplined manner in which he has allowed and conditioned himself to behave in the past and present.

Psychoanalysis does not greatly contribute to therapy because (together with näive behaviorism) it assumes that events and experiences are of paramount importance in a person's life, that he cannot help being traumatized by the unpleasant occurrences of his earliest years, and that if he fully understands the origins of these occurrences he will overcome their noxious influences. Actually, as Epictetus demonstrated some two thousand years ago, humans are not bothered by the things that happen to them but by their *view* of these things. They *bring* to external stimuli a special kind of receiving apparatus that enables them to *create* joys or traumas in connection with the events they experience. Their "experiences," in fact, include both stimuli *and* responses; and if they were, say, Martians or Venutians instead of Earthians, they would doubtless have much different "experiences" than they commonly have when being toilet trained, rejected by their mothers, or threatened with disapproval by their fathers.

A human is primarily a responding or creative individual. He not only perceives external (and internal) stimuli but he concomitantly thinks or conceptualizes about them. He also becomes so prejudiced by his own generalizations and philosophies that he perceives succeeding stimuli (or, if you will, "experiences") in a distorted and distinctly *human* way. So he continually *makes* his own responses—not, to be sure, entirely out of whole cloth (for he is *also* pushed or motivated to some degree by the nature of some stimuli themselves), but partly out of his own predispositions to be strongly biased (or to have what many psychologists vaguely refer to as his "emotions").

When, moreover, he experiences severe psychological upsets, man hardly feels disturbed because he is born with a blank mind which is then traumatized by the events in his early life. On the contrary, he appears to be born with many strong biosocial tendencies to think and act foolishly and thereby to *make himself* maladjusted. They include tendencies toward short-range hedonism, oversuggestibility, grandiosity, overvigilance, extremism, overgeneralization, wishful thinking, inertia, ineffective focusing, and discrimination difficulties, among numerous others. Practically *all* humans, it appears, are strongly burdened with these predilections; therefore, no matter how they are reared, they can hardly help being somewhat self-sabotaging and disturbed. Although Freud vaguely noted this fact, especially in his views on the "pleasure principle," he somehow missed clearly connecting it with emotional malfunctioning—which he stubbornly kept relating to the individual's early experiences instead of to his early and later *interpretations* of these experiences.

Naïve behaviorists make much the same error. They view a set of stimuli and the "conditioned" responses that follow the presentation of these stimuli, and they wrongly conclude that the stimuli "cause" the responses. Obviously, an even more basic "cause" is the *conditionability* of the responding person. For if he were not intrinsically the kind of individual who *does* respond to S_1, S_2, S_3, etc. Then an infinite number of their presentations would hardly affect him. Even Pavlov's famous dog, when he heard the sound of a bell presented in connection with his being fed, did not become conditioned to salivating *only* because he had an inborn tendency to respond to food. He also, surely, had an inborn tendency to hear bells and to connect their sound with other stimuli that were presented to him. If he were born deaf or if he had no innate capacity to connect the hearing of the bell with the smelling of the food, he would hardly have served Pavlov very well.

Both humans and dogs, then, *bring* something important to their conditioning "experiences." Especially in regard to the most common forms of emotional disturbances—such as feelings of inadequacy, worthlessness, and overweening hostility—it is not merely rejection or brutal treatment by a child's parents that makes him feel upset; rather, it is his own innate vulnerability to criticism and pain and his own inborn tendency to internalize others' negative attitudes toward him and to perpetuate self-criticism and damnation of others long after his original tormenters' barbs have ceased.

Humans, in other words, are highly suggestible, impressionable, vulnerable, and gullible. And they are self-talking, self-indoctrinating, self-stimulating creatures. They need, of course, *some* environmental influences to develop into suggestible and self-propagandizing individuals, just as they need external stimulation in order to develop at all. But with a wide variety of stimulation from outside people and events, they will still tend to be exceptionally vulnerable and self-indoctrinating.

If this is true, it follows that feelings of worthlessness do not stem from the attitudes that an individual's parents take toward him, but from his own tendency to take these attitudes too seriously, to internalize them, and to perpetuate them through the years. And if he is to conquer such feelings, a therapist will hardly help him by showing him that his parents *were* castigating and by claiming that *this* is the cause of his present lack of ego strength. The insight that is thus given him through psychoanalytic therapy may be partially correct; but it does not go far or deep enough. For he requires, to get better and to remain better, the insight that, whatever his parents' behavior may have been, he no longer has to take them seriously, to agree with their criticisms of him, and to keep castigating himself.

To acquire a solution to the problem of his own worth, the individual had better see his *own* propensities to exaggerate the significance of others' attitudes toward him; and see clearly that he can vigorously question, challenge, change, and minimize these tendencies toward distorted thinking about himself and others. It is even better if he understands that all measures of self-worth are tautological, definitional, and essentially magical; that though he is born and reared with a strong tendency to rate or value himself, he does not *have to* give in to this tendency; and that he can rigorously and empirically rate only his *traits* and *performances* rather than his *being* or his *self*, and in that manner can truly stop deifying and devilifying himself.

Psychoanalytic methods focus largely on past events rather than the human thinking that gives special *meaning* to these events; and they indirectly, passively, and inefficiently teach the client how to work at *changing* his disturbance-creating meanings. The individual's anxieties, depressions, hostilities, and other symptoms of disturbance are not caused by his *past* misinterpretations of his parents' behavior and attitudes, but by his *present continuation* of these interpretations; and unless these current residuals of his old cognitive errors are vigorously and persistently attacked, there is little chance of his modifying them significantly.

Psychotherapy increases in effectiveness as the therapist works on the premise that his clients are "emotionally" disturbed because of the flaws in their thinking mechanism. If helped to change their thinking, they also change their emotional reactions to external stimuli, past and present. RET therapists have significantly increased their effectiveness over their own previously employed analytic, client-centered, and other modes of therapy. Some of them have been converted to the rational approach because they obtained almost immediately better results when they tried it with several clients who were not responding to other approaches. It has likewise been found that whereas only a small number of clients can be reached with psychoanalytic techniques, all kinds of clients can be helped with the rational-emotive method, including disturbed individuals whose traits include fixed homosexuality, psychopathy, schizophrenic reactions, mental deficiency, and other syndromes that are usually unresponsive to most therapeutic methods.

Furthermore, the main essence of RET—the A-B-C theory of personality disturbance—can be used effectively by non-RET therapists who wish to incorporate it into their own systems. Thus, psychoanalytically oriented therapists, behavior therapists, existential therapists, marriage and family therapists, and various other kinds of therapists often show their clients, following RET principles, that whenever they get upset about an Activating Event (occurring at point A) by reacting with disturbed emotional Consequences (occurring at point C), their upsetness is not directly caused by A but by their Belief System (at point B). They can then (at point D) ideationally and actively Dispute their irrational Beliefs and thereby enormously change or eliminate their dysfunctional emotional Consequences.

Many therapists, of course, still vigorously oppose RET and insist that it is far too simple, and oververbalized, too intellectualized, authoritarian, and brainwashing. Actually, it is none of these, but is complexly philosophic, quickly gets at unconscious and unverbalized material, deals with the individual's basic emotions, and helps him to *act* as well as to *think* in order to change them. It is authoritative rather than authoritarian, and is aimed at inducing people to be less suggestible and more independent in their thinking.

One of the most gratifying aspects of developing the theory and practice of rational-emotive therapy has been the concomitant discovery that many other psychotherapists, most of them originally psychoanalytic in their thinking, have independently divined and applied similar principles in their own work.[1]

A vast amount of data is available to confirm the major hypotheses of RET. For example, the fundamental thesis of RET, that human thinking is a basic cause of emotion, and that healthy and unhealthy emotional reactions are significantly affected by changes in peoples' cognitions, has been experimentally validated by many psychological studies.[2]

Research studies that provide empirical evidence that rational-emotive therapy and similar cognitive therapies actually work have also been appearing with increasing frequency in psychological literature.[3] As for clinical findings, these have also been voluminous.[4]

Is RET a form of behavior therapy? In some ways, yes. Hans Eysenck includes it under "other methods" in his book, *Experiments in Behavior Therapy*. Gerald Davison includes it among the techniques that are taught to the postdoctoral students in behavior modifications at the State University of New York at Stony Brook. Arnold Lazarus, in his book, *Behavior Therapy and Beyond,* shows how he employs it in his own practice. Aaron T. Beck indicates that it is one of the main cognitive therapies that are an important aspect of virtually all behavior therapies. One need not take issue with these views.

Although RET is based on the assumption that humans are born with the tendency to learn one set of responses more easily than another, it also holds that specific patterns of disturbance are learned and that—albeit with some difficulty—they can be unlearned. It therefore not only shows the client what his maladjustment-creating philosophies are, but it directly and actively induces him to attack, challenge, and work against these philosophies and to retrain himself to think and behave more efficiently. It employs many of the time-honored educational and reeducational techniques, including didactic explanation, role playing, reinforcement, desensitization, persuasion, repetition, practice, modeling, and homework assignments. It also includes preventive teaching and may therefore be properly called, instead of by the medically toned term *psychotherapy,* by the education-centered terms, *behavior modification* or *emotional education.* Although RET goes beyond the usual methods of Joseph Wolpe's reciprocal inhibition and B.F. Skinner's operant conditioning, and although it deals with global states of emotional disturbance rather than (as these methods often do) with limited symptoms, it legitimately includes many of the regular conditioning, deconditioning, and self-conditioning techniques, such as those proposed by Lloyd E. Homme and David Premack. Of the main irrational ideas that the client tends consciously or unconsciously to believe, some of these ideas, that the therapist keeps showing him he holds and keeps logically and empirically refuting, include:

1. The idea that it is a dire necessity for an adult human to be loved or approved by virtually every significant other person in his life.

2. The idea that one should be thoroughly competent, adequate, and achieving in all possible respects to consider oneself worthwhile.

3. The idea that certain people are bad, wicked, or villainous and that they should be severely blamed and punished for their villainy.

4. The idea that it is awful and catastrophic when things are not the way one would like them to be.

5. The idea that human unhappiness is externally caused and that people have little or no ability to control their terrors and disturbances.

6. The idea that it is easier to avoid than to face life's difficulties and self-responsibilities.

7. The idea that one's past history is an all-important determiner of one's present behavior and that because something once strongly affected one's life, it should indefinitely affect it.

Assuming that the client, in creating his own disturbance, dogmatically adheres to one or more of these irrational ideas, the rational-emotive therapist incisively inspects his feelings and responses and looks for the specific notions with which he is indoctrinating himself to create his disordered Consequences. He then shows the client how each and every one of his dysfunctional emotions or acts is preceded by such an unscientifically held and empirically unvalidatable hypothesis, and how this unwarranted premise will inevitably cause his ineffective behavior.

Another way of stating this is to say that the therapist shows the client that whenever he becomes emotionally upset, he is invariably devoutly believing in some magical, unverifiable hypothesis; namely, that something is *awful*; that it *shouldn't* exist; and that in order to be in the least happy he *has to* have it changed. There is no way of his ever validating (or invalidating) these mystical hypotheses; since *awfulness* is an indefinable term with surplus meaning (as opposed to *inconvenience* or *misfortune*, which can be defined in terms of empirical referents); since there are no absolute *shoulds* or *shouldn'ts* in the universe (though there are many desirables and *undesirables*); and since the only real reason one *has* to have anything in order to be in the least happy is because one *thinks* one has to have it.

A disturbed human response stems from the individual's illogically and irrationally escalating a desideratum into a necessity; from his hypothesizing that something is sacred rather than desirable; from his deifying or devilifying some aspect of himself, of others, or of the universe around him; from his departing from empirical reality and the logico-deductive method of scientific thinking and resorting to absolutistic, magical, dogmatic, entirely unprovable assumptions to which he then rigidly and uncritically holds. Rational-emotive theory and practice holds that if the individual, instead, stayed rigorously, in his thinking about himself and the universe, with the scientific method, he would probably never have any emotional problems, though he would certainly have many reality problems. Or, stated differently, he would have life problems; but he would not have problems about *having* problems, but would interestedly and absorbedly tackle the issues of today and tomorrow, and usually enjoy this kind of problem solving.

The therapist actively tries to show the client that he tends to have the same self-denigrating philosophy in many aspects of his life—such as in his vocational, social, and sports performances. He is helped to see that he *generally* catastrophizes about the possibility of his failing; and that, if he is to lose his symptom of sexual impotence and also to reduce his basic anxiety-creating proclivities, he'd better change his whole philosophy of life by seeing that *no* failure is truly awful and that he can *never* be a totally worthless individual, no matter how many times he fails.

By inducing the client to generalize to the philosophic source of his present and future symptoms, RET becomes a holistic kind of psychotherapy that helps him to become minimally anxious and hostile in virtually *all* respects. It is, moreover, one of the most humanistic methods of emotional education ever created, since it essentially teaches people to accept themselves and others as inevitably fallible *humans*, and not to expect, in any way whatever, that they or any other person will be perfect, nonerrant, and *super*human. When I expect myself to be superhuman, I become anxious and depressed; when I expect you to be, I become hostile; when I expect the world to be superperfect, I become self-pitying and rebelliously inert. If I am truly human, and expect nothing but humanness from others, I shall practically never upset myself about anything.

The generalized, holistic, humanistic aspect of RET is also prophylactic—for therapies that concentrate on symptom removal are limited because (*a*) the client's symptoms may gradually or suddenly return some time after his treatment ends, and because (*b*) even if his particular symptom does not recur (as Joseph Wolpe claims that it usually does not in deconditioning therapy), it is likely that some other symptom, sometimes of a different order, will erupt later. Thus, an individual who is now relieved of his fear of riding in automobiles may subsequently become afraid of planes, new cities, meeting strangers, failing on his job, and a host of other things.

In successful RET, however, the client essentially learns that *noth-*

ing is truly awful, terrible, or horrible; that he can *never* be rated as worthless (nor as being great); and that *no* human can legitimately be condemned for anything he does. Consequently, the "cured" RET client is not likely to experience a recurrence of his old symptoms or an outbreak of new ones that is so common among other "cured" individuals. Moreover, since he learns a scientific method of dealing with personal problems that he can use for the rest of his days, he will tend, if he keeps applying this method, to become still healthier and to experience more personality growth after he leaves therapy. This is not to say that relapses never occur with clients who are significantly helped by RET. But its basic goal is to help people not merely with their symptoms but with all possible emotional malfunctionings they may experience now or later—and to help them by showing them how they can radically alter their fundamental philosophies of life—which *are* their symptom-creating mechanisms.

Is RET an insight-producing form of therapy? Yes, it is; and on a level that goes deeper, I believe, than that of the usual dynamic psychotherapies. Where these techniques help the client to gain insight into the presumed antecedent causes of his behavior, and often induce him—wrongly!—to focus on the origins of these causes (if, indeed, these can ever truly be known), RET helps him gain three important kinds of insights:

Insight No. 1 consists of the client's seeing that his present dysfunctional behavior not only has antecedent causes in the past but that these causes *still* exist and are *presently* observable. Insight No. 2 consists of the client's acknowledging that the main reason why his early tendencies to disturb himself continue to exist is because he is now *actively* instrumental in perpetuating them. Insight No. 3 consists of the client's acknowledging that there probably is no other way for him to get better but by *his* continually observing, questioning, and challenging his own belief system, and by *his* working and practicing to change his own irrational beliefs by verbal and by motor counterconditioning activity.

The three main insights derived through RET, then, involve the client's seeing that he had better *act* against as well as *understand* the philosophic causes of his disordered behavior. Whereas most psychotherapies, including psychoanalysis and other "depth-centered" methods, give the client what has been wrongly called "intellectual insight" into his problems (or what might more accurately be called his knowledge that he is acting badly and his *wish* to correct his behavior), RET, when it is successful, gives him so-called "emotional insight": meaning, his determination to *work hard* at using his "intellectual insight," so that he finally and forcibly changes—that is, reconditions himself in regard to—that behavior.

Are transference relationships importantly employed in rational-emotive therapy? Not usually—at least not in the sense that transference is generally analyzed in psychoanalytic therapy. The rational therapist is sometimes supportive when a client is exceptionally self downing; and he frequently serves as a good model for the client, in that he tries to follow a sane philosophy of life and to remain minimally anxious and hostile himself, no matter what transpires during the therapy sessions. He also may show the client that if he is in dire need of the therapist's approval, he also probably needs (or *thinks* he needs) others' acceptance; and if he is exceptionally demanding of and hostile toward the therapist, he probably makes the same childish demands of others in his outside life. The therapist thereby uses some of the experiences of the therapeutic relationship to help the client in his regular existence.

But the rational-emotive therapist does not believe that all the client's significant emotions are unconscious transfers from his early attitudes toward his parents; nor that everything he does during the session is indubitably a function of this kind of transference. He does not encourage the establishment of a transference neurosis, and he frequently sees a client for a good many sessions, with few intense transference reactions developing. This is because the rational therapist talks sanely and directively to the client, does not encourage undirected fantasies and free associations, and does not use the sessions mainly for existential encounters (which he might well enter into with his personal friends but which he deems largely inappropriate with a highly disturbed individual who has come to him for help). RET, moreover, is usually done in face-to-face settings, and in as efficient and rapid-fire manner as the client can handle, so that intense emotional relationships between therapist and client are less likely to occur than they are to arise in many other kinds of therapy.

When transference reactions do occur in RET, the therapist quickly shows the client not only that he is acting today as he tended to act years ago, but that he still has the same irrational beliefs which caused him to act that way in the past. Hence, the client is to do something about changing, instead of merely acknowledging, these beliefs. Thus, a client who hates the therapist because he confuses him with his authoritarian father, whom he may have (consciously or unconsciously) abhorred when he was a child, is shown that (a) his original hatred for his father was inappropriate, even if the latter had acted tyrannically, because although it was proper for the client to violently dislike his father's *behavior,* it was irrational for him to conclude that his progenitor was *condemnable as a person* for displaying this behavior; that (b) all hostile reactions are the result of illogical and moralistic thinking; that (c) he does not *have* to condemn anyone, such as his father, for acting the way he does; and that (d) he is foolishly seeing the therapist *as* his father, when the two are obviously discrete individuals. In RET, in other words, not only transference reactions but their philosophic causes are brought to light, and the latter are vigorously attacked, until the client changes them for more tenable attitudes toward past and present significant others.

How about unconscious material, is this used in rational-emotive therapy? It very definitely is! Although there is little evidence that most human motivations are deeply unconscious, in that they were once conscious and were then repressed by the individual who could not face them, nevertheless many ideas which people tell themselves to create their disturbed reactions are preconscious, or just below the level of consciousness.

Are the client's defenses and resistances revealed and analyzed in RET? Yes, they are revealed—but they are attacked and uprooted, rather than merely "analyzed." He is shown that he rationalizes, denies, projects, represses, or uses other kinds of defenses. But he is also shown what irrational ideas he is convincing himself of in order to create this kind of defensiveness, and how he can go about changing these ideas.

Is RET necessarily a short-term form of treatment? No, not necessarily. Usually, it takes from one to twenty sessions of individual and/or twenty to eighty sessions of group therapy. Consequently, many clients are seen for relatively brief periods of time. Ideally, however, clients are to be seen for a total period of about two years, during which time they will have about twenty individual and about seventy-five group sessions—which is considerably less therapeutic time than is spent in psychoanalytic therapy. Some rational-emotive therapists, however, such as Maxim F. Young, are able to achieve unusually good results with exceptionally disturbed individuals whom they see from ten to twenty sessions.

AN ILLUSTRATIVE CASE OF
RATIONAL-EMOTIVE THERAPY

To show how RET works with a somewhat typical client, let me outline treatment procedures that were employed with Rhoda S., a thirty-five-year-old physician who came to therapy because she was unable to form any lasting attachments with males, although she said she was eager to be married. Previous to rational therapy, she had been in psychoanalytic treatment for four and a half years, had made little progress in her emotional relationships, and had mainly been told that she was overly attached to her father, sought out males who resembled him, was afraid of having incestuouslike affairs with them, and was really a latent lesbian. Although she largely accepted these interpretations and had a warm relationship with her male analyst, she was still completely frigid with her boyfriends and frantically ran from them when her attachments seemed to be becoming fairly intense.

It was necessary first to work with Rhoda on her specific problem of frigidity. She seemed to have no interest in having sex with females, but she was terribly overanxious about succeeding with males. She kept indoctrinating herself with the ideas—which she had largely acquired from her college roommates—that (a) it was intolerably frustrating when she failed to reach an orgasm, and that (b) there was something horribly wrong and shameful about *her* and her "femininity" when she did not climax.

During the first RET session, the dialogue went partially as follows:

T: Granted that it is frustrating when you come close to, but do not quite achieve, orgasm, why is there something intrinsically *wrong* with you for not achieving it?

C: Because it *is* wrong—there is something malfunctioning about my sexual mechanism, and it is foolish and unrealistic of me not to acknowledge this.

T: True. There is something wrong with one of the ways, the sexual way, that you *function*. But you are implying, much more holistically, that there is something essentially wrong with *you*. As you know, being a physician, it is possible for you to have a malfunctioning limb or internal organ and not be *generally* ailing. Why, then, could you not be sexually inefficient and not be entirely dysfunctional?

C: I guess you're right. I could be. But I still *feel* that there's something essentially wrong with *me* if I never come to orgasm. How come?

T: Well, first of all, you're doing the usual human thing of confusing the whole of you with the part that is not working too well. That is, you are overgeneralizing. But more importantly, perhaps, your overgeneralizing is aided by another confusion; namely, the idea that if you, as a whole, were behaving poorly, and if you were responsible for this behavior—because you theoretically had some choice in the matter and were not exerting it for your own good—you would also be reprehensible for being responsible.

C: *Wouldn't* I be? If I *could* achieve sexual fulfillment by, say, really working hard to achieve it, and if I were just lazy or lax in this respect and therefore did not achieve what I could, wouldn't I then be reprehensible?

T: No, of course not. You would be self-defeating and foolish. But you would hardly be a sinner or a blackguard for *being* foolish. You would be a human being with failings. But that would not make you, except by arbitrary, moralistic definition, a Failure, with a capital F, who *deserves* to keep defeating herself, and who could not possibly act in any nondefeating way in the future.

C: But *wouldn't* I deserve to keep failing if I didn't lift a finger to help myself succeed?

T: Yes, in the objective sense that not lifting a finger to succeed would normally cause you to reap the consequences of your inertia; namely, repeated failure. But not in the sense that the universe is so justly ordered that anyone who evades work *must* keep failing and *ought to* be punished by the powers-that-be for his iniquity.

C: You mean that, statistically speaking, there is a high probability that I would keep failing to achieve orgasm if I didn't try various methods of attaining it, but that nonstatistically and absolutistically there is no reason why I *have* to keep failing because some fate or God ordains that I must?

T: Yes, that's exactly what I mean. Realistically, the chances are high that you will fail, sexually or any other way, if you don't work and practice to succeed. But there is no necessity that you will. And, of course, we know that many of the women who hardly try at all to reach orgasm easily do so, while many other women who, like you, frantically try to do often never achieve it. So there is no one correlation between trying and succeeding, though there is a correlation significantly above chance between these two variables. We are pretty sure, moreover, that there is no godly fate or presence looking over your (and others') conduct and making sure that the good workers get rewarded and the goofers do not. You may invent such a fate or presence in your head, but that does not prove its objective existence.

C: So even if I don't succeed at achieving an orgasm, you seem to be saying that I deserve to gain any happiness in life that I can obtain, and that I don't have to punish myself.

T: Right! It would be far wiser if you worked, unfrantically and unfrenetically, to achieve sexual fulfillment. But even if you don't, and you therefore never achieve it, you are not a worthless individual—only a bright girl who is acting, in this respect, idiotically. And if you see this, and *don't* condemn yourself as a person for acting in this manner, there then is a good chance that you will correct your future behavior, will focus properly on enjoying sex (instead of only proving what a great partner you can be), and will in fact enjoy it. If you never do, that's too bad—but not catastrophic, and not self-demeaning.

C: You imply that I will actually succeed at sex if I don't condemn myself for not succeeding.

T: Yes, the chances are you will. Maybe you won't, but you certainly will give yourself a higher probability of doing so. For when you focus on "What a louse I am for not trying properly to succeed!" you become as unsexual or antisexual as you can become. While if you forget this nonsense, and concertedly focus on sex, on the possibility of your enjoying it, and on the best methods you can devise to increase that possibility, sooner or later you will probably succeed.

This is what actually happened. I induced Dr. S. to focus on sex enjoyment instead of her own worthlessness, and she soon began to get closer to orgasm and within a few weeks reached it for the first time in her life. At first, she had to use somewhat bizarre, masochistic fantasies to bring on climax during intercourse; but after some further experience and practice, she was able to concentrate on her lover and on her own sensations and fairly easily come to climax.

We then tackled her wider emotional problems with males. We soon determined that she was not getting deeply involved because she still felt traumatized by being rejected by her fiancé a decade prior to her therapy sessions. He had seemed to care for her greatly, but became more and more anxious as their wedding day approached. He went into something of a panic a few days before the ceremony was to take place and went to see a psychiatrist, who advised him not to marry anyone while he was so indecisive. She felt completely crushed by his agreeing to go along with the psychiatrist—with whose views she completely disagreed—and they never saw each other again. Since that time, she remained so afraid to get involved with anyone who might possibly reject her under similar circumstances, or who might even marry her and then withdraw from her emotionally, that she kept having a number of sex friendships but no deep emotional involvements with men.

During the sixth therapy session, this dialogue ensued:

T: What are you really afraid of in regard to marrying?

C: Of rejection, it would seem. Of being left alone once again, after I had built up high hopes of remaining together with a man forever, as I did with my ex-fiancé.

T: That's a surface explanation that really doesn't explain anything. First of all, you are constantly getting rejected, the way you are going on now, because you pick men who aren't marriageable or whom you refuse to wed. Therefore, your hopes of a prolonged, intense involvement are perpetually being dashed—rejected. Secondly, you are really rejecting yourself, all the time. For you are assuming that if you did get refused by some man, just as you once did, you couldn't possibly stand it—weakling that you are! This is a complete vote of nonconfidence in yourself. *You* are therefore truly refusing to accept yourself as you are. *You* are demanding that you be perfectly safe.

C: But isn't it better to be safe than hurt?

T: You mean, isn't it better to have never loved and never lost?

C: O.K. But if losing is so dreadful, *isn't* that better?

T: But why should losing be so dreadful?

C: Oh, loneliness. Not ever getting what you want.

T: But aren't you lonely *this* way? And do you *now* get what you want?

C: No, I don't. But I also don't get what I very much *don't* want.

T: Partly. But not as much as you think.

C: What do you mean?

T: I first of all mean what you mean: that you do not like to get rejected—and who the hell does?—and that you are avoiding this dislikable event by not trying to get accepted. But I mean, secondly, that what you really dislike most about being rejected is not the refusal itself—since that merely gets you what you have when you do not try for acceptance: namely, being alone—but the belief that *this* kind of loneliness makes you a slob, a worthless person.

C: Oh, but I *do* dislike, and dislike very much, the refusal itself. I *hate* to be refused and then have to be by myself.

T: Partly. But suppose you won one of the males you desired and he died, and you lost him *that* way. Would that make you feel as badly as if you won him, he were still alive, and he *then* rejected you?

C: No, I guess it wouldn't.

T: Ah! You see what I'm getting at?

C: That it's not really the loss of the man that I'm concerned about, but his rejection of me.

T: Exactly! It's not the loss of him—but the loss of *you*. *That's* what you're really worried about. If you lose a man by his dying or going away or something like that, you don't like it: for then you're not getting what you want and you feel frustrated. But even if you lose a man by his being available, but his still rejecting you, then you're not only frustrated, but you wrongly conclude that if he rejects you, you must reject yourself. That is to say—you lose yourself as well as him. At least, that's the way you set things up in your mind—that's *your* conclusion, *your* hangup. And what you call "loneliness" is not merely your being alone (which I will grant is annoying and bothersome) but your being alone plus your falsely believing that you're no good for being in that state.

C: Looks like, in this area, I'm doing much the same thing as I did in the sex area. I'm condemning myself for not succeeding; that makes things much worse than my merely not succeeding.

T: Right again! Just as you caused yourself, in large measure, to fail sexually, because you were overly concerned with succeeding, and therefore focused on *how* you were doing instead of the pleasure of *what* you were doing, you are causing yourself to feel terribly rejected by defining yourself as a worthless individual in case you fail in your emotional relations. In fact, not only do you cause the *feeling* of rejection in this manner, but you also often may bring on the rejection itself. For if a man whom you find desirable finds that you are terribly anxious about your winning his approval, he may look upon you as being too crazy for him to become deeply involved with, and he may therefore leave you.

C: I'm afraid that that's just what does happen in many instances. The men, the good ones I mean, seem to be impressed with me at first. But then they seem to view me differently, and to lose interest.

T: Yes. Probably because *you* view yourself so differently. At first, you are intent on them and their traits, since you are interested in finding what you consider to be a good man. But as soon as you find what you think you are looking for, you then focus on yourself: on how many failings you have, on what a phoney you really are, on how he's sure to find you out soon. You then become so anxious, and so little concentrated on him, that he sees that something is wrong, and finally rejects you. Then, of course, you take that rejection as "proof" that you really *are* no good—when, actually, it is only proof that you *think* you are and that rejections occur more frequently when you view yourself in this negative manner. And the vicious circle completes itself.

C: You seem to be describing my case with deadly accuracy. But what can I do about it?

T: Isn't it obvious? Your basic symptom is emotional inadequacy—just as, a few weeks ago, it was sexual inadequacy. Your fundamental *problem,* however, is fear of rejection—just as it was fear of failure. Now, what did you do about that fear that you can do again about this one?

C: I guess I saw, mainly, that it was *not* terrible, although it was still highly undesirable, if I failed at sex. And I focused on doing my best to enjoy it, instead of severely criticizing myself in case I didn't succeed at it.

T: Right! Now, why can't you do the same kind of thing in regard to having deeper emotional relations with men?

C: You mean, concentrating on enjoying my relations with them, instead of knocking myself down if one of them, one of the good ones, that is, rejects me?

T: Yes. And—as you said a moment ago in regard to the sex failure—convincing yourself that it is highly undesirable, but *not* terrible, if you do get rejected. Convincing yourself, in other words, that you will clearly be deprived, but never be a *worm*, if one of the good men you choose indicates that he is not choosing you in return.

C: It's really the same thing, then, that I did before. Only bigger and harder!

T: Yes, bigger and harder—but still the same basic thing, and still far from impossible to do. Why don't you try it and see?

Again, Dr. S. did try to work on her problem of defining herself as worthless in case she was rejected by a desirable male. She had more trouble doing this than she had had with the problem of sexual frigidity—particularly because she could not too easily find suitable males with whom to test herself. Within the next eight months, however, she did find two fairly good candidates, and she boldly threw herself first into an intense relationship with one of them and then with the second when the first did not work out. Although neither of these relationships led to marriage, and one was an out-and-out rejection by the man with whom she was involved, while the other was a keen disappointment because she chose the wrong sort of person, she for once refused to castigate herself for her failures and managed to have strong feelings of love for both these men. As a result of these experiences, she was looking forward hopefully, when she left therapy after twenty-nine sessions, to a more successful love relationship in the future. About three years later she did marry and has, to my knowledge, been devoted to her husband and her work ever since.

LIMITATIONS OF RATIONAL-EMOTIVE THERAPY

All psychotherapy, including RET, has its definite limitations. Human beings are practically never completely uncondemning and tolerant. Even when they are helped significantly by a psychotherapeutic process, they tend to slip back to some degree into their old patterns of undisciplined and overemotional behavior. To remain even reasonably rational and not self-defeating, they have to work hard and long, and they frequently fail to continue to do this. Some of them—such as those who have serious mental deficiencies or exceptionally psychotic behaviors—do not seem to have the capacity to help themselves much. And though most of them do have considerable self-actualizing and regenerative capacities, as Abraham Maslow and Carl Rogers have shown, there is no guarantee that, even with the most effective forms of psychotherapy, they will permanently utilize their own abilities to grow and experience.

RET is unusually effective with clients who acknowledge that they have emotional problems and who are willing to work at understanding and changing their thinking and behavior. It often is useful with individuals with moderate to severe disturbance, with those afflicted with frigidity and impotence, with people with marital problems, and with those with vocational difficulties. Others—particularly those who will not face their problems or who refuse to work at therapy, such as individuals with character disorders and overt psychotic reactions—can be treated with RET, and often considerably helped; but the rates of significant improvement are lower with these individuals than with more willing clients. Like most other psychotherapies, RET is more effective with younger and brighter clients; but it also has been used with good results with those who are mentally retarded, with people over sixty, with those from lower-income brackets, with alcoholics and drug addicts, and with others with whom most forms of psychotherapy show poor rates of improvement.

While originally designed for use with adults, RET has been successfully applied with children. At The Living School, a private school for normal children operated by The Institute for Advanced Study in Rational Psychotherapy, the principles of RET are taught, by a variety of academic and other procedures, to grade-school children, in an effort to prevent them from picking up many of the emotional disturbances which children in our society often acquire.

Usually, RET gets best results when employed by a vigorous, active-directive, outgoing therapist who himself is willing to take risks and to be little concerned about winning his clients' approval. It can, however, be successfully applied by less outgoing therapists, as long as they are sufficiently active to keep challenging and questioning their clients' irrational ideas and as long as they persist at teaching these clients a more scientific method of looking at themselves and the world and of working against their own self-indoctrinations. A bright and well-motivated therapist (including a paraprofessional) can learn the fundamentals of RET in a relatively short time and can begin to practice it, on both himself and others, shortly after he becomes acquainted with its fundamental principles. Even disturbed clients who are undergoing RET can frequently help their friends and relatives by using some of its aspects with these others. RET can also be used to a considerable degree through the employment of bibliotherapy materials, written communications, tape recordings, and programmed materials, in addition to its regular uses in individual and group therapy sessions.

Eventually, behavioral scientists will test, with a large series of randomly selected clients, the efficacy of various other types of therapy: psychoanalytic, client-centered, existential, rational-emotive, and others. Until that time, it seems justifiable to reiterate what was stated as the original two hypotheses in my first major talk, in 1957, on rational psychotherapy, "(a) That psychotherapy which includes a high dosage of rational analysis and reconstruction . . . will prove to be more effective with more types of clients than any of the nonrational or semirational therapies now being widely employed; and (b) That a considerable amount of—or, at least, proportion of—rational psychotherapy will prove to be virtually the only type of treatment that helps to undermine the basic neuroses (as distinguished from the superficial neurotic symptoms) of many clients, and particularly of many with whom other types of therapy have already been shown to be ineffective."

NOTES

[1] Thus, Adler (1927); Beck (1967); Berne (1964); Dorsey (1965); Frankl (1955); Ginott (1965, 1969); Glasser (1965); Haley (1963); Kelly (1955); Lazarus (1971); Lecky (1943); Phillips (1956); Rotter (1964); Satir (1967); Stekel (1950); Stieper and Wiener (1965); and Thorne (1950) have all developed theories and practices of psychotherapy overlapping with RET.

[2] These studies include those by Beck and his associates (1959, 1967, 1970); Becker *et al.* (1960, 1963); Breznitz (1967); Carlson

et al. (1969); Davies (1970); Davison (1967, 1968); Deane (1966); Fritz and Marks (1954); Garfield *et al.* (1967*a*); Geer *et al.* (1971); Glass *et al.* (1969); Jones (1968); Jordan and Kempler (1970); Lang *et al.* (1967); Nisbett and Schacter (1966); Rimm and Litvak (1969); Schacter and Singer (1962); Taft (1965); Valins (1966); Valins and Ray (1967); Velten (1968); and Zingle (1965).

[3] Successful studies in this respect have been done by Baker (1966); Burkhead (1970); Coons and McEachern (1967); di Loreto (1969); Gewirtz and Baer (1958); Gliedman *et al.* (1958); Gustav (1968); Hartman (1968); Kamiya (1968); Karst and Trexler (1970); Krippner (1964); Maultsby (1970*b*); Nuthmann (1957); O'Connell and Hanson (1970); Shapiro *et al.* (1959, 1962); Sharma (1970); and Steffy *et al.* (1970). Research studies that clearly support the efficacy of the type of *in vivo* desensitization, or homework assignments, which are constantly employed in rational-emotive therapy have also been consistently appearing in the literature, including those by Garfield *et al.* (1967*b*); Litvak (1969*a*, 1969*b*); Ritter (1968); and Zajonc (1968).

[4] Thus, successful reports of rational-emotive treatment have been published by Ard (1967, 1968, 1969); Callahan (1967); Diamond (1967*a*); Geis (1969); Glicken (1966, 1968); Greenberg (1969); Grossack (1965*a*); Gullo (1966*a*, 1966*b*); Harper (1960); Hauck (1966, 1967*b*, 1968); Lafferty (1965); Lazarus (1971); Maultsby (1968, 1970*b*); Sherman (1967); Wagner (1966); and Weston (1964, 1970), as well as in several of my own writings.

4

THE A-B-C's OF RATIONAL-EMOTIVE THERAPY

Rational-emotive psychotherapy is a comprehensive approach to psychological treatment and to education that not only employs emotive and behavioristic methods but also significantly stresses and undermines the cognitive element in self-defeating behavior. Humans are exceptionally complex, so that there is no simple way in which they become "emotionally disturbed," and no single manner in which they can be helped to overcome their disturbances. Their psychological problems arise from their misperceptions and mistaken cognitions about what they perceive; from their emotional underreactions or overreactions to normal and to unusual stimuli; and from their habitually dysfunctional behavior patterns, which encourage them to keep repeating nonadjustive responses even when they know they are behaving poorly. Consequently, a three-way, rational-emotive-behavioristic approach to their problems is desirable; and rational-emotive therapy provides this multifaceted attack.

Primarily, RET employs a highly active cognitive approach. It is based on the assumption that what we label our "emotional" reactions are mainly caused by our conscious and unconscious evaluations, interpretations, and philosophies. Thus, we feel anxious or depressed because we strongly convince ourselves that it is not only unfortunate and inconvenient but that *it is terrible and catastrophic* when we fail at a major task or are rejected by a significant person. And we feel hostile because we vigorously believe that people who behave unfairly not only *would better not* but *absolutely should not* act the way they indubitably do and that it is *utterly insufferable* when they frustrate us.

Like stoicism, a school of philosophy which originated some twenty-five hundred years ago, RET holds that there are virtually no legitimate reasons for people to make themselves terribly upset, hysterical, or emotionally disturbed, no matter what kind of psychological or verbal stimuli are impinging on them. It encourages them to feel strong *appropriate* emotions—such as sorrow, regret, displeasure, annoyance, rebellion, and determination to change unpleasant social conditions. But it holds that when they experience certain self-defeating and *inappropriate* emotions—such as guilt, depression, rage, or feelings of worthlessness—they are adding an unverifiable, magical hypothesis (that things *ought* or *must* be different) to their empirically based view (that certain things and acts are reprehensible or inefficient and that something *would better* be done about changing them).

Because the rational-emotive therapist has a highly structured and workable theory, he can almost always see the few central irrational philosophies which a client is vehemently propounding to himself and through which he is foolishly upsetting himself. He can show the client how these cause his problems and his symptoms; can demonstrate exactly how the client can forthrightly question and challenge these ideas; and can often induce him to work to uproot them and to replace them with scientifically testable hypotheses about himself and the world which are not likely to get him into future emotional difficulties.

The cognitive part of the theory and practice of RET may be briefly stated in A-B-C form as follows:

At point A there is an ACTIVITY, ACTION, or AGENT that the individual becomes disturbed about. Example: He goes for an important job interview; or he has a fight with his mate, who unfairly screams at him.

At point rB the individual has a RATIONAL BELIEF (or a REASONABLE BELIEF or a REALISTIC BELIEF) about the ACTIVITY, ACTION, or AGENT that occurs at point A. Example: He believes, ''It would be unfortunate if I were rejected at the job interview.'' Or, ''How annoying it is to have my mate unfairly scream at me!''

At point iB the individual has an IRRATIONAL BELIEF (or an INAPPROPRIATE BELIEF) about the ACTIVITY, ACTION, or AGENT that occurs at point A. Example: He believes, ''It would be catastrophic if I were rejected at the job interview.'' Or, ''My mate is a horrible person for screaming at me!''

Point rB, the RATIONAL BELIEF, can be supported by empirical data and is appropriate to the reality that is occurring, or that may occur, at point A. For it normally *is* unfortunate if the individual is rejected at an interview for an important job; and it *is* annoying if his mate unfairly screams at him. It would hardly be rational or realistic if he thought; ''How great it will be if I am rejected at the job interview!'' Or: ''It is wonderful to have my mate scream at me! Her screaming shows what a lovely person she is!''

Point iB, the IRRATIONAL BELIEF, cannot be supported by any empirical evidence and is inappropriate to the reality that is occurring, or that may occur, at Point A. For it hardly would be truly catastrophic, but only (at worst) highly inconvenient, if the individual were rejected for an important job. It is unlikely that he would never get another job, that he would literally starve to death, or that he would have to be utterly miserable at any other job he could get. And his mate is not a horrible person for screaming at him; she is merely a person who behaves (at some times) horribly and who (at other times) has various unhorrible traits.

His iB's, or IRRATIONAL BELIEFS, moreover, state or imply a *should, ought,* or *must*—an absolutistic *demand* or *dictate* that the individual obtain what he wants; for, by believing that it is catastrophic if he is rejected for an important job, he explicitly or implicitly believes that he *should* or *must* be accepted at that interview. And by believing that his mate is a horrible person for screaming at him, he overtly or tacitly believes that she *ought* or *must* be nonscreaming. There is, of course, no law of the universe (except in his muddled head!) which says that he *should* do well at an important job interview, or that his mate *must* not scream at him.

At point rC the individual experiences or feels RATIONAL CONSEQUENCES or REASONABLE CONSEQUENCES of his rB's (RATIONAL BELIEFS). Thus, if he rigorously and discriminately believes, "It would be unfortunate if I were rejected at the job interview," he feels concerned and thoughtful about the interview; he plans in a determined manner how to succeed at it; and if by chance he fails to get the job he wants, he feels disappointed, displeased, sorrowful, and frustrated. His actions and his feelings are *appropriate* to the situation that is occurring or may occur at point A; and they tend to help him succeed in his goals or feel suitably regretful if he does not achieve these goals.

At point iC the individual experiences IRRATIONAL CONSEQUENCES or INAPPROPRIATE CONSEQUENCES of his iB's (IRRATIONAL BELIEFS). Thus, if he childishly and dictatorially believes, "It would be catastrophic if I were rejected at the job interview. I couldn't stand it! What a worm I would then prove to be! I *should* do well at this important interview!" he tends to feel anxious, self-hating, self-pitying, depressed, and enraged. He gets dysfunctional psychosomatic reactions, such as high blood pressure and ulcers. He becomes defensive, fails to see his own mistakes in this interview, and by rationalization blames his failure on external factors. He becomes preoccupied with how hopeless his situation is, and refuses to do much about changing it by going for other interviews. And he generally experiences what we call "disturbed," "neurotic," or "overreactive" symptoms. His actions and feelings at point iC are *inappropriate* to the situation that is occurring or may occur at point B, because they are based on magical demands regarding the way he and the universe presumably *ought to be*. And they tend to help him fail at his goals or feel horribly upset if he does not achieve them.

These are the A-B-C's of emotional disturbance or self-defeating attitudes and behavior, according to the RET theory. Therapeutically, these A-B-C's can be extended to D-E's, which constitute the cognitive core of the RET methodology.

At point D, the individual can be taught (or can teach himself) to DISPUTE his iB's (IRRATIONAL BELIEFS). Thus, he can ask himself, "*Why* is it catastrophic if I am rejected in this forthcoming job interview? How would such a rejection *destroy* me? Why couldn't I *stand* losing this particular job? Where is the evidence that I would be a *worm* if I were rejected? Why *should* I have to do well at this important interview?" If he persistently, vigorously DISPUTES (or *questions* and *challenges*) his own iB's (IRRATIONAL BELIEFS) which are creating his iC's (INAPPROPRIATE CONSEQUENCES), he will sooner or later come to see, in most instances, that they are unverifiable, unempirically based, and superstitious; and he will be able to change and reject them.

At point cE the individual is likely to obtain the COGNITIVE EFFECT of his DISPUTING his iB's (IRRATIONAL BELIEFS). Thus, if he asks himself, "Why is it catastrophic if I am rejected in this forthcoming job interview?" he will tend to answer: "It is not; it will merely be inconvenient." If he asks, "How would such a rejection destroy me?" he will reply, "It won't; it will only frustrate me." If he asks: "Why couldn't I stand losing this particular job?" he will tell himself: "I can! I won't like it; but I can gracefully lump it!" If he asks: "Where is the evidence that I would be a worm if I were rejected?" he will respond: "There isn't any! I will only feel like a worm if I *define myself as* and *think of myself as* a worm!" If he asks, "Why *should* I have to do well at this important interview?" he will tell himself: "There's no reason why I should *have* to do well. There are several reasons why *it would be nice. It would be very fortunate* if I succeeded at this job interview. But they never add up to: 'Therefore I must!' "

At point bE the individual will most likely obtain the BEHAVIORAL EFFECT of his DISPUTING his iB's (IRRATIONAL BELIEFS). Thus, he will tend to be much less anxious about his forthcoming job interview. He will become less self-hating, self-pitying, and enraged. He will reduce his psychosomatic reactions. He will be able to become less defensive. He will become less unconstructively preoccupied with the possibility or the actuality of his failing at the job interview and will more constructively devote himself to succeeding at it or taking other measures to improve his vocational condition if he fails at it. He will become significantly less "upset," "disturbed," "overreactive," or "neurotic."

On the cognitive level, then, rational-emotive therapy largely employs direct philosophic confrontation. The therapist actively demonstrates to the client how, every time he experiences a dysfunctional emotion or behavior or CONSEQUENCE, at point C, it only indirectly stems from some ACTIVITY or AGENT that may be occurring (or about to occur) in his life at point A, and it much more directly results from his interpretations, philosophies, attitudes, or BELIEFS, at point B. The therapist then teaches the client how to scientifically (empirically and logically) DISPUTE these beliefs, at point D, and to persist at this DISPUTING until he consistently comes up, at point E, with a set of sensible COGNITIVE EFFECTS, cE's, and appropriate BEHAVIORAL EFFECTS, bE's. When he has remained, for some period of time, at point E, the individual has a radically changed philosophic attitude toward himself, toward others, and toward the world, and he is thereafter much less likely to keep convincing himself of iB's (IRRATIONAL BELIEFS) and thereby creating iC's (INAPPROPRIATE CONSEQUENCES) or emotional disturbances.

In addition to its cognitive methods, RET has exceptionally important behavioristic techniques that it consistently uses. It especially uses activity homework assignments, which the therapist or the client's therapy group assign to him during various sessions, and later check to see whether he is doing them. Such assignments may consist of the client's being asked to initiate contacts with three new people during a week's period, to visit his nagging mother-in-law instead of trying to avoid her, or to make a list of his job-hunting assets and of several means of his looking for a better job. These assignments are given in order to help the client take risks, gain new experiences, interrupt his dysfunctional habituations, and change his philosophies regarding certain activities.[1]

A third major emphasis in RET is on emotive release. Thus, the rational-emotive therapist usually takes a no-nonsense-about-it direct confrontation approach to the client and his problems. He forces or persuades the client to express himself openly and to bring out his real feelings, no matter how painful it may at first be for him to do so. Frequently, he ruthlessly reveals and attacks the client's defenses—while simultaneously showing him how he can live without these defenses and how he can unconditionally accept himself whether or not others highly approve of him. The therapist does not hesitate to reveal his own feelings, to answer direct questions about himself, and to participate as an individual in rational marathon encounters. He does his best to give the client unconditional rather than conditional positive regard and to teach him the essence of rational-emotive philosophy; namely, that no human is to be condemned for anything, no matter how execrable his acts may be. His *deeds* may be measureable and heinous, but he is never to be rated or given a report card *as a person*. Because of the therapist's full acceptance of him as a human being, the client is able to express his feelings much more openly than in his everyday life and to accept *himself* even when he is acknowledging the inefficiency or immorality of some of his *acts*.

In many important ways, then, RET uses expressive-experiential methods and behavioral techniques. It is not, however, primarily interested in helping the client *feel* better, but in showing him how he can *get* better. In its approach to marathon group therapy, for example, RET allows the participants plenty of opportunity to encounter each other on a gut level, to force themselves to stay in the here and now, to face their own emotional and sensory reactions to themselves and to other members of the group, and to be ruthlessly honest with themselves and others. Instead, however, of beginning and ending on a purely basic encounter or sensitivity training level—and thereby risk opening up many people without showing them how to put themselves together again—the rational-oriented marathon also shows the participants exactly what they are telling themselves to create their negative feelings toward themselves and others. They are further told how they can change their internalized and uncritically accepted iB's (IRRATIONAL BELIEFS) so that ultimately they can feel and behave spontaneously in a less self-defeating manner and can actualize their potential for happy, nondefeating lives.

Basically, RET is an extension of the scientific method to human affairs. People, for biological as well as environmental reasons, tend to think superstitiously, unrealistically, and unscientifically about themselves and the world around them. In science, we teach them to set up hypotheses about external reality and then to vigorously question and challenge these hypotheses—to look for empirical evidence for and against them, before they are cavalierly accepted as truths. In rational-emotive therapy, the therapist teaches his client to question scientifically and to dispute all self-defeating hypotheses about himself and others. Thus, if he believes—as, alas, millions of people tend to believe—that he is a worthless person because he performs certain acts badly, he is not taught merely to ask: "What is truly bad about my acts? Where is the evidence that they are wrong or unethical?" More important, he is shown how to ask himself: "Granted that some of my acts may be mistaken, why am I a totally bad *person* for performing them? Where is the evidence that I must always (or mainly) be right in order to consider myself worthy? Assuming that it is *preferable* for me to act well or efficiently rather than badly or inefficiently, why do I *have* to do what is preferable?"

Similarly, when an individual perceives—and let us suppose that he correctly perceives—the erroneous and unjust acts of others, and when he makes himself (as he all too frequently does) enraged at these others and tries to hurt or annihilate them, he is taught by the rational-emotive therapist to stop and ask himself: "Why is my hypothesis true that these error-prone people are absolutely no good? Granted that *it would be better* if they acted more competently or fairly, why *should* they have to do what would be better? Where is the evidence that people who commit a number of mistaken or unethical acts are doomed to be forever wrong? Why, even if they persistently behave poorly, should they be totally damned, excommunicated, and consigned to some kind of hell?"

Rational-emotive therapy teaches the individual to generalize adequately but to watch his *over*generalizing; to discriminate his desires, wants, and preferences from his assumed needs, necessities, or dictates; to be less suggestible and more thinking; to be a long-range hedonist, who enjoys himself in the here and now *and* the future, rather than merely a short-range hedonist, who thinks mainly of immediate gratification; to feel the appropriate emotions of sorrow, regret, annoyance, and determination to change unpleasant aspects of his life, while minimizing the inappropriate emotions of worthlessness, self-pity, severe anxiety, and rage. RET, like the science of psychology itself and like the discipline of general semantics, as set forth by Alfred Korzybski, particularly teaches the client how to *discriminate* more clearly between sense and nonsense, fiction and reality, superstition and science. While using many behavioristic and teaching methods, it is far from being dogmatic and authoritarian. Rather, it is one of the most humanistically oriented kinds of therapy, in that it emphasizes that man can fully accept himself just because he is alive, just because he exists; that he does not have to prove his worth in any way; that he can have real happiness whether or not he performs well and whether or not he impresses others; that he is able to create his own meaningful purposes; and that he needs neither magic nor gods on whom to rely. The humanistic-existentialist approach to life is therefore as much a part of rational-emotive psychotherapy as is its rational, logical, and scientific methodology.

RET, like many other modern forms of psychotherapy, is backed by a good many years of clinical experience by the present author and various other rational-emotive therapists.[2] It is supported by several studies demonstrating its clinical effectiveness under controlled experimental conditions.[3]

Rational-emotive psychotherapy has a great many therapeutic applications, some of which are unavailable to various other modes of psychotherapy. For one thing, it is relevant and useful to a far wider range of client disabilities than are many other therapies. Robert Harper, Cecil H. Patterson, and others have shown that many techniques, such as classical psychoanalysis, can only be effectively employed with a relatively small number of clients and are actually contraindicated with other individuals (such as with schizophrenics). Rational-emotive therapy, however, can be employed with almost any type of person the therapist is likely to see, including those who are conventionally labeled as psychotic, borderline psychotic, psychopathic, and mentally retarded. This is not to say that equally good results are obtained when it is employed with these most difficult individuals as are obtained with less difficult neurotics. But the main principles of RET can be so simply and efficiently stated that even individuals with very serious problems, some of whom have not been reached by years of previous intensive therapy, can often find significant improvement through RET.

Prophylactically, rational-emotive principles can be used with many kinds of individuals, to help prevent them from eventually becoming emotionally disturbed. At a school for normal children operated on the principles of rationality, the pupils from the first grade onward are taught a rational-emotive philosophy by their regular teachers, in the course of classroom activities, recreational affairs, therapy groups, and other games and exercises. They are taught, for example, not to catastrophize when they do not achieve perfectly, not to enrage themselves against others when these others act badly, and not to demand that the world be nicer and easier than it usually is. As a result of this teaching, they seem to be becoming remarkably less anxious, depressed, self-hating, and hostile than other children of equivalent age.

Rational-emotive ideas also have application to politics, to problems of the generation gap, to the treatment and prevention of violence and murder, and to various other areas of life. Because it is deeply philosophic, because it realistically accepts individuals as they are and shows them how they can obtain their fuller potentials, and because it is not only oriented toward individuals with emotional disturbances but toward all types of people everywhere, RET is likely to be increasingly applied to the solution of many kinds of human problems.

Is RET really more effective than other forms of psychotherapy? The evidence is not in that will answer this question. Clinical findings would seem to indicate that it benefits more people than do most other methods; that it can obtain beneficial results in surprisingly short order in many instances; and that the level of improvement or cure that is effected through its use is more permanent and deep-seated than that obtained through other methods. But this clinical evidence has been haphazardly collected and is now being substantiated through controlled studies of therapeutic outcome. My hypothesis is that RET is a more effective procedure for clients and therapists because it is active-directive, it is comprehensive, it is unusually clear and precise, and it is hardheaded and down to earth.

More important, rational-emotive therapy is philosophically unambiguous, logical, and empirically oriented. This can be especially seen in its viewpoint on the most important of therapeutic problems: that of human worth. Nearly all systems of psychotherapy hold that the individual is worthwhile and can esteem himself because he discovers how to relate well to others and win the love he needs and/or learns how to perform adequately and to achieve his potentials for functioning. Thus, Sigmund Freud held that man solves his basic problems through work and love. Alfred Adler emphasized the necessity of his finding himself through social interest. Harry Stack Sullivan stressed his achieving adequate interpersonal relations. William Glasser insisted that he needs both love and achievement. Nathaniel Branden demanded competence and extreme rationality. Even Carl Rogers, who presumably emphasized unconditional positive regard, actually has held that the individual can truly accept himself only when someone else, such as a therapist, accepts him or loves him unconditionally; so that his self-concept is still dependent on some important element outside himself.

RET, on the contrary, seems to be almost the only major kind of psychotherapy (aside, perhaps, from Zen Buddhism, if this is conceptualized as psychotherapy and not exclusively as a philosophy) that holds that the individual does not need *any* trait, characteristic, achievement, purpose, or social approval in order to accept himself. In fact, he does not have to rate himself, esteem himself, or have any self-measurement or self-concept whatever.

It is not only undesirable but it is impossible for the individual to have a self-image, and it is enormously harmful if he attempts to construct one. Ego ratings depend on the summation of the ratings of the individual's separate traits (such as his competence, honesty, and talents, for example), and it is not legitimate to add and average these traits any more than it is legitimate to add apples and pears. Moreover, if one finally arrives, by some devious means, at a global rating of the individual (or of his "self"), one thereby invents a magical heaven (his "worth," his "value," his "goodness") or a mystical hell (his "worthlessness," his "valuelessness," his "badness"). This deification or devilification (note that this word is devil-ification, not de-vilification) of the individual is arrived at tautologically, by definition. It has no relation to objective reality; it is based on the false assumption that he *should* or *must* be a certain way and that the universe truly *cares* if he is not what he *ought* to be; it refuses to acknowledge the fact that all humans are, and probably always will be, incredibly *fallible*; and it almost always results in the self-rating individual's harshly condemning and punishing himself or defensively pretending that he is "worthy" and "good" in order to minimize his anxiety and self-deprecation. Finally, since self-ratings invariably involve ego games wherein the individual compares his self-esteem to that of others, they inevitably result in his deifying and damning other humans in addition to himself; and the feelings of intense anxiety and hostility that thereby occur constitute the very core of what we usually call "emotional disturbance."

Rational-emotive therapy, by solidly teaching the individual to avoid *any* kind of self-rating (and only, instead, to measure his characteristics and performances, so that he may help correct them and increase his enjoyment), gets to the deepest levels of personality change. It offers no panacea for the termination of human unhappiness, sorrow, frustration, and annoyance. But it importantly reveals, attacks, and radically uproots the major sources of needless self-defeating and socially destructive behavior.

NOTES

[1] Eysenck (1964); Pottash and Taylor (1967); and Lazarus (1971) have indicated that the RET homework assignments overlap significantly with some of the methods of behavior therapy. In any event, they are an integral and important part of RET.

[2] Among them, Ard (1966, 1967, 1968); Callahan (1967); Diamond (1967a, 1967b); Glicken (1966, 1968); Greenberg (1966); Grossack (1965a, 1965b); Gullo (1966a, 1966b); Hauck (1967a); Lazarus (1971); and Wagner (1963, 1966).

[3] These studies include those of Burkhead (1970); di Loreto (1969); Grossack, Armstrong, and Lussiev (1966); Karst and Trexler (1970); Krippner (1964); Lafferty *et al.* (1964); Maultsby (1970a, 1970b; Sharma (1970); and Zingle (1965).

Furthermore, RET has been empirically confirmed, in terms of some of its major theoretical hypotheses, by a great many experimental studies. These include the studies of Argabite and Nidorf (1968); Barber (1969); Berkowitz *et al.* (1969); Carlson *et al.* (1969); Conklin (1965); Cook and Harris (1937); Davies (1970); Geis (1969); Hartman (1968); Jones (1968); R. S. Lazarus (1966); Maultsby (1970b), Miller (1969); Mowrer (1964); Schacter (1964); Schacter and Singer (1962); Taft (1965); Valins (1966); and Velten (1968).

5

A COMPREHENSIVE APPROACH
TO PSYCHOTHERAPY

A proliferation of schools of psychotherapy has punctuated the American and, to an extent, the world scene during the years since the Second World War. They differ from one another in essential respects, yet have much in common. Most of the approaches reject classical psychoanalysis; many of them embrace, in one form or another, a technique that is called "active-directive." Among such active-directive methods, rational-emotive psychotherapy is the subject of increasing interest. My colleagues and I have practiced RET since the mid-fifties, and we acknowledge our indebtedness to many forerunners who used active-directive methodology, as, for example, Adler. In previous works, I have described and explained rational-emotive therapy. Now, drawing upon a wealth of experience of many coworkers and myself, I shall delve into many of the theoretical and practical aspects of this new psychology, showing its points of agreement and those of disagreement with other therapies, and where there is disagreement, developing the arguments that support the view here propounded.

One might start with a statement that RET is a *comprehensive* approach to therapy, in that it actually attacks the individual's problems from a cognitive, an emotive, and a behavioristic standpoint. Nevertheless, it is true that all leading systems of psychotherapy are somewhat comprehensive. Thus, the expressive-experiential-existential school of therapy includes a coniderable amount of cognitive and behavior methodology.[1] The practitioners of behavior therapy wittingly or unwittingly embrace many emotive and cognitive techniques.[2] And, as R. R. Pottash and J. E. Taylor have indicated, cognitive therapists include a good many aspects of behavioristic and emotive procedure in their individual and group therapy sessions.[3]

Rational-emotive psychotherapy is one of the few existing methods which not only openly and avowedly employs cognitive, emotive, and behavioristic approaches, but also does so on theoretical grounds. For it hypothesizes that human beings normally think, emote, and act in an interrelated and inevitably pluralistic manner, and that they do not get what are usually called *emotional reactions* unless they are simultaneously using their perceptual-cognitive and overt motor faculties. It particularly holds that what we term *emotional disturbances* are concomitants of their appraising or evaluative cognitions and of their habituated motorial responses. Consequently, rational-emotive therapy, in quite consciously and openly attempting to be a comprehensive system of psychotherapy, employs at least three major and interacting techniques.

Some of the cognitive, emotive, and behavioristic aspects of RET are illustrated in a typical case of a person who came for assistance. The client was a thirty-year-old male who was exceptionally shy, who had not been able to speak up in front of even a small group of people, who was entirely virginal because he lacked the courage to date and to make sexual overtures to girls, who thought that he might be basically homosexual, and who was making no progress in his would-be career as a novelist because he rarely sat himself down at his typewriter to do any actual writing. Five years prior to coming to see me he had suffered a so-called nervous breakdown and had been hospitalized in the psychiatric ward of a general hospital for one month; and he had then had nine months of psychoanalytically oriented psychotherapy, which had not been very helpful to him. He was referred to me by one of my former clients, who taught in the same school as he did, and who had had several heart-to-heart talks with him about his problems. This client was seen by me for a total of five individual sessions and forty-two group therapy sessions.

RET experiential-emotive techniques. The main experiential-emotive methods that I employed with this shy teacher were as follows:

1. I began with the client's feelings and active-directively probed and reflected until I got him to see that he mainly felt that he was an inadequate, worthless individual who was born defective and who could not possibly succeed at anything, including teaching, writing, and social-sexual relations with females. I also induced him to express his intense, though at first covered-up, hostility toward me, toward other members of his therapy group, and toward difficult and rejecting females. In group, he was directed to speak sharply to one of the females, about whom he previously had made only some indirect but caustic remarks, and to admit that he really hated her guts.

2. The members of his therapy group, with my participation, kept the client mainly in the here and now. Whenever he tended to go off on an extended narration of the dismal events of his past life, and to blame his parents and their overprotecting attitudes for his present state of inhibition, we said something like: "That's all very well, but it's quite irrelevant to the way you feel and act *today*. So you once felt that you had to give in to your parents' overprotecting ways. But you're a big boy now, and *you're* the one who's carrying on this state of inhibited feelings today. What are you feeling *right now*? Suppose, for example, you went out on a date with Judy, who's sitting next to you, and you thought she would possibly react favorably to a sexual pass. How would you feel about approaching her?''

3. Directly and forthrightly, I instructed the client to encounter others, to take emotional risks, and to do verbal or nonverbal exercises during the therapeutic sessions. On one occasion, I induced him to take the hand of a female member of his group and to try to talk her into kissing him. During his very first session of group therapy, I forced him to speak up about his basic problems, even though he was

most reluctant to do so and wanted to wait several more sessions, until he knew the members of the group better and felt safer with them. On another occasion, the group gave him the homework assignment of taking a promotion exam, which frightened him.

4. Often, I used dramatic techniques—such as role playing, story telling, humor, and strong language—to make therapeutic points with the client in an intense, forceful, emotive manner. Once, I deliberately forced him to interrogate another member of his therapy group who was not writing the plays he said he wanted to write, and got him to laugh uproariously at this other member's attempts to evade his questioning with flimsy excuses for his not actually writing. Other group members and I joined the laughter. In the course of this session, the client confessed that he had written three novels but was having trouble in getting agents or publishers to consider them. He seemed to come out of himself while talking to the other group members and confessing his own problems (some of them for the first time in group). But, at the next session, shamefacedly yet honestly, he confessed that he had made up in its entirety the story about finishing three novels himself; actually, he hadn't even been able, yet, to finish a single chapter of one novel, but only had done fragments of chapters. After this really honest confession, he was able, for the first time in his life, to do some concerted writing on a novel.

5. Sometimes I employed pleasure-giving methods with this client, to help him feel better, give him learning experiences, and to make him more receptive to the harder-hitting, work-oriented aspects of therapy. Thus, I got him to go to a masseuse for several massage treatments, to show him that he could enjoy a female's working on his body and could easily become sexually aroused by this procedure.

6. At times I emotively attacked the client's defense system, in order to shake him up. On one occasion, during an individual therapy session, I mimicked his evasive and namby-pamby manner with girls and had him hilariously laughing at himself. Subsequently, whenever he attempted to revert to this defensive position, he tended to remember my mimicking session and to challenge his own defensiveness and force himself to be more assertive with girls he dated.

7. I revealed many of my own authentic and personal feelings,

desires, and responses, to show him that I could empathize with his emotions and serve as a good model for him. Thus, I revealed that I myself had been very shy with girls up to my early twenties, and that I had to force myself to pick them up in public places and make overtures toward them. I also showed him, during group therapy sessions, that I was not afraid to open myself up, take chances in being attacked by other group members, and persist in doing whatever I felt like doing even though at times there were unpleasant consequences.

8. In spite of his poor performances, I consistently tried to give the client unconditional positive regard; to fully accept him with his failings, and to refrain from denigrating him as a person. I showed him on many occasions that although I deplored his *behavior,* I never held him in low esteem for displaying this behavior. Rather than despise him, I could always accept him as a human being, even when he did not accept himself.

RET behavioristic techniques. Some of the main behavior therapy methods employed with this inhibited client were the following:

1. I kept reinforcing his good or efficient changes during his time in therapy by verbally approving of them whenever he showed evidences of their occurring; and at the same time, I consistently helped extinguish his poor or inefficient reactions by showing him that they were unfortunate and that they would only produce self-defeating results. Whenever he made progress in asserting himself with a girl, I told him that that was very good (but not that *he* was therefore a good *person*); and whenever he fell back on passive behavior, I showed him that that was bad and that he could do better (but that this did not make him a bad person).

2. I used role-playing with him, both in individual and group therapy sessions, to stimulate someone's criticizing him severely, and to train him in stopping his supersensitive reactions to criticism. During one group session, I helped desensitize his catastrophizing about rejection by having three female members of his group successively reject him, tell him his method of approach was terrible, and severely berate him, while he tried to maintain his equilibrium. As a result of

this and other desensitizing experiences during therapy, he became much better able to handle rejection by girls.

3. The therapy group and I continually gave him activity homework assignments to carry out in the course of his real-life situations. These *in vivo* assignments constitute one of the most important aspects of rational-emotive therapy; virtually all clients treated with this method are given a number of such assignments. There was, for example, the task of taking the promotion exam. At the group's behest, he overcame his fears and did very well on the examination. In addition, he was at various times given writing assignments, such as that of finishing ten pages of a novel every week. He was also given a series of graduated homework assignments in regard to dating women: (*a*) making a date each week with at least one; (*b*) holding a woman's hand in the movies; (*c*) petting with one in a car; (*d*) trying to get a female's clothes off while petting; and (*e*) attempting to have intercourse. After eight weeks of assignments of this type, he was able to engage in coitus for the first time in his life. He then gave himself the additional assignment of spending an entire weekend with the same female, and was quickly able to carry it out successfully.

4. I taught the client David Premack's principle of reinforcement, or how to permit himself easy and immediately rewarding behaviors only after he had forced himself to perform more difficult and subsequently rewarding acts. For example, when he had difficulty studying for the promotion exam that his group induced him to take, I discovered that he greatly enjoyed going swimming almost every day in a pool that was near his residence; and I got him to allow himself to indulge in a half hour of swimming each day only on condition that he had previously spent at least two hours that day studying for the exam. Under these conditions, he was able to study persistently and to pass the examination.

5. I forced this client to keep practicing new behaviors, particularly in the course of group therapy, until he began automatically and enjoyably to experience them. Thus, I forced him to keep speaking up about his own and others' problems in the course of group sessions, even though at first he was reluctant to do so. After about ten group sessions of this kind of forced performances, he found natural enjoy-

ment in being an active group member, and became, in point of fact, one of the most frequent and spontaneous talkers in the group.

RET cognitive techniques. Although rational-emotive therapy employs many pronouncedly experiential-emotive and behavioristic methods, it is best known for its frankly cognitive techniques. Some cognitive approaches used with this shy client were these:

1. I actively showed the client that behind his emotional reactions and his ineffective overt behavior lay a strong self-perpetuating value system or set of irrational philosophic assumptions and that he largely created his own disordered emotions and actions by his vigorous, rigid beliefs in these assumptions. Thus, I showed him that his main premises were: (*a*) "If I make a serious error in public, as in speaking up inadequately before a group of people, I am a worthless individual and I will never be able to act adequately under similar circumstances." (*b*) "I should be able to be perfectly successful in any overtures I make toward women; and if I am so imperfect in this respect that any girl rejects me, that means that I am sexually inferior and that I shall never be able to succeed with a female." (*c*) "If I haven't succeeded with a woman during my first thirty years of life, I am most probably a homosexual who was born to fail with females." (*d*) "I have to be quickly one of the greatest novelists who ever lived and cannot risk writing a novel for fear that I will turn out to be a terrible bust in this respect." (*e*) "Almost any kind of risk taking will result in my experiencing awful trouble and pain, so I'd better not take any speaking, sexual, writing, or other risks; and in that way I will lead a happier existence."

2. I showed the client how and why his philosophic premises were illogical, inconsistent, and contradictory. I demonstrated how his making serious errors in speaking or in sex relations could hardly make him a totally worthless individual: that this conclusion was a *non sequitur.* I explained how his conclusion that he experienced horrible pain from risk taking and that therefore he had better not take risks consisted of circular thinking: His pain did not follow from the risk taking itself but from the definitional statement that he couldn't stand failing at risk-taking experiences; hence if he changed this

definition, this "pain" would no longer exist and would not "cause" him to avoid future risk taking. I showed him that if he gave up taking any speaking, sexual, writing or other risks he might, indeed, lead a safer but hardly a happier existence: since he would thereby make his life quite drab and boring, and he would then become frustrated for failure to achieve that which he feared attempting to achieve.

I also pointed out to this shy client how his philosophic hypotheses were supported by no empirical referents and how they were invariably nonvalid or nonvalidatable. Thus, there was *no evidence* that he was a worthless *individual* because his public speaking *performances* were inadequate; this is an essentially tautological, magical proposition. And there was no reason why he *should* or *must* be perfectly successful in his overtures toward women; though there might be several good reasons why *it would be better* if he were successful in this respect. These, again, are definitional, unempirically based statements, which could never really be proven or disproven factually.

3. I taught this client how to question and challenge, logically and empirically, his own self-defeating hypotheses about himself, about others, and about the world; and how to employ the scientific method in regard to himself and the solving of his own problems, just as a physical or social scientist would in the solving of problems external to the self. I taught him how to locate his own magical, tautological propositions—his *should, ought,* and *must* statements—and how to question and challenge them vigorously. I showed him how to ask (*a*) "*Why* am I a worthless individual if I speak up inadequately before a group of people?" (*b*) "*Who says* that I should be perfectly successful in any overture I make toward a woman?" (*c*) "*Where is the evidence* that if I haven't succeeded with a female during the first thirty years of my life, I am therefore probably a homosexual?" (*d*) "*Why is it necessary,* even though it may be desirable, that I be a first-rate novelist?" (*e*) "Why *must* I experience terrible trouble and pain if I try risk-taking experiences?" In this manner, I gradually taught the client the scientific method of thinking and experimenting, and how to apply this method to his own life.

4. I demonstrated why and how it was possible for the client to change significantly his thoughts, feelings, and performances, and thereby create in himself basic personality change. On one occasion, I taught him how to fantasy or imagine his actually being successful in his overtures toward a woman; and during the following week, partly as a result of this kind of imagery, he was able to go further in taking off her clothes than he had ever done before—a step on the road to his loss of virginity. On another occasion, I showed him that if he thought of failing sexually, he would easily lose an erection he had already achieved; while if he thought, ''What a great piece of ass this woman is,'' he could quickly achieve an erection when he didn't have one. In one of the group therapy sessions, several members of the group and I demonstrated to him that he was specifically convincing himself that it would be awful if he said the wrong thing in the group and that therefore he was saying nothing; and that when he stopped to convince himself that it would merely be inconvenient, but not in the least awful, if he said the wrong thing, he immediately lost most of his difficulty in speaking and actually began to enjoy speaking up.

5. The group members and I discussed important questions of philosophy, morals, and politics with the client and helped him clarify to himself (a) what some of his ethical views were; (b) what his purposes in living were; (c) what kinds of goals and vital absorbing interests he would like to set for himself; and (d) what kind of a world he would prefer to live in. During one session, he revealed that he didn't want to get involved with a woman for fear that he would later reject her and thereby gravely hurt her. But the group showed him that as long as he was honest with her, it was perfectly ethical for him to reject her after first caring for her, just as it would be ethical for her to reject him, since no one could promise to love anyone else forever. As for his hurting this female terribly, the group showed him how: (a) people are continually getting deprived or frustrated in love affairs, but that's their moral prerogative: to risk frustration in order to achieve possible fulfillment; and (b) he could certainly deprive her of satisfaction by first loving and then rejecting her, but if she became terribly upset or hurt in the process, this would not be the result of his

frustrating her but of the nonsense she told herself about how horrible, how catastrophic it was for her to be frustrated; and she, therefore, would really be unduly and foolishly hurting herself.

On another occasion, I showed this client that he was terribly afraid that he was homosexual not because being homosexual would be unfortunate—which it might well be in his case—but because he erroneously was viewing it as a great moral sin. I convinced him that fixed homosexuals were not depraved or rotten; that at worst they were emotionally disturbed individuals; and that he would hardly be an enormous sinner if he ever did become homosexual. Immediately after the session during which we had this discussion, the client lost almost his entire fear of becoming a fixed deviant.

6. His therapy group and I gave this client relevant information, not only about psychology but often about sociology, anthropology, law, education, and related fields. Thus, we explained how and why human beings usually become emotionally disturbed; how statistically normal many of his problems were; why he was not likely to harm himself by masturbation; what some of the laws about homosexuality were; and how he could go about acquiring some better study habits. Although this information was not usually designed to help the client solve some of his basic personality problems, it was intended to have a supportive and palliative effect in the process of his therapy, and it often appeared to help him significantly.

7. I used various supplementary aids in teaching this client some of the principles of human behavior in general and of rational-emotive psychotherapy in particular. I gave him various pamphlets and books to read; he attended several lectures and workshops on rational therapy, and he purchased a couple of tape recordings. Finally, at my suggestion, he brought along his own cassette tape recorder and recorded a few of the individual sessions he had with me, and then listened to these sessions a good many times at home. These various supplementary teaching devices were found to be helpful to the client, especially—he thought—the repeated listening to the recordings of his own sessions and several readings of the two books.

8. On many occasions, both the client's group and I went over with him the A-B-C's of personality formation and change which are the

essence of the theory of rational-emotive therapy. He was specifically shown that whenever he experienced any disordered emotion, behavior, or psychosomatic symptom at point C, this did not stem from the events or conditions that were occurring in his life at point A, but from his irrational beliefs, attitudes, meanings, and philosophies at point B. More specifically, he was taught to distinguish clearly between the rational or appropriate ideas he was telling himself at point rB and the irrational or inappropriate ideas he was telling himself at point iB.

In one instance, for example, the client became very angry at his parents, when he remembered how they had overprotected him during his childhood and thereby helped him to become shy and inhibited. He was shown, by me and his group, that his anger at this point did not stem from his parents' overprotection (or from his remembrance of this overprotection) at point A. Rather, it resulted from the sane idea at point rB, "What a handicap it was for them to overprotect me like that! I wish to hell they hadn't done so!" and from the absurd ideas at point iB, "They *ought* not to have been so overprotective! I can't *stand* thinking about what they did to me! They are horrible people for having acted in that way. They deserve to be punished for their behavior and I hope they drop dead!"

These ideas, at point iB, we showed the client, were irrational because: (*a*) There was *no* reason why his parents ought not to have been so overprotective, even though it would have been lovely if they had not been. (*b*) He *could* very well stand thinking about their overprotectiveness, although he might never like it. (*c*) They were *not* horrible people for having acted the way they did, but merely poor, fallible human beings who unfortunately made a mistake in overprotecting him. (*d*) Even if their behavior was benighted, they hardly deserved to be killed, or otherwise severely punished, for having been born and raised to act the way that they did.

When the client finally accepted the irrationality of his own iB ideas, his anger against his parents completely vanished, and he began to get along with them remarkably better than he had ever previously done. He also began to accept more and more the basic tenet of rational-emotive therapy: as Epictetus stated two thousand years ago,

"Men are disturbed not by things, but by the views which they take of them." And whenever he thereafter became upset or acted self-defeatingly at point C, he tended quickly to look for the iB statements he kept telling himself to create this reaction, and to challenge and question these statements until he stopped foolishly believing in them.

In many ways, such as those just delineated, this shy and sexually backward client was emotively, behavioristically, and cognitively treated in the course of his rational-emotive individual and group therapy sessions. Within less than a year of starting treatment, he lost most of his shyness, became adept at speaking up in front of both small and large groups, had sexual affairs with three girls and began to have steady relations with one of them, entirely lost his fear of being a fixed homosexual, and was halfway toward completing his first novel. At times, he was still anxious and guilty, especially when stressful situations arose; but his feelings of self-acceptance appreciably increased, and his hostility toward his parents and other individuals became minimal. All the members of his therapy group agreed that he was able to quit treatment and get along by himself. During the year following the termination of therapy, I had two letters from him and spoke to him briefly when he attended some workshops. From this contact and information, I received the impression that he appeared to be holding his gains and even strengthening himself further in some areas.

Progress of this sort does not always follow. Even though rational-emotive therapy is a comprehensive form of treatment that includes several important cognitive, emotive, and behavioristic approaches to basic personality change, it is hardly a miracle cure, and does require a considerable amount of effort and practice on the part of the client. Hence, it is hardly the therapy of choice for individuals who want to be coddled, who think they require immediate gratification within the therapy sessions, who believe that they will magically be cured by some kind of sudden insight, or who refuse to work at helping themselves. It is also not exactly appealing to the therapist who primarily wants to gratify himself during therapy, who is in dire need of his

clients' approval, who prefers to be passive during most of the therapeutic process, and who is enamored of discovering many fine details
of the events of his clients' past or present existence.

RET, however, can be used with a large variety of clients, including individuals who are severely neurotic, borderline psychotic, and
overtly psychotic; those who are bright, those somewhat retarded;
those who are from high socieconomic and educational backgrounds,
those from culturally deprived homes; and those who come for many
or for only a few sessions. The active-directive, cognitive-oriented,
homework-assigning methods that have been vigorously espoused
since the mid-1950's have now begun to be increasingly incorporated
into other, originally more monistic, systems of psychotherapy, so
that a comprehensive system of therapy appears to be evolving, too
slowly it is true, but surely, nevertheless.

NOTES

[1] See, for example, the work of Bach and Wyden (1969); Gendlin
(1964); May (1967); Otto (1968); Perls *et al.* 1951); Rogers
(1951, 1961, 1967); Schutz (1967); Stoller (1967); and Whitaker
and Malone (1953).
[2] The reader is referred to Cautela (1966); Davison (1968);
Wolpe (1958); and Wolpe and Lazarus (1966).
[3] Reference can here be made to the work of Adler (1927, 1932);
Berne (1964); Kelly (1955); Phillips (1956); Phillips and Wiener
(1966); and Wiener and Stieper (1965).

6

A RATIONAL APPROACH
TO INTERPRETATION

Practically all schools of psychotherapy take a distinct approach to interpretation, even if they mainly caution against it. In the practice of rational-emotive psychotherapy, the therapist takes a definite stand on many problems of interpreting the client's verbalizations and behavior so that the latter comes to understand much more fully what he is thinking and doing and uses his insight into his own (and others') behavior to change fundamentally some of the aspects of his functioning and malfunctioning. Interpretations made in RET are in some respects similar to, or overlap significantly with, the approaches of other schools; but many of them are also radically different.

Several kinds of interpretation, however, are usually *not* emphasized in rational-emotive psychotherapy, although they are highly important in psychoanalytic and neopsychoanalytic therapies.

1. The rational therapist for the most part ignores connections between the client's early history and his present disturbances. He does not believe that the client was made neurotic by his past experiences,

but by his own unrealistic and overdemanding *interpretations* of these experiences. He therefore spends little time in digging up and interpreting past occurrences and events; rather, he *interprets the interpretations* of these events. Thus, instead of showing the client that he feels angry at dominating women today because his mother dominated him when he was a child, he shows him his irrational thinking processes that made him, when he was young, *demand* that his mother not be dominating, and that in the present are still leading him childishly to demand that women be passive or warm rather than ruling and cold. The rational therapist consistently keeps interpreting the client's *responses* to his history, rather than that history itself and its hypothesized intrinsic connections with his current behavior.

2. Most analytic schools of therapy spend considerable time interpreting deeply unconscious or repressed material to the clients. The rational-emotive school holds that there is no such entity as *the* unconscious or *the* id; and that although thoughts, feelings, and actions of which the individual is partly unaware frequently underlie his disturbed behavior, practically all the important attitudes that exist in this respect are not deeply hidden or deliberately kept out of consciousness because the client is too ashamed to acknowledge them, but are just below the level of consciousness, or (in Freud's original formulations) in his preconscious mind, and are relatively easy for the client to see and accept if the therapist will forcefully, persuasively, and persistently keep confronting him with them. The rational therapist, therefore, probably does more interpreting of unconscious or unaware material to the client than do most other therapists; but he does so quickly and directly, with no mysticism or mumbo jumbo, and no pretense that this material is terribly hard to discover and face.

3. Most contemporary psychotherapists appear to aggrandize the significance of the transference relationships between themselves and their clients, and expend much energy interpreting to the latter their deep-seated feelings for themselves. The rational therapist believes that the client's relations with other human beings are normally far more important than his relations with the therapist, and that how he likes or hates the therapist has little to do with his basic problems,

though it may well be an illustration of his difficulties. He therefore ignores most of the feelings which the client has about him and selectively uses only those aspects of these feelings that truly seem important and that may be employed to teach him how to relate better to others and to people in the outside world. Instead of interminably analyzing the client's attitudes toward him (and his own attitudes toward the client), he interprets and attacks the general philosophy that the client employs to *create* his transference reactions: namely, his irrational belief that he *needs* the therapist's approval and that he cannot accept himself without it.

4. A great many therapists concentrate on interpreting to their clients their resistances and defenses: showing them how they rationalize, project, repress, compensate, and resist getting better. The rational-emotive psychotherapists probably overlap with analytic therapists more in this than in any other respect, since they particularly show clients the rationalizing, inconsistent, and illogical modes of thinking. Going much further than most other therapists in this regard, however, the RET therapist directly and vigorously *attacks* the clients' illogical thought processes and evasions, and forces them, by giving them activity homework assignments, into positions where they no longer employ self-defeating mechanisms or irrational thinking.

5. Many schools of therapy today, such as the Freudian and the Jungian, emphasize the interpretation of dreams. The rational therapist does not believe that the dream is the royal road to the unconscious, nor that it usually gives important aspects of the patient's thoughts and wishes that are not easily available from an examination of waking life and fantasies. He consequently spends little time on dream analysis and prefers, instead, to examine the client's current nondreaming thought and behavior, to see how it reveals—as it almost invariably does—the underlying irrational philosophies and self-defeating attitudes toward himself and others. By the same token, the rational-emotive therapist rarely interprets the client's obscure symbolisms, whether these occur in sleeping or waking life, because he believes that there are too many allowable interpretations to many symbolic processes, and that it is often impossible to define exactly

what a given symbol means. He would rather focus on specific events in the client's life and his concrete responses to these events; and from these (and especially from the responses) he can determine exactly what the client's basic postulates about himself and the world are, how irrational are these postulates, and what can be done about changing them or eliminating their irrationality.

6. Some schools of psychotherapy, particularly the experiential and the Gestalt schools, emphasize the desirability of interpreting to the client the meanings behind his physical gestures and postures. The rational therapist does some of this kind of interpretation, but in a minimal way in most instances, because he is more interested in attacking the ideas behind the client's gestures rather than in demonstrating their mere existence. Thus, if he sees that the client is holding himself back physically or is speaking in a stilted manner, he will not only point this out, but will try to get him to see that this posture or gesture is a direct result of his believing that he dare not let himself go because then people would find out what he really was like and would hate him. The rational therapist questions and challenges this hypothesis that the client holds about himself, rather than emphasizing the symptomatic results, such as postural inhibitions, that result from it.

7. The psychoanalytic, experiential, and expressive schools of therapy tend to interpret almost *all* the client's expressions, fantasies, and behaviors as significant and to show him the unconscious meanings behind these manifestations. Thus, they will make an issue of his being late to the therapy session, or his slips of the tongue, or his writings or drawings, and will find notable underlying meanings in all these kinds of productions. The rational therapist will ignore much of this activity and expression and will, in a most selective manner, interpret what he considers to be the most meaningful aspects of the client's life: such as, his procrastination at work or at school, his problems relating to others, and his evaluation of himself. It is not that he thinks various of the client's behaviors unmeaningful, but that he selects some of them as being much *more* significant than others, and prefers to concentrate the therapeutic work, in the interests of efficiency, on these more important areas.

So much for what the rational-emotive therapist tends to de-emphasize or not do in the realm of interpretation. What, now, does he tend to emphasize and do?

His main interpretations are invariably philosophic rather than expository or even explanatory. If the client, for example, is unaware that he is overly dependent on others, the rational therapist not only shows him that he is, but also shows him that dependency is the result of an idea, a belief, or a value system; namely, the belief that he *must* have other people's help or approval in order to like himself. The therapist then forces him to question and challenge this hypothesis, to prove to himself how invalid it is, and to replace it with another hypothesis—e.g., that it is fine to have other people's approval but that he is a perfectly valuable person in his own right *whether or not* he does have it.

The main philosophic ideologies that the rational-emotive therapist keeps showing the client are the underpinnings of his disturbed behavior are the irrational ideas that (*a*) he must totally condemn himself and others for wrong or inefficient conduct; (*b*) he must attain a high degree of perfectionism in his and others' eyes; (*c*) he must be absolutely sure that certain desirable events will occur and other undesirable events will not; (*d*) he (and others) are utter heroes when they follow a proper line of conduct and complete villains when they do not. The rational therapist, in other words, continually shows the client that he is an absolutist, a bigot, a moralist, a perfectionist, and a religious dogmatist; and that only by accepting reality, uncertainty, and tolerance is he likely to surrender his emotional disturbances.

The therapist who takes a rational approach to interpretation keeps showing his client that there are highly probable consequences to his irrational premises: that if he believes that others must approve him, he probably *will* become anxious and depressed; that if he intolerantly condemns people for their mistakes and failings, he very likely will become incessantly hostile and suffer pains in his own gut. He continually proves, by the laws of logic, that certain unrealistic philosophies of life *do* result in self-defeating symptoms, such as phobias, obsessions, and psychosomatic disorders; and that only if the client changes these philosopies is he likely to get significantly and permanently better.

Instead of interpreting to the client the historical causation of his present aberrations, the rational therapist shows him that *he* is in the saddle seat ideologically, that *he* brought on that original inappropriate responses to failure and frustration, and the *he* is continuing to respond destructively in the same basic manner in which *he* chose to respond years ago. The therapist fully acknowledges that the client's biological inheritance as well as his sociological conditioning make it very easy for him to get into certain dysfunctional habit patterns and to continue to behave in self-sabotaging ways. But he shows the client that *difficult* does not mean *impossible*; that he *can* change, with sufficient work and practice on his part; and that he'd *better* force himself to do so if he wants to live with minimal anxiety and hostility.

The rational therapist, in other words, interprets to the client the essential *two*-sidedness which underlies his past, present, and future behavior. He demonstrates how, on the one side, the client is biosocially prediposed to allow himself to sink into neurotic pathways; and how, on the other side, he has a special faculty, called reason, and a unique ability, self-propelled effort and practice, which he can employ to overcome largely his oversuggestibility, short-range hedonism, and rigid thinking. He interprets to the client not only how he got the way he is, but exactly what kinds of irrational beliefs he keeps reindoctrinating himself with to keep himself that way; and how he can logically parse, reflectively challenge, and ruthlessly uproot these beliefs. His interpretations, therefore, go much deeper and make wider inroads against disturbed ideas, emotions, and actions than do the interpretations of many other therapists.

The rational-emotive therapist also interprets and teaches the general principles of scientific method and logic to his clients. He shows them that false conclusions, about either objective reality or oneself, stem from (*a*) setting up false premises and then making reasonably logical deductions from these premises; or (*b*) setting up valid premises and then making illogical deductions from them. He shows his clients exactly what are their false premises and illogical deductions from valid premises. He teaches them to accept hypotheses as hypotheses, and not as facts; and to demand observable data as substantiating evidence for these facts. He also shows them how to experiment, as much as is feasible, with their own desires and activities, to discover what they truly would like to have out of life. He is in many such ways a scientific interpreter who teaches his clients—who in many ways resemble the students of other science teachers—how to follow the hypothetico-deductive method and to specifically apply it to their own value systems and emotional problems.

The rational therapist interprets to clients how their ideas and motivations are unconsciously influenced by their actions, and how they can consciously change the former by forcefully changing the latter. He urges them not only to question and challenge their irrational philosophies of life on theoretical or logical grounds, but he gives them practical homework assignments, so that they can *work* against reimbibing these false and inimical values. In the course of so doing, he interprets to them what happens in their heads when they overinhibit their activities—for example, when they withdraw from social relations because of their inordinate fears of rejection- -and what likewise happens in these same heads when they force themselves to do things that they have been afraid to perform. Instead of endlessly interpretively connecting the client's past with his present, he more often focuses on connecting his present with his present: that is, his current inactivity with his contemporary uncritical acceptance of unvalidated hypotheses. And he tries for reciprocal change in the client, by inducing him to modify two-sidedly both his thinking and his motor behavior.

In several important respects, then, rational-emotive psychotherapy encourages interpretation which is rather different from the kinds that occur in most other forms of therapy. The RET practitioner tends to interpret in the following ways:

1. Interpretation is usually made in a highly direct, not particularly cautious, circumlocutious, or tortuous manner. The rational therapist feels that he knows right at the start that the client is upsetting himself by believing strongly in one or more irrational ideas; and he usually can quickly surmise which of these ideas a particular client believes.

As soon as he does see this, he tends to confront the client with his irrational notion, to prove to him that he actually holds it, and to try forcefully to induce him to give it up. Where the majority of other therapists tend to be passive and nondirective in their interpretations, the rational-emotive therapist is almost at the opposite extreme, since he believes that only a direct, concerted, sustained attack on a client's long-held and deep-seated irrationalities is likely to uproot them.

2. Most analytic therapists follow Lewis Wolberg's rule that "it is important to interpret to the patient only material of which he has at least pre-conscious awareness," but the rational therapist has no hesitancy in trying to show him, from the first session onward, material of which he may be totally unaware, and that even may be (on occasion) deeply repressed. He frequently directly confronts the client with two conflicting behaviors or values, to show him that the position that he says he consciously believes in or follows obviously is coexistent with an opposing, and presumably an unconsciously held, position which he also follows. The rational therapist is not intimidated by the client's possibly becoming temporarily more upset when he in confronted with some of his own covert thoughts and feelings, since he then immediately goes to work on showing the client how he is *creating* his own upsettedness, and precisely what he can do to calm himself down again by changing the ideas with which he is creating this state of disorder.

3. Most psychotherapists only dare to make deep interpretations when, as Wolberg again states, "the therapist has a very good relationship with the patient." The rational-emotive therapist, however, usually starts making direct, depth-centered interpretations from the very first session, long before any warm or intense relationship between him and the client may be established. He is frequently highly didactic and explicatory, and relies much more on the client's potential reasoning powers than on his emotional attachment to the therapist to induce him to accept his teachings and explanations.

4. While rarely being warm, fatherly, or loving to the client, the rational therapist consistently has what Carl Rogers calls "uncondi-

tional positive regard" for him, in that he is quite nonjudgmental. The core of rational-emotive therapy consists of teaching the client that no one is to be blamed, condemned, or moralistically punished for any of his deeds, even when he is indubitably wrong and immoral—because he is a fallible human, and can be accepted as such even when he makes serious blunders and commits crimes. The therapist, following this philosophy that an individual does not have to be evaluated *as a person* though his *performances* may be measured and rated, fully accepts all his clients, even when he has to point out to them that their deeds are irresponsible and reprehensible. Giving then unconditional positive regard, he can afford to actively-directively confront them with all kinds of undesirable aspects of their behavior, since his interpretations in this connection are quite consonant with his own tolerance for *them*, as individuals, in spite of their deplorable *ways*.

5. Because, again, the rational emotive therapist keeps forthrightly and ceaselessly attacking, not the client but his feelings of guilt and shame, he does not have to watch the timing of his interpretations too carefully. He does not wait for the client to be ready for major interpretations; usually instead, he *makes* him ready, by presenting the realities of the client's presumably shameful ideas and feelings, and concomitantly fighting against the belief that they need be shameful. Occasionally, with an especially anxious client, the rational-emotive practitioner may have to wait to make certain revelatory interpretations; but most of the time he quickly jumps in with them, and not only gets them, but the irrational ideas that induce the client to keep himself from facing them, out of the way.

6. Much of the time, the rational therapist puts his interpretations in the forms of questioning rather than of declarative statements—not because he is afraid to upset the client by being more direct, but because one of his prime goals is to teach the client to question himself and his own thinking. Thus, instead of telling the client what he is saying to himself to make himself anxious, the therapist will say to him: "What could you be telling yourself? Why would you think this event, if it occurred, would be terrible? What evidence is

there that it would be catastrophic if you failed at this task?'' By these leading questions, the client is led to make his own interpretations of his behavior—and, more importantly, to *keep* making these interpretations when the therapist is no longer present.

7. Like many other therapists, the rational-emotive practitioner frequently makes the same interpretation repetitively. He deliberately does this, knowing that the client has been repeatedly overlooking this interpretation, or pushing it out of his mind, or making some false interpretation instead. He therefore wants to give the client an opportunity to go over the same ground, again and again in some instances, until he begins to see that the interpretation is really true and workable, and not merely to overlook it or give it lip service.

8. The rational-emotive therapist is unhesitatingly vigorous about many of the interpretations he makes. He believes that the client clings relentlessly to his self-defeating irrationalities partly because he has very strongly continued to reindoctrinate himself with them over the years, and that he is not going to give them up unless he strongly and courageously gives himself some alternative ideas. The therapist therefore vigorously shows him that he *cannot* be happy with some of his absurd values, that he'd better give them up if he wants to become minimally anxious, and that *there is no other way* than steady work and practice on his part if he is truly to surrender his superstitions and become less disturbed.

The rational therapist, therefore, quickly and persistently interprets to most of his clients the philosophic sources of their disturbances; namely, the specific irrational ideas that they keep telling themselves, to create and maintain their psychological aberrations. He explains exactly what these ideas are and how they are biologically rooted as well as sociologically instilled. Thus, he shows the client that he is born with a tendency to desire approval from others and to believe mistakenly that he absolutely *must have* that approval and is a worthless individual without it; and that, in an other-directed society, such as our own, he is raised to accentuate rather than to minimize this belief, and is conditioned to feel that prestige and popularity are all-important. Thus, again, the therapist shows the client that he is physiologically predisposed to be a short-term hedonist (or to adhere to what Freud called the pleasure principle, and to strive for immediate satisfaction rather than future gain), and that in our culture, and with his particular set of parents, he is usually also socially conditioned to believe that he *must* have what he wants and that it is catastrophic when his desires are not fulfilled.

The rational therapist indicates to the client what these biosocial irrational beliefs inevitably *do* to the person who believes them, how illogical and self-defeating these ideas are, and how they can be attacked and uprooted by the client's challenging and questioning them, in theory as well as in practice, and working against them to the best of his ability in ideomotor ways. Because of his theory of human disturbance and its philosophic causation, his content and manner of interpretation is in many respects quite different from that of most other psychotherapists.

His interpretations do not ignore the unconscious, but are largely concerned with material that is conscious, and not always deeply repressed; not overly involved with transference phenomena; directly attacking in regard to resistances and defenses; little concerned with dreams and obscure symbolic processes; highly selective in regard to what is significant in the client's life; very concerned with the fundamental irrational ideas which underlie the client's disturbed emotions; emphasizing of the inevitable consequences of his false premises and illogical deductions from sensible assumptions; strongly favoring general principles of scientific method; and distinctly involved with impelling the client into action that will help him change his value system. Because of their strong philosophic flavor, rational-emotive interpretations are usually made in a manner that is exceptionally direct, independent of the therapist's warm relationship with his client, conducive of a nonjudgmental attitude on the part of the therapist, not particularly dependent on any kind of special timing, largely given in the form of forthright questioning, quite repetitive in many cases, and unhesitatingly vigorous. Both the content and the form of rational-emotive interpretation unquestionably have dangers and drawbacks and may be pragmatically and experimentally modified as time goes by.

7

A RATIONAL-EMOTIVE APPROACH
TO LEADERSHIP AND HOSTILITY

To the considerable literature on leadership that has appeared in recent years, one finds a general consensus, or at least an overlap, as to
what constitutes leadership and as to the traits necessary for the
emergence of leadership ability.[1] A leader is generally defined as
one who effectively directs, commands, or guides some group or activity. If this definition is accepted, then without too much trouble
one can select a known group of leaders—such as one hundred individuals who started without any amount of money or influence and
who worked their way to the top of a sizable organization—and can
then discover the main traits that they seem to have in common.

Although this kind of study does not seem actually to have ever
been done with any definitiveness—Anne Roe's study of eminent
scientists being perhaps closest to the mark—it has been approx-
imated by the work of many students of leadership who have gone
through the biographies of numerous outstanding individuals and
have generally, if not overrigorously, culled from the data the main

characteristics for which many or most of them were noted. It has also been done, on more of a firsthand basis, by many reporters and writers who have personally encountered a good number of industrial, academic, military, and other leaders, and who have reported their impressions of the traits possessed by these individuals.

Over a period of some twenty-five to thirty years of practice as a psychotherapist and marriage and family counselor, I have probed in detail into the lives, and particularly the current lives, of well over five thousand individuals, about 5 percent of whom were acknowledged leaders in one or more fields. This has afforded me the opportunity to talk, frequently over some period of time, with approximately two hundred fifty outstanding individuals. Many of them, of course, were severely disturbed; otherwise they would not have come to a therapist. Hence they can hardly be considered to be typical of leaders in general (though, since it is fairly well known that a high percentage of outstanding individuals, these days, go for some form of therapy, it is also possible that these members of the sample were not so different from the average leader). A good many of the leaders I have seen, however (I would roughly say from one-quarter to one-third of them), were not seeing me because of their own severe problems, but because they were intimately involved with a wife, a girl friend, a child, a sibling, or another associate who did have personality problems, and therefore they participated with me in trying to help this other individual.

From this study of patients and clients, it appears that leaders definitely do tend to have certain traits; and the impression seems strong that they usually—although not invariably—become leaders precisely because they have these traits.

What kind of characteristics do leaders tend to have? Very briefly, the main ones appear to be:

1. A high level of drive or ambition and a distinct direction in which this drive is channeled.

2. Firmness in making decisions and the ability not to get sidetracked or spend time in bemoaning their fate even when they believe that their decisions may be wrong.

3. A high degree of work confidence. This by no means implies that they necessarily have self-confidence, self-acceptance, or what Carl Rogers calls "unconditional positive regard." For they may condemn themselves severely when they fail, and hence not fully accept themselves. But they usually feel that in the long run, and often in the short run as well, they definitely are going to succeed.

4. Intelligence that is decidedly above the average and that frequently is outstanding.

5. Persistence, practice, and consistent disposition for hard work.

6. Good knowledge of the field in which they become leaders, and frequently of other fields as well.

7. Lack of overweening anxiety; sufficient calmness and stability to keep them moving along the lines in which they effectively want to move.

8. Tolerance of others, at least in their main field of endeavor.

In addition to the good many proven leaders whom I have met over the past quarter of a century, it has also been my job to try to help a great many more individuals—and now I would say the number has been from a thousand to fifteen hundred—who have had indubitable ability and intelligence, but who have been dramatic underachievers in some field of endeavor. Many of these individuals, if they ever overcame their emotional disturbances, would in all probability become real leaders. Rational-emotive psychotherapists endeavor to show these people how to remove their emotional blocks and how to achieve their leadership potential; and in a good number of instances, with success. As a result, there is hardly a major field of activity, be it art, science, teaching, industry, the ministry, medicine, or psychiatry or psychology, which today does not include at least a few outstanding and well-recognized leaders who have probably been helped to reach their goal as a result of rational-emotive active-directive therapy.

What happens, in terms of leadership, when people with high leadership potential condemn (*a*) themselves for being imperfect, (*b*) others for behaving badly, and (*c*) the world for not being easy or rewarding enough? A great deal happens—and nearly all of it negative. For practically every leadership quality begins to become disrupted and to disappear when the individual with the theoretical potential to actualize these qualities keeps feeding himself foolish assumptions about himself and the world. Specifically:

1. The person who is demanding that he *must* succeed, and *has* to condemn himself if he doesn't, tends to lose his drive and direction: for wouldn't it be awful, he convinces himself, if he remained ambitious in a given area and did *not* outstandingly achieve! Consequently, his ambition tends to flag.

2. The self-condemning individual who is afraid of failure, and who would define *himself* as a worthless person if he did fail to be a great leader, finds himself unable to make and to stick firmly to major decisions: for suppose he decided incorrectly—or suppose another possible decision would be even better than the one he has already made?

3. The perfectionistic, superdemanding person soon loses work confidence. Even when he succeeds, he is sure that he has not done well *enough*; and when he does not succeed, he is certain that he will *never* be able to do so.

4. The potential leader who has a high degree of intelligence, but who insists that he has *got* to do the right things in life and that others *have* to approve him, begins to focus so much on success and on pleasing others that he fails to use his intelligence, and often behaves quite stupidly. In addition, he who condemns others for their errors and who cannot tolerate the world when it puts difficulties in his path deflects himself from intelligent problem-solving and winds up preoccupied with all kinds of irrelevant hostilities and self-pityings.

5. Leadership usually requires persistence, practice, and consistent hard work. But the person who is preoccupied with blaming himself and others largely persists at *this* form of behavior, and at little else. He is what is called "self-centered" instead of "work-centered"; and his leadership activities consequently suffer.

6. The individual who suffers from extreme anxiety and hostility as a result of his definitional, unrealistic value system often fails to gain the specialized knowledge of a given area that would be necessary for him to have if he were to become a leader. He cannot concentrate too

well on school work, in many instances; he does not have enough time for reading; he is procrastinating and disorganized in the studying that he does do; and in various other ways he remains relatively ignorant.

7. Proven leaders usually have a lack of overweening anxiety; do have sufficient calmness and stability to keep them moving along the lines in which they effectively want to move. But individuals with highly moralistic, condemnatory philosophies generally are terribly anxious and angry; and in many ways, as we have just been seeing, their anxiety and anger deflect them from effective leadership.

8. It is preferable that leaders have a capacity for tolerance of others, at least in their main field of endeavor. But those who blame themselves, others, and the world at large, are of course quite intolerant, and directly pick fights with their associates or indirectly get into brawls with them because they are so upset about the so-called injustices and horrors that are happening to them outside their specific field of endeavor.

Almost every possible trait of leadership that one can imagine, therefore, can seriously be interfered with or destroyed by the potential leader's proneness to become emotionally upset. This does not mean, of course, that no acknowledged leaders are emotionally disturbed, for clearly a good many of them are. Some, such as Savonarola and Hitler, probably became leaders of their groups *mainly* because they were exceptionally bigoted, grandiose, and obsessed. Usually, however, severe disturbance does not abet leadership; and a case can be made for the hypothesis that when it does, it is much more prone to do so under conditions of violence and terrorism than in peaceful times.

It can also be held, of course, that the kind of leader that is represented by a Hitler, a Stalin, or a Rasputin, is not exactly the kind of individual that a therapist or a social scientist would be interested in producing. Whatever may be their talents, their "leadership" qualities, in practically all instances that have been recorded, are achieved at the expense of, rather than through, help to others.

There is also some amount of evidence—though it must be admitted that it is hardly conclusive—that the leaders of the world who have tyrannized others were not particularly happy in their own right, and that in many ways they were miserable. Certainly, like Hitler, they can at times literally jump for joy as they cram another predatory victory under their belts. But much or most of the time they seem to be underlyingly depressed, brooding, anxious, hostile, and paranoiac. What is perhaps also important, and frequently overlooked, is that for every antisocial leader who rises to eminence because of his ruthless, monomaniacal thoughts and actions, probably a thousand or ten thousand individuals with highly similar thoughts and feelings wind up in mental hospitals, prisons, psychologists' offices, political or social exile, and paupers' or suicides' graves. The fact that a Hitler is enabled to rise to power over scores of millions of people not only shows something about his own genius for leadership but also about the nation that elevated him to a dictatorship position and then permitted him to reign for over a decade. In any truly sane kind of milieu, it is to be doubted whether this kind of "leadership" would long be permitted to flourish.

Assuming that a leader, in a truly realistic sense of that term, is defined as an individual who not only stands at the head of and directs the activities of a certain group but who also manages this group for its benefit as well as for his own, it would appear that this type of leader is much more likely to achieve and to maintain an outstanding position if he is minimally emotionally disturbed. This means that he would better be (1) distinctly free of self-deprecation (and hence afflicted with little anxiety, guilt, and depression), and (2) notably tolerant of others (and hence prone to little hostility, grandiosity, and low frustration tolerance).

In one of the pioneer works on leadership, Ordway Tead noted that would-be leaders were likely to sabotage their own efforts by allowing themselves to possess several unfortunate personality traits, including compensation, sublimation and suppression, rationalization, transference, projection, obsession, and delusions. He was doubtless correct about this; but he was too influenced by the psychoanalytic theories of his day and therefore did not realize that most of the sabotaging traits he mentioned were defenses against underlying disturbances. These defenses have been beautifully described by leading analytic writers (as Otto Fenichel, Sigmund Freud, and Anna Freud); but these same writers failed to delineate the basic disturbances which lie behind and cause the defenses, since they themselves have been obsessed with libidinal hypotheses (especially that of the Oedipus complex) which seem to have little substantiation and which are derivative rather than truly causative of disturbances.

Why, for example, do so many individuals use the defense of rationalization when they have palpably done some stupid or wrong act? Because, if they did face the truth, and fully admit that they committed this act and that they were truly responsible for committing it, they would feel impelled to castigate themselves. It is their tendency, therefore, to condemn themselves for their sins and errors that causes, and in many instances practically assures, their becoming defensive. Similarly, even the Oedipus complex itself is not truly *a cause* but a *result* of human disturbance, if and when it actually exists. For it is not the boy's lusting after his mother—his Oedipal *feelings*—that causes his complex; rather, it is his *blaming himself* for having these feelings.

If leaders, therefore, are defensive, it is largely because they have a strong tendency to condemn themselves. One can vaguely, as the Freudians do, call this tendency their "superego" or conscience; but that only names it rather than more clearly describes it. What it really seems to be is the early acquired predisposition of a human being to make the empirical observation, "I have made a mistake and that is unfortunate, since I and others will probably have to suffer from unpleasant consequences as a result of this mistake," and for him *also* to make the overgeneralized, nonempirical conclusion about his behavior, "Because I made this mistake, I am a *bad person* who deserves to suffer *more* than the mere consequences of making this error, and who will doubtless be damned by God, man, and the universe (and perhaps eternally roasted in Hell) for making it."

In order to be only slightly disturbed or undisturbed emotionally, an ideal leader would probably have to be a minimally condemning individual. For if he were to be maximally tolerant of himself and others he would, first, be able to lead effectively—that is, organize, manage, and direct the activities of some group of individuals—at no undue cost to himself. He would not irrationally upset himself when he blundered (as even the most talented and capable individuals of course often do). He would not inordinately worry about the future. He would not be afraid to make very important decisions. And he would not work under undue stress, and perhaps bring on psychosomatic problems, while he was carrying out his leadership activities.

Secondly, this ideal leader would be minimally resentful of others, including his close associates. He would not have to prove to himself and everybody else that he was the greatest person who ever existed. He would not have childish temper tantrums when others treated him or his causes unjustly. And he would not be likely to lead his group or his nation into a major war or other kind of holocaust because of his inability to tolerate frustration and difficulty.

This last point is one of increasing importance in today's highly complex, industrialized, and atom-powered world. In the old days, when rulers of the stamp of Caligula, Nero, Genghis Khan, Robespierre, and Napoleon reigned supreme, there was much bloodshed and needless suffering, but it still tended to take a limited toll: for the means of human destruction were relatively limited, and it took years or decades before a million or more men could be sacrificed to a leader's hostility and callousness. Today, of course, matters have changed enormously, so that a few sullen, supersensitive, impatient commanders could much more easily give the go-ahead signal to certain button-pushers; and the amount of death and destruction that would soon ensue would be immediate and phenomenal.

How, then, is this kind of a very real cataclysm to be averted? No one truly knows; and as Abraham Maslow has aptly pointed out, perhaps the most valuable thing any psychologist could do in the near future would be to come up with a solution to the problem of how we are going to be able to control human hostility. It would appear to me that one of the better answers would be the producing, by all the nations of the world, of a group of leaders who would be truly informed, responsible, and unhostile.

Is this ideal possible to attain? Yes, at least in theory. For although man seems to have deep-seated biological as well as sociological roots to his aggressiveness—as Konrad Lorenz, Desmond Morris, N. Tinbergen, and other ethologists have indicated, and as psychologists and psychiatrists like Hans Eysenck and Anthony Storr are also beginning to admit—he still has an uncommonly large cerebral cortex and is uniquely, among all animals, able to think about his thinking. Conscequently, whatever his "natural" prejudices and his ease of making himself extremely impatient and hostile, he definitely has the power, if only he wishes to work at using it, of minimizing and at times even eliminating hostility.

This, alas, is not the common position of today's leading psychotherapists. Most of the practitioners of the Freudian school, the experiential school, and the Reichian school seem to agree that there are two basic possibilities as far as the feeling and expression of hostility is concerned: either (1) the individual feels hostile to others and suppresses or represses his feelings, in which case he becomes quite emotionally disturbed and probably heir to ulcers, high blood pressure, or other psychosomatic complaints; or (2) he feels hostile to others and honestly acknowledges, deeply feels, and forthrightly expresses his hostility, in which case it does not lead to harmful results and he is able to live healthfully with it.

What these psychotherapists almost completely forget and ignore is a third, and radically different view, of hostility, that was first propounded some two thousand years ago by the Roman philosopher Epictetus and his chief follower, Marcus Aurelius, and that is now an integral part of rational-emotive psychotherapy. This view states that hostility does not stem simply from (*a*) our inborn tendency to become angry, and (*b*) some noxious or frustrating stimulus, but also from (*c*) our tendency to think crookedly about the stimulus and *our persistent refusal to work against this tendency.*

Becoming enraged, in this regard, is very much like becoming overweight. In order to get fat, the individual must have (*a*) an inborn tendency to take on weight if he overeats, and (*b*) sufficient food presented to him so that he is able to overeat. If he is biologically inclined to remain thin no matter what he eats and/or he is unable to acquire much food, he clearly will not overeat and become fat. If the stimulus (plenty of food) is always available and his organism is inclined to fatness, he still will not make himself overweight unless he pointedly ignores these realities and fails to discipline himself by refusing to keep stuffing the food in his mouth. For no matter how easily he gains weight nor how much food is available to him, he still must actively go through an overeating process before he gains superfluous weight.

So with intense anger. The stimulus (frustration and unfairness) is almost always available to us—since the world we live in obviously is a frequently depriving, restraining, unfair place. The inborn tendency of humans (and other animals) to become enraged when they are frustrated is clearly observable, as pointed out by John Dollard and his colleagues. But in order for us to erupt into actual rage, we still have to focus actively on the stimulus, give an exaggerated meaning to it, and insist that it is not only unfortunate or unfair but that it *should* not exist and that we cannot *stand* its existence.

Hostility, in other words, does not stem from frustration but from our childish, grandiose, unrealistic refusal to accept the fact that we are being frustrated. Just as the overeating individual unrealistically tells himself, "I *should* be able to eat all I want and still not gain too much weight," the angry individual often says to himself, "I *should* be able to remove immediately all the deprivations and injustices in my life and not be inconvenienced by them at all." Since the overeating person is *not* able to eat to his heart's content and remain slim, and the enraged individual is *not* able to remove all frustrations or to live very comfortably with them, these two individuals are demanding the impossible and hence are unnecessarily disturbing themselves. But although both these individuals naturally *tend* to react the way they do—since that's the way humans are and very few of them *easily* stop themselves from overeating or foolishly enraging themselves—there is no *necessity* to remain as they are. If they use their powers of thinking (and of thinking about thinking), they can, after some amount of work and practice, radically change their propensities. In fact, if they keep concertedly and persistently questioning and uprooting their self-defeating beliefs which lead them to overeat and to make themselves enraged, they tend, after a sufficient period of time, automatically and "naturally" to have other beliefs and to easily curb these responses.

More specifically, the leader who is enraged by the frustrating or unfair behavior of others is not really incensed by frustration or unfairness but by his own unrealistic, immature attitudes toward these stimuli. Thus, if he is the head of a government and he is dealing directly with the head of another government who appears to be acting dishonestly or unjustly, he first tends to tell himself sanely, "How unfortunate that this other leader is acting that way! I wish that he would behave more honestly and fairly. However, since he is not doing so, let me see what I can do either (*a*) to try to induce him to treat us more decently or (*b*) to try to coexist with him and to keep peace between our countries even though he continues to behave improperly." By telling himself these kinds of statements (and, of course, by truly *believing* them), this leader creates in himself feelings of displeasure, disappointment, and the determination to be reasonably serene—though hardly ecstatic!—in spite of the adverse situation under which he is operating.

Secondly, this leader then adds to his irrationalities a set of further beliefs, along these lines: "Not only is this other leader acting badly but (especially in view of the high stakes involved in our agreeing or disagreeing) he has no right to act that way! He *shouldn't* be so horribly dishonest and unfair! How can he possibly behave in that execrable manner? I think that he is a rat for being the way he is. If it's the last thing I do, I'm going to fix his wagon!"

By convincing himself of these propositions, this leader is creating—and I mean literally creating—strong feelings of rage, horror, and vindictiveness. With these feelings, he will hardly be in any clearheaded position to continue negotiating with the head of the other government for the mutual peace and prosperity of their countries. On the contrary, he will make himself, in most instances, so biased and condemning that almost every action, thereafter, that the other leader and his cohorts take will be viewed in a jaundiced and unfriendly manner.

How can this governmental head get rid of, or at least minimize, his "natural" feelings of rage and enmity which arise as soon as he perceives the dishonesty and unfairness of the head of another state? By going back to his own statements to himself, by rigorously analyzing and parsing them, and by contradicting the nonsensical, magical, and unempirically based beliefs of which they consist. Thus:

1. He has told himself, "Not only is this other leader acting badly but (especially in view of the high stakes involved in our agreeing or disagreeing) he has no right to act that way!" But this essentially means that although he might possibly allow the other leader to make a small mistake or one that had minor consequences, he cannot possibly allow him to make a large one or one that has major consequences. But why can't he? And how is he to stop this other leader from making huge errors instead of making only small ones? Obviously, the leader of the rival government *is* prone to make momentous mistakes. And why has he no right, as a fallible human being, to be as fallible as he indubitably is? *It would be nice* if he had fewer or less serious failings; but how does that prove that he has *no right* to have just as many as he has?

2. The enraged leader has told himself, about the other head of state, "*He shouldn't* be so horribly dishonest and unfair!" But why is this dishonesty and unfairness so *horrible?* Certainly, it is highly inconvenient. But what is so *awful* (that is, full of awe, terrifying) about something that is highly inconvenient? Furthermore, even if dishonesty and unfairness on the part of the head of a government were truly dreadful and frightening, why *should* he not be dishonest and unfair? Is there an inalienable law of the universe that says that moderately bad things should exist but extremely terrible things should not? Who passed this so-called law; who polices the world to see that it is enforced?

3. The "good" leader is saying to himself, in regard to the "bad" leader, "I think that he is a rat for being the way he is." But how can a human being be a rat? Maybe, if we want to stretch things a bit (and be rather unfair to rodents), we could justifiably state that he acts rattily. But how does that make him, as a whole person, a rat? How can one take *a person* who has a bad trait (let us say, a man who lies to the head of another state) and make him into a *bad person* (meaning, one who must *always* lie and who is to be perpetually damned for

lying)? Moreover, if a person really were an incorrigible and complete liar (which would be very difficult to prove, short of discovering his entire history up until the very day of his death), why would he be condemned for being what, alas, he has been born and raised to be? If anything, being as handicapped as he is, one should presumably tend to sympathize with him, help him in every possible way, and let him live comfortably with the fact that he is an inveterate liar.

4. The leader who upsets himself terribly about another leader's dishonesty and unfairness is telling himself, "If it's the last thing I do, I'm going to fix his wagon!" But this is irrational because (*a*) he is being vindictive against another human being who just happens to be more fallible, and hence presumably more pitiable, than others are; (*b*) he is giving himself needless pain because this other person happens to be the unfortunate way he is; (*c*) he is not concentrating on the serious problem at hand—which is, how can he keep his own government from impending trouble or disaster—but on a completely irrelevant problem: how to punish another person.

In almost all possible respects, then, the leader who becomes angry and who insists on remaining angry, at another leader (or, for that matter, at almost any other person or thing) is sabotaging himself and his own cause, and is consequently not acting as a very sensible or effective manager. If he were wiser and saner, he would be looking, primarily, not at the execrable behavior of the leader of another state, but at his own nonsense, which he devoutly believes and keeps indoctrinating himself with, *about* the behavior of others. In that manner, he could give up his irrational assumptions and return to his reasonable statements, which would normally enable him to work for the best possible solution to the difficult problem raised by the other leader's childishness.

Can leaders really be taught to think, feel, and act in a more rational and less anger-producing way? Yes—but not easily, not quickly. Once they have been born with a strong tendency to overgeneralize and to overreact to frustrating stimuli, and once they have been reared in a milieu that encourages this kind of impatient, angry behavior, it is extremely difficult for them to conquer their rage-creating tendencies. Nonetheless, rational-emotive psychotherapists have been able to achieve, in many instances, a great deal of change in their proneness to anger.

A city official who was suffering from high blood pressure and who had had several minor strokes, probably as a result of his "righteous indignation" against his incompetent associates, came for therapy. Once he began to see, as a result of the psychotherapeutic teaching, that innumerable people *are* incompetent and that there is no reason whatever why they should not be, his blood pressure decreased remarkably, he stopped having strokes, and he actually enjoyed his political activity for the first time in his life.

In the case of business executives, Dr. Milt Blum, Dr. Len Haber and I, have had even more success. In our Rational Training Institute (which is affiliated with the Institute for Advanced Study in Rational Psychotherapy), we have seen groups of business leaders who came to training sessions not because they had severe personal problems but because they wanted to work more effectively in their own firms. We found that one of their main problems was their becoming much too upset, on many occasions, about the ineffectual and nasty behavior of their employees and associates. Once we began to show them that it was not this behavior, but their own immature reactions to it, that caused their rage and inefficiency, a high proportion of them were able to make distinct changes in these reactions, and in time automatically to react quite differently. What had once been extreme rage on their part came to be feelings of acute disappointment and regret, with emphasis on doing something to rectify the unfortunate situations their employees and associates were creating, rather than on moaning and fuming about these situations.

So it can be done. Leaders, for the most part, are able to discover how they themselves are causing their temper tantrums when others behave poorly; and a good proportion of them are willing to work at changing their self-enraging philosophies and at replacing them with sensible substitutes. There is every reason to believe, therefore, that if leadership training included emotional education, as well as academic and practical instruction, a great deal could be done to show business executives, government officials, military officers, educational administrators, and other leaders how to stop berating themselves when they were imperfect, how to stop making themselves angry at people when they act fallibly, and how to accept the difficulties of living in a world that will probably always be less than ideal in many respects.

Not that nothing is being done, today, in this respect. The last decade has seen an enormous increase in emotional education as far as executives, labor officials, school administrators, and many other kinds of leaders are concerned. Unfortunately, however, the great bulk of this emotional training has taken the form of basic encounter, sensitivity training, Esalen-type "feel-in" groups, and other forms of group therapy that tend to "open" people up without "closing" them again, and that assume that experiencing or "feeling better" automatically leads to reorganizing one's philosophy of life or "getting better." If this type of group encounter were mixed with or supplemented by a more hard-headed, cognitively oriented, active-directive therapy, there is reason to believe that it would be much more effective.

Emotional education, moreover, would better be started much earlier than when the individual reaches college or when he is being trained for leadership functioning. Preferably, it should be instituted throughout all his school life, since there is evidence, from Freudian and other sources, that it will probably be neglected (or taught very badly) in his home environment. My main hypothesis is, in fact, that if human beings are taught unconditionally to accept themselves, to stop condemning others, and to stop whining about the inevitable rigors of reality (after making concerted and persistent attempts to change what they can change in this respect), and if this teaching becomes an integral part of our entire educational and job-training system, not only will we be able to bring out leadership qualities in many individuals who now have great potential in this respect but are not likely to actualize it, but we will also be able to produce the kind of leaders who thoroughly enjoy themselves and their work and who remain maximally free from emotional disturbance. This kind of a so-cietal-organized, cradle-to-the-grave program would, it seems to me, be a truly rational approach to leadership and to living.

NOTES

[1] For some of this literature on leadership, see the works of Dubin *et al.* (1965); Gellerman (1965); Lewis and Pearson (1966); Schell (1965); and Tead (1964).

8

REASON AND EMOTION IN THE INDIVIDUAL PSYCHOLOGY OF ADLER

Rational-emotive therapy owes a great debt to Alfred Adler, so much so that it is reasonable to inquire whether RET could not have developed within the Adlerian framework, becoming something of a revisionist approach in this system.

Rational-emotive therapy is not only a theory of personality development and change, as is individual psychology, but it is also a specific methodology. In the latter respect, it tends to differ radically from Adlerian methods, as well as from those of all other major schools of therapy. Philosophically, moreover, RET takes a rather extreme, and unique, stand on human worth and self-evaluation that differs significantly from that taken by individual psychology (and from virtually all other therapeutic psychologies). Where Adler presented, in many ways, a true ego psychology and showed human beings how to esteem themselves in spite of their innate and acquired limitations, RET is essentially an antiego psychology, which makes a determined effort to induce the individual to recognize rather than evaluate himself, and hence minimize ego games rather than play them successfully. Moreover, RET places less specific emphasis on social interest and more on self-interest than does individual psychology. Although the original formulation of RET was deeply influenced by the work of Adler, as well as that of various important neo-Adlerians—such as Wilhelm Stekel, Karen Horney, Erich Fromm, and Harry Stack Sullivan—the focus in the development of a new technique was primarily on the differences between these new views and those of various other therapists.

Consciously and unconsciously, then, Alfred Adler was certainly one of the main mentors in the formulation of RET; and it is highly probable that without his pioneering work, the main elements of rational-emotive therapy might never have been developed. Nevertheless, RET therapists, including myself, feel a little uncomfortable about referring to themselves as Adlerians. This offers a real advantage: we can now revere many or most of Adler's writings and find much theoretical substance and practical usefulness in them, while at the same time highlighting their distinct limitations and unhesitatingly try to construct ideas and techniques to overcome these limitations and to help make individual psychology—and, if you will, rational-emotive therapy—more precise, more empirically founded, and more valid.

Adler's view of emotion, and of its cognitive or reasoning correlates, was unusually incisive, perceptive, and to my way of thinking correct in regard to the interrelationship between ideation and emotion. Freud had originally devised, in his typically brilliant way, the theory that emotional disturbance, or neurosis, is basically *ideogenic*. Unfortunately, however, this great idea got lost in the shuffle about the Oedipus myth, or who chopped down Jocasta's cherry tree while Laius's body lay smoldering in the grave.

Adler was much more tenacious in holding to the hypothesis that a person's emotional reactions—and in fact his entire healthy or neurotic life style, directly correlated with his basic ideas, beliefs, attitudes, or philosophies—are, in essence, *cognitively* created. For example, Adler stated:

It is very obvious that we are influenced not by "facts" but by our interpretation of facts . . . Everyone possesses an "idea" about himself and the problems of life—a life-pattern, a law of movement—that keeps fast hold of him without his understanding it, without his being able to give any account of it. [1]

Again:

We orient ourselves according to a fixed point which we have artificially created, which does not in reality exist, a fiction. This assumption is necessary because of the inadequacy of our psychic life. [2]

Still again:

The individual . . . does not relate himself to the outside world in a predetermined manner, as is often assumed. He relates himself always according to his own interpretation of himself and of his present problem . . . It is his attitude toward life which determines his relationship to the outside world. [3]

The very core of Adler's theory of emotion, therefore, is his statement that "in a word, I am convinced that *a person's behavior springs from his idea*" (italics in original). [4] This is also the central theme of the philosophy of Epictetus and Marcus Aurelius, of Spinoza, of Bertrand Russell, of V. J. McGill, and of many other ancient and modern thinkers. It has been vigorously espoused by many outstanding modern psychotherapists. [5]

More specifically and importantly, Adler realized that the individual's deep-seated feelings of inadequacy, inferiority, or worthlessness are also of cognitive origin. Thus, in this connection he noted that we shall find:

many people who spend their whole life fighting for their lives and others to whom life is a vale of sorrows. We must understand that they are the victims of a mistaken development whose unfortunate consequence is that their attitude toward life also is mistaken. . . . The most important and valuable fundamental thesis for our communal life is this: *The character of a human being is never the basis of a moral judgment, but is an index of the attitude of this human being toward his environment, and of his relationship to the society in which he lives.*[6]

In these passages, Adler shows that he clearly grasped the most important idea which was later to be promulgated, and probably in somewhat clearer form, by rational-emotive therapists: namely, that the value or worth of an individual cannot really be scientifically or empirically measured. It is largely a definitional or tautological concept that depends upon his *thinking* and *convincing himself* that he is a "good person" or a "bad person," is "worthwhile" or "worthless." As Adler wrote:

Let us be very modest then, in our judgment of our fellows, and above all, let us never allow ourselves to make any *moral* judgments, judgments concerning the moral worth of a human being![7]

Although this sounds very much like the writings of rational-emotive therapists, it is still much too vague and too easily misinterpreted by emotionally aberrated individuals whom a therapist is trying to help. For such people, according to both Adlerian and RET theories, are biologically prone as well as environmentally conditioned to think distortedly about themselves and the world; and consequently they had better be very precisely and strongly reeducated to think more clearly and thereby to emote more appropriately. In RET, therefore, we attempt to show the individual how to differentiate rigorously his measurements and evaluations of his *acts* and *deeds* from his judgments and ratings of *himself* or what Adler calls his "moral worth."

That is to say, it is usually beneficial for a person to observe his behavior and to acknowledge, for example, that his study habits are poor, reactions of anger are too easily provoked, and socializing with others leaves much to be desired. But it is exceptionally foolish and harmful for him to conclude, "Therefore, I am a rotten person, I have no moral worth." Because, although his *acts* are measurable, *he*, a total human being, is not; and if he does rate *himself*, he will sooner or later tend to (1) feel depressed and inadequate; (2) become obsessed with his self-rating instead of with bettering his performances; (3) act *less* efficiently; and (4) ultimately become falsely convinced that he *cannot* perform adequately. Adler generally saw this difference between the person's rating his traits and rating himself; but he did not too precisely show his clients exactly how they were doing this and how they could challenge and dispute their self-evaluations until they rarely rated themselves at all.

Let us now examine Adler's view of some of the more specific negative emotions, such as anger, depression, and anxiety, to see how he accurately perceived and counterattacked them and in what ways his methods can be developed and improved. In regard to feelings of anger, he most perceptively and pioneeringly stated:

Anger is an affect which is the veritable epitome of the striving for power and domination. This emotion betrays very clearly that its purpose is the rapid and forceful destruction of every obstacle in the way of its angry bearer. Previous researches have taught us that an angry individual is one who is striving for superiority by the strenuous application of all his powers. . . . We must designate all irascible, angry, acrimonious individuals as enemies of society, and enemies of life. We must again call attention to the fact that their striving for power is built upon the foundations of their feelings of inferiority. . . . Temper tantrums are much more frequent among children than among adults. Sometimes an insignificant event is sufficient to throw a child into temper tantrums. This arises from the fact that children as a result of their greater feeling of inferiority, show their striving for power in a more transparent manner. An angry child is striving for recognition. Every obstacle he meets appears exceptionally difficult.[8]

It is probably true, as Adler states here, that "anger is an affect which is the veritable epitome of the striving for power and domination." Not that the angry individual *consciously* craves to be godlike and indominatable; but if we are thoroughly honest about it, which we rarely are about our feelings of anger, resentment, and hostility, we had better admit that virtually every time we become irate, we at least temporarily believe that someone else *should* not be acting in a certain manner or that some aspect of the world *ought* not to be the way it indubitably is. But to demand or dictate that people or things *must* be the way we want them to be *is* to be grandiose: since only God, obviously, has that power; and these days, even he is having one devil of a time exercising it!

As far as is scientifically known, there *are* no shoulds, oughts, or musts in the universe; and the world *doesn't* really, nor ever will, give a fig about us. The universe simply *is*; and it just doesn't think we are special, care whether we live or die, or insist that things go our way. To believe otherwise is clearly to aspire to be godlike. Anger, therefore, is obviously a grandiloquent *insistence,* like that of a child, that we get what we want.

There is good reason, however, to reject the Adlerian concept that all angry demanders, in their striving for power over others and the universe, are fundamentally overwhelmed by feelings of inferiority and that their grandiosity is a compensation for these feelings. Adler notes:

In paroxysms of rage, the whole gamut of inferiority and superiority appears with utter clarity. It is a cheap trick whereby the personal evaluation is raised at the cost of another's misfortune.[9]

This may be *sometimes* true; but there is no evidence that it is *always* so.

On the contrary, observation of normal and neurotic children and adults would tend to indicate that humans frequently are grandiose on the side of, or in addition to, their feelings of inadequacy. The young child strongly craves another child's toys and is furious when he cannot have them, not necessarily because he thinks he is inferior and impotent (which on other occasions he may also think) but simply because he is naturally the kind of creature who has low frustration tolerance: who easily believes that he *should* have what he wants. Similarly, very powerful adults—such as kings and millionaires—who have relatively few feelings of inadequacy, still childishly think that they *must* not be balked and become terribly enraged when, even in some minor way, they are.

Anger, in other words, invariably stems from grandiose distorted thinking: from the false conclusion that because one *wants* something very much and because one *could* theoretically obtain it, one *ought* to be endowed with it. It is doubtful if there is any feeling of resentment, rage, hostility, fury, or temper that does not directly stem from some consciously or unconsciously held belief in a *should, ought,* or *must.*

Adler also notes that "there are occasions when anger is largely justified," and I think he again errs here because he fails to discriminate clearly between rational and irrational beliefs. When, at point A, some action of an unjust or frustrating nature occurs, the individual can react to it with a rational belief at point B. This would take the form of internal reasoning: "Isn't it unfortunate that this injustice or frustration happened?" In which case, he will feel, at point C, the emotion of annoyance or irritation—but not anger! But if, at point B, he reacts with an irrational belief, and convinces himself: "It is awful that this injustice occurred! It *should* not have happened! I *can't stand* its occurrence!" he will then experience at point C the emotion of anger, hostility, or rage. What Adler, therefore, calls "justifiable" anger is in all probability annoyance or irritation; and this kind of "anger" can be very effective in helping the individual tackle the injustices and frustrations he encounters, and possibly minimizing or eliminating them. Real anger, however, that is either felt or expressed, seems invariably to have the additional magical element, or irrational belief at point B: "Injustice and frustration *should* not exist; and I can't stand the way that reality includes their existence!"

The second negative or destructive emotion that Adler discusses in detail is what he calls "sadness". What emerges is a confusion between sadness, depression, and despair—which are really qualitatively much different entities. Thus, Adler writes:

> The affect of sadness occurs when one cannot console himself for a loss or deprivation. Sadness, along with other affects, is a compensation for a feeling of displeasure or weakness, and amounts to an attempt to secure a better situation. In this respect its value is identical with that of a temper paroxysm. The difference is that it occurs as a result of other stimuli, is marked by a different attitude, and utilizes a different method. The striving for superiority is present, just as in all other affects, whereas an irate individual seeks to elevate his self-evaluation and degrade his opponent, and his anger is directed against an opponent . . . The sad person complains and with his complaint sets himself into opposition to his fellows. Natural as sorrow is in the nature of man, its exaggeration is a hostile gesture against society.[10]

Adler makes some very important, and again pioneering, points here. But unfortunately, he is imprecise and hence is unable to give any elegant solution to the problem of sadness and depression. In rational-emotive terms, this problem might be solved as follows:

At point A, an action occurs: The individual gets rejected by, say, his girl friend. At point B, his belief system intervenes to interpret what has happened to him at point A. First, he has a rational belief:

"Isn't it unfortunate that I got rejected; this is really too bad." If he stuck rigorously with this rational belief, he would have, as Adler points out, the feeling of sadness at point C, the consequence. He would feel terribly sorry about his loss, and because of his feeling of displeasure would attempt to secure a better situation—for example, to win his girl back or to get another girl friend.

But the individual does not stay with his rational belief about the action that has occurred at point A. Instead, he immediately tends to lap over to the additional, magical, irrational belief at point B: "Isn't it awful that I got rejected! What a worthless being I am! I'll probably never be able to get a suitable girl friend again!" This irrational belief leads to the inappropriate or neurotic consequence at point C—deep-seated feeling of anxiety and depression, withdrawal, and inertia in regard to trying to find another girl.

What is more, Adler indicates, the individual may have some other irrational beliefs at point B. He may conclude that now that he has lost his girl friend, he is no longer the king of lovers that he thinks he *should* be. He may feel so inadequate because of this belief that he may then feel forced to compensate and to gain false superiority again by trying to degrade his girl friend, showing extreme hostility to her, and making a real enemy of her. So his irrational beliefs at point B may cause him to be, at one and the same time, inappropriately self-deprecating and hostile to others.

It would be appropriate to question the implications of Adler that the depressed or despairing individual must feel both inferior *and* angry about his loss; though, statistically speaking, it is true that he often will. But he will frequently be self-condemning. And it is his irrational *ideas* of self-condemnation that *create* his depression.

If Adler's theories of anger and depression are correct, and if they are concretely translated into rational-emotive terms, the solution to these two important and ubiquitous problems becomes almost crystal clear. The angry individual would better vigorously Dispute—at point D—his irrational beliefs that it is *awful* that injustice occurred, that it *should* not have happened, and that he *can't stand* its occurring, until he fully acknowledges that it is not *awful* but only *inconvenient* if others treat him unfairly, that *it would be better* if these others treated him justly, but that is no reason why they *should*, and that he *can* tolerate, though never like, the injustices of life. At this point, he will arrive at E, the therapeutic Effect, which is to feel annoyed and irritated but no longer angry and upset about the injustices that occurred at point A.

In other words, the Adlerian position shows the individual that he ideologically created his own feelings of anger and depression, but it is somewhat vague as to what, exactly, he did to create these feelings and how, precisely, he may go about changing them. The rational-emotive position shows him concretely what irrational beliefs he subscribes to that create his feelings of anger and depression, and specifically how to dispute, to question and challenge, these ideas, until they are surrendered and until the feelings they engender not only temporarily abate but become, in time, much less likely spontaneously to arise again. For in RET, the individual is clearly shown how to differentiate his irrational from his rational beliefs, how to empirically and logically attack and uproot the latter, and how to carry out activity "homework" assignments that will help him depropagandize himself from his unscientifically held and self-defeating beliefs and how to acquire a basically sensible philosophy of living.

Let us consider one more profoundly dysfunctional emotion which Adler analyzes—that of anxiety. He writes:

> The mechanism of *anxiety* does not directly demonstrate any superiority—indeed it seems to illustrate a defeat. In anxiety one seeks to make oneself as small as possible, but it is at this point that the conjunctive side of this affect, which carries with it at the same time a thirst for superiority, becomes evident. The anxious individuals flee into the protection of another situation, and attempt to fortify themselves in this way until they feel themselves capable of meeting and triumphing over the danger to which they feel exposed. . . . In this case we are dealing with individuals who demand support from someone, who need someone paying attention to them at all times. As a matter of fact it amounts to nothing more than the institu-

tion of a master-slave relationship, as if someone else had to be present to aid and support the anxious one. Investigate this further and one finds many people who go through life demanding particular recognitions. They have so far lost their independence (as a result of their insufficient and incorrect contact with life) that they demand exceptional privileges, with extraordinary violence. No matter how much they seek out the company of others, they have little social feeling. But let them show anxiety and fright, and they can create their privileged position again. Anxiety helps them evade the demands of life, and enslaves all those about them. Finally it worms itself into every relationship in their daily lives, and becomes their most important instrument to effect their domination.[11]

Again, Adler is unusually perceptive in this passage; but there appears to be a quite unjustified concentration on the notion that superiority and inferiority feelings *have* to go together, and that consequently even the most anxious individual, who thinks that he needs everyone's approval, is also attempting to win the power struggle and to dominate others. There seems to be a confusion here between the *need* to dominate and the action the individual takes to effectuate that presumed need. The former can be extremely strong, while the latter can be virtually nonexistent.

Adler incisively sees that superiority strivings and inferiority feelings are almost invariably connected, but this still leaves us with the necessity of seeing *how* they are connected. If an individual devoutly wishes and ardently thinks that he needs to be almost perfect—as I think practically all of us do—he will almost certainly end up by thinking of himself as inferior or inadequate. For he is incredibly *fallible*; and he simply cannot get these particular wishes or so-called needs fulfilled. Once, moreover, he starts feeling inadequate, he will often (since he still has the overweening demand that he be adequate) rationalize and compensate for his failings, and he may not only then *desire* to be godlike but may actually begin to *behave* like God. But often, of course, does not mean always; and much more frequently, in fact, he will first demand that he be noble and great; then feel terribly inferior because he cannot achieve that demand; and then berate himself mercilessly for his feelings of inadequacy. In the process, he will not only give up his underlying *striving* to be superior but may even surrender his *desire* to be.

Adler, in zeroing in on that minority of individuals who feel inadequate and who *therefore* "demand exceptional privileges, with extraordinary violence," forgets that the majority feel inadequate without making such demands. Certainly, as he points out, *some* "spoiled brats" dominate those they love by immensely needing their help. But many nonspoiled brats dominate no one and end up feeling almost totally worthless.

Fundamentally and basically, Adler made great contributions toward the understanding of anxiety. He saw anxiety as a destructive emotion. In RET terms, we can develop this by stating that anxiety starts at point A, when an individual may not receive approval or achieve some goal he wishes to attain. At point B, his belief system, this individual then rationally tells himself, "Isn't it unfortunate if I fail! I shall be terribly sorry about failing. Let me see what I can do to succeed." If he sticks rigorously to this rational belief at point B, he will almost immediately experience, at point C, the emotional consequence of concern or caution; and he will thereby be helped to achieve the approval or goal that he desires.

If, however, this same individual irrationally tells himself, at point B, "Isn't it awful if I fail! I shall be an utter worm, a worthless person if I do! I absolutely *must* succeed!" he then, as a result of this irrational belief, starts experiencing anxiety, overconcern, and panic. No matter how much he rationalizes, compensates, or rules others by his overweening anxiety, he still underlyingly feels it: because he is still an essentially fallible human who will at times fail and he still, definitionally and foolishly, is convinced that it is awful to fail and that he *must* succeed.

When the problem of anxiety is concretely stated in these ideological, rational-emotive terms, the basic solution to it becomes crystal clear. The individual had better Dispute, at point D, his irrational Beliefs, by asking himself: "*Why* would it be awful if I fail?

Where is the evidence that I would be an utter worm if I do? Why *must* I succeed?'' If he keeps logically and empirically questioning his magic assumptions at point B, he will then almost always be able to answer himself: "It is not awful, but merely inconvenient, if I fail. There is no evidence, nor ever can be, that I am an utter worm if I do. I don't *have* to succeed, although it would be lovely if I did." He will then experience, at point E, the behavioral and emotional Effects of his disputing his irrational Beliefs: namely, a significant drop in his anxiety.

All this is implicit in individual psychology. Adler thought that disturbed humans guided their lives by fictions and by unrealistic and conflicting goals and purposes, and that, in order to become less disturbed, they must change these fictions and goals. He never seems to have concretely outlined, however, just what the basic irrational, disturbance-creating ideas of people usually are, and what precisely can be done about disputing and changing them. This is the task of rational-emotive therapy. In significant respects, therefore, individual psychology and RET importantly complement each other.

Nevertheless, Adler himself, as he developed his view of man and his philosophic-therapeutic outlook, may have been reaching toward answers not unlike those later developed by RET. Thus, in 1928 Adler came out with a paper, "Brief Comments on Reason, Intelligence, and Feeble-Mindedness," in which he distinguishes between private intelligence and reason or common sense. The latter is associated with social interest (meaning, an openness toward the world and empathy), while the former is characterized by lack of social interest. While, at this time, he did not completely abandon his earlier attempts to place the crux of psychological disorders on overwhelming inferiority feelings and grandiose compensation attempts, he did shift his emphasis to "the individual's distance from the . . . reasonable, generally human solution of a life problem" and he noted that all failures in life "are characterized by lack of social feeling,"[12] that is, lack of common sense.

In 1936, Adler also gave an interview to Dudley Barker of the London *Evening Standard,* in which he notes that "it is always the child who has no social interest who shuts himself up in himself, who develops imaginary grievances.'' And in this same interview, he disavowed some of his previous near-obsessiveness with what he originally called the "inferiority complex." Barker reports: '' 'That is only a phrase,' he insisted. 'All the world uses it now, but I seldom use it myself.' ''

Heinz Ansbacher notes that a careful reading of a new translation of Immanuel Kant's *The Classification of Mental Disorders* indicates that the great philosopher, a century before Adler, made a clear-cut distinction between private intelligence and common sense: "The only feature common to all mental disorders is the loss of common sense (*sensus communis*), and the compensatory development of a unique, private sense (*sensus privatus*) of reasoning." Ansbacher therefore concluded:

> To the present writer it is comforting to know that when he uses the Adlerian pair of opposites, ''private sense'' and ''common sense,'' he actually goes back to Kant, and that there is most likely a direct line from Kant to Adler. This last knowledge should remove all doubt, if some people still had any, that Adler belongs among the phenomenological, cognitive, understanding, Gestalt and field psychologists such as Spranger, Stern, Wertheimer, Lewin, all of whom can be said to have developed under the influence of Kant. On the other hand, Freud was never influenced by Kant.

Adler's antithesis between private intelligence and common sense or reason is much closer to RET views and practices than are some of his other notions about inferiority and grandiosity. For, mirroring my idea that there are no shoulds, oughts, or musts that we can scientifically prove and that the world does not really give a fig about us, Adler notes: "The belief that the cosmos ought to have an interest in the preservation of life is scarcely more than a pious hope."[13] And in line with the contention of RET adherents that the individual need not experience low frustration and anger just because he is severely deprived, Adler writes that the sensible (or should I say "common sensible"?) individual feels "at home on this earth with all its advantages and disadvantages. This feeling at home is directly a part of social interest . . . [The normal person] regards the adversities of life not as an injustice inflicted upon him."[14]

Adler's later view still leaves some important differences between Individual Psychology and rational-emotive therapy. For example, where the latter speaks of the irrationality of the individual, and implies that he has both false premises and illogical deductions from these premises, Adler contends only that his basic premises and goals are false but that he actually proceeds quite logically once he assumes that these premises are true. Adler and the Adlerians thereby seem to gain some therapeutic advantage, since the disturbed individual is not asked by them to change completely but only to change an error in his premises and goal. They can honestly show him that he is quite intelligent, but that he is merely starting with wrong assumptions; while the rational therapist might have to state or imply that since both his assumptions and his deductions are wrong, the client is really pretty stupid.

Although the Adlerian position does have some practical advantages, rational-emotive therapy seems to be confirmed more by empirical data. We have learned from Adler that the disturbed individual's basic premises and goals are false or fictional; but more concretely than Adler, we try to show him exactly *why* they are, and that all of his premises and goals, when logico-empirically parsed, are theological or unvalidatable statements.

As for the individual's tendency, when he is disturbed, to think illogically as well as to make irrational assumptions, this can be clinically and experimentally validated. Thus, Beck found that depressed patients differed significantly from nondepressed medical patients in that they produced many more cognitive distortions, including arbitrary inference, selective abstraction, overgeneralization, magnification and minimization, and inexact labeling. J. E. Overall and D. Gorham found that schizophrenic individuals showed disruption of formal thought processes, including such characteristics as irrelevant responses, disconnected ideas, vagueness, and peculiar word usage or syntax. My own studies show that in addition to nonveridical premises, all kinds of disturbed individuals tend to engage more frequently than do nondisturbed persons in various kinds of illogicalities, including short-sightedness, extremism, unthinkingness, wishful thinking, ineffective focusing, discrimination difficulties, and overgeneralization. Unless, therefore, a therapist fully faces the reality of human illogicality and crooked thinking (as well as the reality of the human proneness to accept false premises and goals), he will tend to be somewhat handicapped in his encounters with seriously disturbed people.

Adler's latter-day formulations regarding private intelligence and common sense reasoning distinctly improve upon his earlier overemphasis on the inferiority-grandiosity model of human behavior. RET, enriched by Adlerian thought, has gone forward, providing an improved model of psychotherapeutic understanding and practice.

There are essentially three different views of the origins of human emotions and how they can be changed. The first view is that of the behaviorists and of the Freudians; namely, that emotional reactions are primarily caused by external stimuli, events, or experiences—either in the individual's past or present life. The second view is that of the anti-intellectualists, many of whom are now represented in the modern encounter group and sensory awareness movement; namely, that emotions are sacrosanct unto themselves and essentially spring from themselves. The third view is that of the stoics and the phenomenologists; namely, that emotions are the result of human evaluations, appraisals, interpretations, and cognitions. Adler was largely in this third camp. He unequivocally stated:

> No experience is a cause of success or failure. We do not suffer from the shock of our experiences—the so-called *trauma*—but we make out of them just what suits our purposes. We, are *self-determined* by the meaning we give to our experiences; and there is probably something of a mistake always involved when we take particular experiences as the basis for our future life. Meanings are not determined by situations, but we determine ourselves by the meanings we give to situations.[15]

This seems to me to be an essentially rational and sensible view of human emoting and experiencing. It is the main view, moreover, which profoundly and distinctly shows what man can do to change his disordered and inappropriate emotionalizing.

Although Adler at times was not too clear about how, in detail, man's self-defeating emotional reactions can be modified, he was very definite about the general method of changing them; namely, education. He above all other modern therapists pioneered in advancing the concept that psychotherapy is education and that education would better be psychotherapeutic.

NOTES

[1] Adler, 1964a: 26-27.
[2] Adler, 1927: 72.
[3] Adler, 1964b: 67.
[4] Adler, 1964a: 19.
[5] For example, Berne (1964); Dubois (1907); Kelly (1955); Low (1952); Phillips (1956); Rotter (1954); Thorne (1950); and many others.
[6] Adler, 1927: 157, 189.
[7] *Ibid.*: 157.
[8] *Ibid.*: 267-270.
[9] *Ibid.*: 269.
[10] *Ibid.*: 270.
[11] *Ibid.*: 275.
[12] Adler, 1964b: 53.
[13] Adler, 1964a: 272.
[14] Adler, 1964b: 43.
[15] Adler, 1958: 14.

9

SELF-AWARENESS AND PERSONAL GROWTH OF THE PSYCHOTHERAPIST

Asking a modern psychologist whether he thinks it advisable for therapy to lead to the continuing self-awareness and personal growth of the psychotherapist is like asking a good Christian whether he is against sin. Few recent authorities have failed to emphasize that one of the main goals of psychological treatment is to help the therapist as well as the patient to develop into a more creative and self-fulfilled individual. Even the Freudians—who in the old days seemed to be intent on taking themselves *out* of the therapeutic process and putting only the client himself on stage for literally hundreds of sessions—have in the last couple of decades focused with equal intensity so much on the analyst and *his* problems that *countertransference* has become the most sacred term in the analytic literature.

The new view of transference finds its rationale in the well-being of the client. It is based on the theory that if the therapist spies on himself with sufficient perspicacity and if he eliminates the grandiose distortions through which he normally—or is it abnormally?—sees the client's problems, he will stop introducing into the therapeutic relationship his own neurotic motivations and will thereby be able to help the client more successfully. This seems sensible enough; but what the theory fails to note is that some of the things that the therapist *will* introduce into the sessions with the client if he keeps intensely meditating on himself are not only of dubious merit but are likely to be highly iatrogenic.

Another theory in defense of emphasizing the therapist's awareness of himself in the course of his relationship with the client, is that of some modern existentialists, experientialists, and phenomenologists.[1] According to their view, the therapist must really be *himself*, must be quite self-congruent, if he is to have an authentic encounter with the client; consequently, if that is the way he happens to feel, he should stand on his head, masturbate, tell the client he hates him, or do just about anything he pleases during the therapeutic hour, as long as he truly believes in what he is doing and feeling and is not being in any way artificial. This theory seems to be straightforward enough if it is taken to mean that the therapist is an individual, too, with his own right to live and have a ball, and that in any existential encounter he is entitled to be himself and to get as much out of the therapeutic relationship as he possibly can.

The first difficulty with this theory is that it assumes that the client-therapist relationship is and should be an existential encounter. If it truly is, then why is the client paying for it and the therapist being rewarded by anything more than the encounter itself? Moreover, are authentic existential encounters actually feasible or possible when one of the collaborators has distinct disturbances—is highly paranoid for example—and is not truly capable of relating to another human being, but is only seeking what Helmuth Kaiser called fusion, what I call the dire need to be loved, and what others call dependency? Thomas Szasz can wail from now till doomsday that mentally ill people are not really ill, but that they are merely judged so by an overly blaming society. But he is still, in my opinion, on the wrong track when he refuses to face the increasingly obvious reality that schizophrenics are born as well as made, and that they have a deficiency in relating that often makes a farce out of any attempt by a therapist to have an authentic existential encounter with them.

As therapists, moreover, we'd better realistically admit that many or most of our clients are simply not the kind of people we personally would choose for close friends; and as Schofield has pointed out, we give them only a special mode of paid friendship. It seems ridiculous, therefore, to speak of authentic encounters between two individuals, one of whom is usually considerably brighter, better educated, less disturbed, less dependent, and less interested in being friendly than is the other. This is not to say that worthwhile existential dialogues or I-Thou relations *could* not occur between some clients and some therapists; they can and at times they undoubtedly do. The question is: how *often* are they likely to take place? And the honest answer, considering the limitations that the therapeutic relationship normally imposes, would seem to be: seldom.

If this is so, then the notion that therapy is supposed to be a collaborative encounter where the therapist derives just about as much fun and frolic out of the relationship as does the therapee is hardly tenable, and it is folly to pretend otherwise. The existentialist position, therefore, in the last analysis, boils down to the same point as the psychoanalysts make; namely, that if the therapist is truly himself in the course of the time he spends with the client, he will thereby increase the latter's chances of being improved or cured. On the surface, this seems to be a fairly good argument: since if the therapist has the courage to be himself, he may well serve as a good model for the client, who presumably has much less courage in this direction, and may by this kind of behavior help teach the client how to take more risks in his own right and how to get over some of his fears of living.

Again, however, the theory sounds better than its practical application may be. For one thing, it is merely an assumption that if the therapist leads a fully committed, swinging kind of existence, and the client is inhibited and depressed, the latter will take heart from the former's example and begin to become a swinger himself. The facts, sadly enough, often prove otherwise: for the client, even before he comes to therapy, usually has encountered some friends or relatives who are much happier and effective than he. Rather than being constructively moved by their example, he has on the contrary usually told himself that just *because* these people are alive and productive, and just *because* he is not, he is undoubtedly worthless himself, and he might just as well give up entirely on trying to emulate them.

I often find exactly the same thing happening in therapy. My clients are almost all sad sacks, distinctly less creative and productive than they are potentially capable of being. When they realize that I do not get upset by any of their tricks and testings, and that I blithely continue to see them and other clients and to have quite an enjoyable time seeing them, and at the same time turn out a significant number of books, articles, speeches, radio and TV appearances, they frequently tell me that my activity makes them feel worse than they did before: because they believe that they *should* be able to work on my kind of level, and they obviously as yet cannot. Until, therefore, I am able actively to depropagandize these clients, and vigorously convince them that they need *not* follow my personal lead in order to have a high estimation of themselves, I find that my being a good model to them frequently boomerangs.

Furthermore, it is likely that most clients, even before they arrange to see a given therapist, assume that he is more effective in his way of life than they are; and it should hardly come as a great surprise to them when this actually proves to be the case. If they thought he was *as* incompetent and error-prone as they are convinced that they themselves are, they would hardly seek his aid in the first place; and when they find that he is not this inadequate, they may be gratified to know that the possibility of human effectiveness, which they previously assumed existed, actually does exist. There is no reason to believe that they are startled into changing their behavior significantly by this gratifying discovery.

The theory that the client is significantly helped by finding a good life model in the therapist is limited by the fact that he may actually be the reverse. He may be—and in fact, not infrequently is—one of the worst possible models, and if he really is himself while he is with the client (rather than playing the role of the sensible person he would like to be, but in real life definitely is not), he may serve as the kind of model that a neighborhood gangster all too frequently provides to a growing boy.

On several counts, then, the theory that the therapist should be his authentic self in order that he may (*a*) have a real, worthwhile encounter, or (*b*) provide a model image with which the client can identify and into which he can help change himself, has serious limitations. This is not to say that it is of no value whatever; but merely that all available evidence leads one to suspect that, at the very least, its validity should be considered dubious.

"Well, that may be so," you may interject, "but that hardly gainsays the fact that the therapist's self-awareness is a highly desirable thing, and that one of his main goals in therapy should be continually to develop this trait. After all, *any* technician is better off if he is consciously aware of what he is doing and openmindedly prepared to use his insight into himself to change his ways and correct his shortcomings. How could this kind of self-sensitivity *not* be very helpful to him and his client?"

Self-awareness is a nice sounding word; but behind its mellifluously polished bell peals a more than slightly tarnished clapper. One pernicious aspect of self-awareness, for example, is self-consciousness. For a human being to know what he is doing, it is frequently necessary for him to focus sharply on his own performances; and this is by no means all to the good. In fact, as Knight Dunlap pointed out some decades ago, extreme introspection, dangerously encouraged by psychoanalysis, is one of the very cores of neurosis. Dunlap said of the analytic client:

> In repeated periods of treatment his attention is kept fixed
> on himself, and he examines himself, and examines his circumstances, always with self-reference. In most cases he is
> instructed to introspect when away from the place of treatment, to carry introspection as a habit into his daily life.
> That this procedure intensifies a pathological trait already
> established there is no doubt. It seems also to develop the

trait of introspection in persons not previously afflicted with it.

Dunlap doubtless exaggerates here—since calm and nonblaming introspection may be of decided help to disturbed people. But his point is not entirely ill taken, because the neurotic (and, especially, the psychotic) client is frequently overaware of his own thoughts and feelings when he comes to treatment. To spend many sessions making him still more aware of himself, without concomitantly actively depropagandizing his self-condemning tendencies, is irresponsible, and has probably been instrumental in driving not a few psychotherapy patients into more aggravated states of confusion, anxiety, and depression.

By the same token, the therapist who deliberately makes himself acutely aware of all his own reactions during the therapy sessions is risking turning himself into an obsessive-compulsive or some other kind of extreme neurotic, and thereby may be encouraging his client to do likewise. The more he monomaniacally ruminates on what he thinks and feels about himself, and the more he discusses his own inner demons with this client, the more is the latter likely to feel encouraged to reflect continually over his own cerebrations—and to remain as sick as, or to get even sicker than, before.

This mode of analytic self-rumination, moreover, serves as a most fascinating though pernicious kind of diversion for both the therapist and his therapee. For the main goal of almost every client is not really to work hard at changing the philosophic assumptions that make and keep him sick—especially the assumptions that he must perform perfectly and be loved by every significant figure in his life if he is to consider himself worthwhile—but to manage to live fairly comfortably while persisting in these untenable beliefs. And the main goal of the therapist, if he is efficient, is to help to knock these ideas out of the client's head and induce him to make more plausible, reality-centered premises and value systems around which to build his life. When, however, the therapist is intensely preoccupied with contemplating his own contemplations, he is going to have little time and energy to spend persuading the client to give up *his* delusions; and both will easily tend to play games with each other and to "enjoy" an *égoisme à deux*—or even a *folie à deux*—relationship which maintains the gruesomely existent staus quo and helps no one.

The client's basic disturbance is that he usually overreacts to an undesirable situation with too much negative feeling, and then he keeps focusing and refocusing on his own feeling. The one thing he practically never concentrates on is the real *cause* of this feeling; namely, the irrational, self-defeating ideational premises that he keeps indoctrinating himself with in order to generate it and keep it viciously alive. The therapist would better continue showing the client that the disordered emotions—the guilt, anxiety, depression, and hostility—that he keeps experiencing are only of symptomatic importance; it is the cognitive nonsense, the internalized sentences behind these emotions, that are truly significant, that have to be clearly seen and actively challenged by the client before he can modify them and get himself better. But if the ultra-self-aware therapist is reveling in his own transference-countertransference feelings during the therapeutic sessions, he is at least inferentially espousing a condition of self-indulgence that will hardly help, and will frequently harm, the already too-indulgent and frustration-intolerant client.

Human feelings, moreover, are poor criteria of truth and reality. The fact that I strongly feel that there is a kindly God watching over me or that I am really the Queen of Sheba and everyone is against me and no one wants to acknowledge my real identity hardly is any proof that these allegations are true. Unless I soundly check the premises and beliefs behind these feelings, I am not likely to prove a single thing by having them—except that I am out of my mind. If I bring these feelings to a therapist, and he spends a large part of my sessions telling me *his* feelings about *me*, and relating these to mine about him, the emotions that we thus unburden onto each other may be just as rooted in reality as were my original grandiose or self-deprecatory feelings. Even if our feelings are true reflections of the external world—if he tells me, for instance, that he hates me because he thinks I am behaving quite obnoxiously, and I tell him that I loathe him because he doesn't seem to be helping me—there is no reason to believe that our mutual expressions of these feelings will be particularly helpful. The real therapeutic point *still* is: Which of our basic value systems *caused* the feelings, and what can we do to *change* these values? It is hard to imagine a way to obscure this point better than my therapist and I reveling in hatred for each other.

A further pernicious aspect of self-awareness is its propensity for self-indulgence. If the therapist is heavily engaged in feeling, expressing, and analyzing his own emotions during the hour that is presumably reserved for the client, he can easily deflect the latter—not to mention himself, as well—from the fundamental question of what caused these feelings and what can be done about *un*causing them in the future. It so happens that the *work* attached to asking and answering this kind of question is often deemed to be highly onerous by human beings—and particularly by those whom we call mentally ill. Whereas these same individuals will work their heads off at creating all sorts of needless phobias, fits, compulsions, and other manifestations of their disturbances, they will rarely try very hard to undo the results of their negative efforts. Although it is quite easy and enjoyable for a man to emote, and even to ruminate about the fact that he is emoting, and although it may also be satisfying for him to turn up interesting (and often highly implausible) psychodynamic explanations for his emotions, it is much more difficult for him (*a*) to track down the concrete, simple, exclamatory sentences that he tells himself to create his feelings; and (*b*) to keep consciously questioning and challenging these sentences until he finally dispenses with them, and changes them into saner philosophies of action.

In any event, by emphasizing his own self-awareness during the therapy sessions, the therapist may indulge himself in several different ways: 1. Forget that his main, and highly specific job, is to help the client rather than himself. 2. Ignore the fact that therapy is largely work, both on his own and the client's part, instead of pleasure. 3. Go for immediate gratification rather than long-range gain: try to help the patient *feel* better rather than *get* better. 4. Fail to teach the client, by his own good example, the value of a self-disciplined, well-ordered life. 5. Give up too easily and too quickly on the slow, plodding, retraining effort that is usually necessary to get most clients, especially the borderline and outright psychotics, to change their poor thinking and immature behaving.

Quite directly, then, the therapist who is overconcerned about his self-awareness may shirk some of his therapeutic responsibilities. What is more, by this kind of avoidance, he tends to set up a sabotaging paradigm for his client to follow.

Still another deleterious factor in the therapist's overemphasizing self-awareness may be the evaluative aspect that he gives to his countertransferring activities once he presumably discovers them. The main reason why self-rumination is baneful is not because, as Dunlap seemed to think, it is harmful *per se*, but because almost all humans who engage in it do so in a worrisome, self-depreciating manner. The man who keeps thinking about the ineffective way in which he asked his boss for a raise, or the spectacle he made of himself when he was impotent with his sweetheart, is not just viewing and reviewing the *events* surrounding his failures, he is invariably evaluating him*self* in terms of these events. In other words, he irrationally involves his entire ego with his performance, and thinks that because the latter was poor, *he* is no good *in toto*. And it is his negative *evaluation* of himself that makes his rumination about his misdeeds so dreadful.

This is what the therapist who obsessively makes himself aware of his therapeutic errors is likely to do. Rather than just *seeing* that he has, let us say, been jealous of his client for making more money than he makes and consequently advising this client to retire at an early age and commit himself to nonprofitable pursuits, he may savagely excoriate himself for being thus prejudiced. In so doing, he may transmit his own guilt (or some of the consequences thereof) to his client, and may in fact help the latter to be just as illogically guilt ridden as he is himself. Or he may be so ashamed that the client will discover his prejudice that he may deal with him in an overreactive, love-giving manner, and thereby do him as much harm as good. Or he may, at the very least, be so preoccupied with his own self-castigation that he will supremely fail to engage in what is most probably the most therapeutic of all methods; namely, vigorously and directly counterattacking the client's self-blaming tendencies, until he is forced to give them up.

An overemphasis on the therapist's self-awareness may easily lead to a degree of self-centeredness that goes beyond desirable limits. Enlightened self-interest is almost certainly a fine trait for both therapist and client to aim at; the first and foremost law of human morality is probably: To thine *own* self be true. Self-centeredness, however, goes far beyond self-interest, in that the self-centered individual not only thinks that he has a right to be as happy as anyone else, but also that the world should really revolve around him and provide him with a special kind of happiness, whatever fate may befall others. He grandiosely believes that the world owes him a living, and should provide it with little effort on his part; and he consequently does little but inconsiderately go after his own satisfactions, wail like a banshee when he is deprived in any way, and either totally ignore the feelings of others or actually gratuitously do them in. Self-centeredness, then, does not consist of a healthy focusing but of a distorted *over*focusing on oneself and one's problems. It is frequently a *demand* that others be of service, and a wild attempt to get their approval because it is felt that their love is *absolutely needed*. In the terms of David Riesman, self-centeredness therefore is integrally related to other-directedness instead of self-directedness; and in some other ways is conspicuously misnamed, since the "self" that the self-centered individual is concentrating upon is by no means necessarily a truly accepted one, but is quite dependent on the help and approval of others.

Just as self-awareness can lead to some of the other evils we have been examining in this chapter, it can also result in self-centeredness. For the therapist who keeps asking himself what *he* (rather than his client) is doing wrong can easily become callous and essentially uninterested in that client. Under the guise of changing himself to help the other, he can irresponsibly forget his main task and devote himself almost solely to self-enhancement. Even if he to some extent succeeds in this respect, and becomes a happier person because of the work he does on himself during the therapeutic hour, he is still taking advantage of the client's helpless situation and is demanding that he be especially rewarded for being the great therapist that he supposedly is. In this way, he is insisting that the universe serve him, rather than that he do very much to serve himself in the world. By being childishly grandiose, the therapist is not helping himself grow, and is acting as a poor model to his client—who himself usually has some serious problems of refusing to accept grim reality and demanding that the cosmos be unusually kind to him.

In many ways, then, the emphasis by the therapist on his own awareness, during the course of his sessions with the client, has potentially destructive aspects. This is not to say, of course, that the increased consciousness of his own thinking and feeling processes is all to the bad, for it does have obvious advantages. It enables the therapist to see and correct his own therapeutic mistakes; it can be projectively used by him to give him additional insight into his client; it sometimes helps the therapist in his personal growth, which in turn may eliminate his countertransference reactions and help him serve as a better model to the client; and it may be beneficial in other ways. The main point that I am making, however, is that increased self-awareness on the part of the therapist has its distinct hazards; and it is unscientific and inefficient of us to deny this.

However, it is not merely countertransference that must be warned against, it is transference itself, the efficacy of which is at best a matter of considerable doubt. Partially I can go along with the contention of Carl Rogers that the therapist's unconditional positive regard for the client is a necessary condition for good therapy. Most clients accept themselves only conditionally, and blame themselves mercilessly for their shortcomings; therefore, they are considerably helped by a therapist who shows them, in his actions as well as his words, that he believes that people can be of value to themselves and lead happy lives just because they exist, and not because they do anything well or unusually please others. But when the Rogerians, along with the Freudians, Sullivanites, experientialists, existentialists, and other kinds of therapists, insist that effective therapy must also involve an intense interpersonal relationship between the therapist and client, or a warm acceptance or a deep emphatic understanding of the latter by the former, then they may be injecting their own dire need for the client's love and approval into their theories of therapy and their actual relationships with their therapees.

Actually, quite effectual therapy, leading to a basic personality change, can be done without any relationship whatever between client and therapist. It can be accomplished by correspondence, by readings, and by tape recordings and other audiovisual aids, without the client having any contact with or knowing practically anything about the person who is treating him. It can also be effected, if you are a therapist utilizing the more usual kind of face-to-face sessions, with clients who think that you dislike them, who actively hate you, who feel that you are only lecturing at them, who blindly follow exercises that you give them, and who otherwise maintain a minimal, and often unpleasant, relationship with you. This has been amply proved not only by rational-emotive psychotherapists, but by the behavior and conditioning therapists as well. Stranger still, if reports out of Princeton are to be believed, encounters between schizophrenic children and a talking typewriter, with no therapist whatever in the picture, have been shown to be therapeutically effective.

The idea that specific relationship difficulties *have to be* the basic reason why human beings become emotionally disturbed, and that therefore transference and countertransference *must be* the primary approach to helping them overcome their disturbances, is a most dubious hypothesis. It ignores several fairly obvious facts that provide contradictory evidence. First, if human beings are so easily upset by their negative and double-binding relationships with their parents and other significant figures in their early lives, they must be born with a distinct tendency to be so affected; and if so, it is highly likely that some are born with more vulnerability than others. Second, anyone who is emotionally destroyed because his parental figures did not treat him properly clearly must have some cognitive expectations or philosophic assumptions behind his supersensitiveness; namely, the unrealistic assumptions that people, and particularly his parents, *should* treat him better and that he *must* have their approval in order to like himself. Third, anyone who becomes upset by his poor relations with those significant to him during his childhood, and who remains appreciably disturbed forever after, must patently be repeating to himself, when he is an adult, the same silly views about the world which he was born and raised to believe when he was young. It is his own constant reiterations of these childish beliefs, rather than the early misperceptions that helped him acquire the beliefs, that *now* nourish and keep alive his disturbance. Fourth, since it is, in one way or another, always the individual's *ideas* about the necessity of his receiving approval from others during his childhood and his adulthood that make him disturbed when he has a relationship difficulty, and since it is his own uncritical acceptance of and self-defeating perpetuation of these ideas that keeps him neurotic or psychotic today, *any* means of getting him to challenge, question, and change these philosophic premises will be therapeutic.

One of these means, of course, may be through his having a good interpersonal relationship with a therapist. For he may thereby conclude that if the therapist warmly accepts him, he can unconditionally accept himself, and no longer be so concerned as to whether his parents or others treat him kindly. On the contrary, however, he may even more easily come to the false conclusion that if the therapist loves him, he is *therefore* not the worthless thing he formerly thought he was, and that he can now more successfully go about winning the approval of others. In this case, he has not really changed his love-needing philosophy one iota; he is just as sick as he was before, but is now a "happier" or "better adjusted" invalid because he is convinced that he *can* get the love which he so wrongly still thinks that he absolutely must have.

The transference hypothesis of the cause and cure of emotional disturbance, then, is a highly limited and superficial view. It ignores the biological and the philosophic origins and underpinnings of transference phenomena; and it fails to see the great importance of the rational and persuasive element in psychotherapy, emphasized in recent years by Donald Ford and Hugh Urban, Donald R. Stieper and Daniel N. Wiener, and others. Some of the most effective methods of therapy, such as direct explanation, didactic training, logical parsing, and homework assignments—which are highly efficacious in rational-emotive psychotherapy—are neglected or counteracted by therapists who overemphasize relationship methods.

This is not to say that support, warmth, ego bolstering, emphasizing the patient's assets, helping him solve his practical problems, showing personal respect for him, and similar actions and attitudes, are not legitimate aids in psychotherapy. Sometimes they are, and at times these supportive methods work where virtually no other techniques will. But not always! And in many or most instances, their main value may well be that of propping up the client until he finally is induced to tackle his basic philosophic premises and to *change* his ways of thinking and emoting, rather than to learn to live pseudosuccessfully with these inefficient ways.

Assuming that transference and countertransference have their distinct advantages and limitations in the therapeutic armamentarium, and that heightened self-awareness on the part of the therapist is both a good and a bad thing, can it also be said that continuing personal growth by the therapist also has its distinct drawbacks? Yes and no—for the answer to this question depends on what kinds of personal growth one is talking about and how it is used to help the client.

Real personal growth and maturity on the part of the therapist, it would appear, is almost always beneficial to the client, because it involves the acceptance by the therapist of the unvarnished reality that doing therapy is not invariably a thing of beauty and joy; that some clients are obnoxious and distressing, but that's the way they are; and that, believe it or not, the main function of therapy is to *try* (though not necessarily to succeed) to help the client to get better. Or, to use an old term of Carl Rogers, the sane therapist has to be largely client-centered in his goals, even if his methods are, as are my own, very much inner-directed, theory-based, and authoritative, and hence are *not* directly inspired by the client's productions. His subsidiary goal may well be to enjoy and help himself during the therapeutic session, but his main goal would better be that of helping the client. If it is not, I would strongly advise him to work for greater maturity—or else to cease the practice of therapy and become a teacher, researcher, experimenter, or find some other outlet for his talents and training.

Like all human beings, the therapist had better be primarily true to, and interested in, himself, rather than be masochistically self-sacrificial. He can thereby engage in therapy because he *likes* to do so, because he *enjoys* helping others help themselves. If he likes being a therapist because he prefers the status of his profession, desires to direct the lives of others, is interested in digging up gossip about his neighbors, delights in the detective game of putting the jigsaw puzzle pieces of his clients' lives together, wants to earn a good living doing physically unstrenuous work, or for various other reasons of this sort, he is entitled to his preferences. But if he is to be both a good therapist and a good force for himself, he'd better like helping people solve their problems for their sake as well as his own.

In addition, the mature therapist should preferably possess several other traits if he is to be of maximum help to his therapees. He can try to be self-directed rather than dependent and in dire need of others' approval; tolerant and uncondemning when people act the way he does not like them to act; accepting of uncertainty and chance, and willing to exist in a nonperfectionistic, unabsolutistic way; flexible, unbigoted, and open to change at all times; objective, rational, and scientific in his thinking; committed to some vital absorbing interest in something outside of himself, whether it be in people, things, or ideas; able to take risks and gracefully to accept failure when it occurs; unqualified self-respecting, and capable of accepting himself just because he exists, whether or not other people approve his performances.

If the therapist continues his personal growth in *these* directions he will be of considerably greater help to his clients than if he remains dependent, intolerant, perfectionistic, inflexible, irrational, alienated, anxious, and self-depreciating. Why? Because he can then serve as a better model of mental health to his clients, can risk losing their approval when he tries some methods they do not relish, can accept them unconditionally even when they behave execrably toward him and others, can have more energies to throw into his therapeutic activities, and can more experientially comprehend the rules of straight thinking that he has to teach them if they are to overcome their own irrationalities. All of this is hypothetical, based on a commonsense assumption and on a theoretical approach to psychotherapy that would lead one to believe that healthier therapists do more effective work with their clients than do many of the very unhealthy persons who seem to inhabit the field.

Presuming that the therapist's personal growth *is* a good thing for both him and his client, would this aim not be enhanced by his becoming increasingly aware of himself during therapy? Again: yes and no. If he unblamefully and nonperfectionistically became aware of his poor performances—such as his projections and his grandiosity—he might well work his head off at changing these performances, and thereby help himself and his therapees. But if he severely castigates himself for his countertransference reactions and becomes negatively obsessed with these aspects of his personality, he will only sabotage himself and his patients.

To be therapeutically helpful, then, the therapist's self-awareness had better be more philosophical than observational, and include his not merely seeing *what* he is doing during therapy, but what are the *ideas, beliefs, and value systems* which lie behind and cause his disruptive countertransference reactions. He comprehends these ideas are exactly the same as the disturbance-creating nonsense that the client tells himself—the irrational beliefs, for example, that he *has to be* successful as a therapist, that he *must be* loved by his clients, that he *must be* the greatest therapist who ever lived. Unless he clearly sees these philosophic premises, and most actively, directly, and thinkingly attacks and eradicates them, he will be doing the most superficial kind of therapy with himself no matter *how* aware of his countertransferences he is.

Ordinary insight, whether it be into the client or into the therapist himself, is far, far from enough. The therapist, like the therapee, will obtain three different kinds of insight if he is truly to eliminate his self-defeating and patient-defeating countertransference attitudes. First, he will realize that his countertransferences have concrete philosophic antecedents—that behind every negative emotion is a corresponding irrational belief. Second, he will see that these philosophies now exist not because he acquired them early in life, or was conditioned to have them by his parents, but only because *he* continues to uncritically accept them and continues to convince himself that they are true. Third, he will understand fully, and I mean *fully,* that there is no other way but constant work and practice, continual counterattacking, cogitation, and action, if he is to uproot and eradicate the self-indoctrinations that made him and now keep him the irrational person and the inefficient therapist that he is.

Psychotherapy today is, in many instances, one of the most wasteful, ineffective modes of treatment ever invented—mainly because it tries to help most clients function more effectively with their ill-founded philosophies of life instead of compelling them to face reality and give up these views. It largely helps people feel better rather than get better. The special kind of psychotherapy that we call analysis of the countertransference usually falls into the same booby trap that most other therapy does: it helps the therapist feel good because he now sees some of his own errors and can pat himself on the back for achieving such remarkable insight. It does not show him the philosophic mentality behind his transference and counter-transference reactions, nor what to *do* about these irrational pre mises. It thereby leads the therapist up the same garden path through which he conducts most of his own clients; and the more psychoanalytic he is, the longer and more futile is his tour. It is a mar-velous kind of poetic justice, but one which neither the client nor the therapist deserves, and which both can and had better avoid.

NOTES

[1] As Perls (1969); Maslow (1962); Rogers (1961); and Whitaker and Malone (1953).

10

THE GOALS OF PSYCHOTHERAPY

My main goals in treating any of my psychotherapy clients are simple and concrete: to leave the client, at the end of the psychotherapeutic process, with a minimum of anxiety (or self-blame) and of hostility (or blame of others and the world around him); and just as importantly, to give him a method of self-observation and self-assessment that will ensure that, for the rest of his life, he will continue to be minimally anxious and hostile. Does this mean that I think human anxiety and hostility are invariably self-defeating and that there is no good reason why a presumably well-adjusted person *need* experience these emotions in an intense and sustained manner? It definitely does.

To avoid confusion, it is desirable that such terms as anxiety and hostility be operationally defined. Human beings, in order to preserve themselves in a difficult and alien world, must to some extent be fearful, cautious, or vigilant. If they did not have inborn tendencies to learn easily to look before they leap, they would quickly kill themselves. Operationally defined, therefore, fear consists of the following idea or attitude or internalized sentence: "It would be unfortunate if I hurt myself or got killed; therefore I'd better watch my step, e.g., look before I leap, see whether other people are going to attack me, mind my p's and q's when I am being observed by my teacher or boss, etc." Fear, in other words, is prophylactic, and includes the notions: (1) something or someone is dangerous to me; (2) therefore I'd better *do something* to protect myself against this dangerous thing or person.

Anxiety is quite different from fear in that it invariably includes a third idea, namely, "Since I am inherently an inadequate, incompetent, and worthless individual, and since such an individual *cannot* satisfactorily meet any real danger that threatens him, I therefore cannot possibly cope with this dangerous person or thing with which I am confronted; there is consequently nothing I can do to save myself, and I *must* be destroyed." Anxiety, in other words, adds to the ideas of danger and action against this danger, the superfluous, and essentially metaphysical (that is, unprovable) ideas that the threatened individual is intrinsically or innately unable to cope with the potential or existing danger; that he will absolutely *never* be able to do so; that his cause is consequently *hopeless*; and that by demonstrating that he cannot cope adequately with a *present* danger (or possibility of danger) he indisputably proves that he can *never* properly handle a similar kind of threat.

Stated still differently—since it is most important that we understand what anxiety truly is before we try to eliminate it—anxiety includes not only the person's estimation of the real danger involved in the *situation* which he is in, but also his objective appraisal of his probable *ability* to cope with this situation, and his guesses as to which *solutions* might be best to get him out of this presumably dangerous situation. Going further, anxiety includes the individual's moralistic, negativistic, highly pessimistic evaluations of *himself*, and his implied or stated conclusion that *he* will never be able to handle this or any other similar dangerous situation. Anxiety, moreover, invariably includes an unprovable overgeneralization: namely, that because the individual *has* not as yet figured out a good solution to the danger that he thinks is threatening him, and perhaps because he *has* not been able to cope satisfactorily with similar dangers in the past, he *never* will be able to do so, and therefore is a rotten *person.*

Because anxiety—unlike fear, which is situation appraising and action inducing—is self-appraising and action inhibiting, it practically always leads to unfortunate results. Instead of observing his presumably dangerous circumstances and trying to meet them today or prevent their occurring tomorrow, as an appropriately fearful person would do, the anxious individual mainly observes his own hopeless ineptness to meet the assumed danger. He consequently meets it badly or runs away from meeting it; he usually creates an even more dangerous, or presumably dangerous, situation; he then blames himself even more for being a hopeless incompetent; and he winds up, of course, by becoming more and more anxious. His self-blame impedes performance; he once again wrongly concludes that he cannot cope (instead of *has* not coped) with danger; and he becomes increasingly self-blaming, and increasingly unable to cope with danger. Anxiety, therefore, is dysfunctional and impedes performance, whereas fear may be functional and enable the individual to deal properly with a dangerous situation.

Hostility, like anxiety, also has two parts, a sane and an insane part, when it is operationally defined. The first, or sane, part of hostility consists of what may be called discomfort, displeasure, annoyance, or irritation with an unpleasant situation or a difficult person. Thus, when it rains just as you are about to go on a picnic, or when someone censures you unjustly, you irritatedly may say to yourself: "I definitely don't like this annoying situation (or person); now let me see how I can go about changing it (or dealing with it or him) so that it (or he) is no longer annoying." This sentence, like that which accompanies fear, has two main ideas: (1) Something or someone is unpleasant or irritating to me, and (2) therefore I'd better *do* something to change this thing or person and thus minimize my irritation.

Hostility, like anxiety, is radically different from displeasure or annoyance in that it invariably includes a third idea, namely, "Since this thing or person that is bothering me is noxious, and since the thing theoretically *could* not exist, or the person theoretically *could* not be the way he is, it is logical for me to conclude that this thing *should* not exist and that this person *should* not be the way he is.'' Or, another way of stating this idea is to say that the angry person grandiosely and falsely concludes that ''Because I don't *like* this thing (or person), it (or he) *shouldn't* exist.'' This anger-creating idea, of course, is a metaphysical or unprovable assumption because there is simply no provable reason why a thing that I dislike *shouldn't* exist just *because* I don't like it and because it *could* be different.

Anger, like anxiety, is dysfunctional in that, where the annoyed or irritated individual frequently does something effective to remove the source of his irritation, an angry or hostile person mainly stews in his own juice, spends most of his time and energy cursing the source of irritation rather than doing anything to change it, usually encourages the people at whom he is angry to turn against him and to become even more irritating, and finally ends up in the center of a vicious circle of self-created and self-perpetuated hostility. Moreover, since anger (like anxiety) is generally an unpleasant feeling, he needlessly stirs up his own guts by bringing it on. Unlike anxiety, anger does have some advantages, since the hostile individual can despise others and feel ''superior'' to them, thereby giving himself some amount of satisfaction. But the real gains to be derived from hostility are rarely worth the enormous costs it generally entails; and it is therefore (unlike irritation and annoyance) an emotion that is sanely to be fought and conquered.

Both anxiety and anger frequently, though not always, include another metaphysical notion that connects them with each other, and tends to make the anxious person angry and the hostile person anxious. Thus, the anxious individual, after convincing himself that he *himself* is a worthless slob who cannot possibly cope adequately with the dangerous situations that arise in his life, also often tells himself: ''Because I am so helpless and hopeless in the face of danger, it is *unfair* that situations and people should threaten me instead of helping me. These situations and people *should* be different from the way they are, because I *need* them to be.'' He thereby makes himself hostile as well as anxious.

Similarly, the hostile individual, after convincing himself that people *shouldn't* be the way they are, frequently also tells himself: "I can't *stand* things and people the way they are; I just can't *cope* with their being this awful way." He thereby makes himself anxious or self-hating.

Moreover, since blaming oneself, and thus becoming anxious, will normally lead to the kind of confused thinking that will also, quite easily, induce one to blame others; and since blaming others for being the way they are will frequently irradiate to similarly irrational, self-blaming thoughts, anxiety and hostility will more often than not tend to go together. The essence of both of these negative emotions is blaming, moralizing, or denigrating a person's worth when he is behaving in a typically fallible, human manner.

My therapeutic goals, therefore, invariably consist of trying to help my clients become minimally anxious and hostile, without, at the same time, trying to help them become rash and uncautious or pollyannish and unirritated. Although it is not possible for human beings to become *totally* unanxious or unhostile, since they have distinct inborn, biological tendencies to think unclearly about their own and others' behavior, and hence to confuse anxiety and fear, hostility and annoyance, they can laboriously learn, or train themselves over a considerable period of time, to be anxious or hostile only intermittently and moderately, instead of (as they normally do in our society) to be persistently and intensely angry at themselves and others.

Unlike many other therapists today, I am not primarily interested in getting my clients to *express* or *abreact* or *act out* their anxiety and hostility. I try to get them to admit that they are self-blaming or angry; and then, as quickly as they are able to do so, to *work against, change,* and *eradicate* their anxious and hostile feelings. If, in the process, they express previously suppressed or repressed negative attitudes toward themselves or others, fine. I use the material they express, and work with it—or get *them* to work with it. But the expression of their feelings *per se* is of little interest to me, and I am convinced, in fact, that therapists who encourage such expression frequently help their clients either to adjust to their anxiety and hostility (that is, to feel more comfortable with it), or to enhance it—both of which results I consider to be undesirable.

Virtually all anger and anxiety can be and would better be purged from human affairs—not reality-based annoyance and fear, but needless hostility and self-blame that invariably exist over and above, and are unwittingly or consciously *added* to, normal irritation and vigilance. And these senseless additions can be subtracted again, if the client is clearly and concretely shown exactly *how* he is unconsciously creating aggression out of frustration, panic out of alertness. This is what I aim to do with my clients; unmistakably show them exactly how they *are* adding idiotic and unprovable assumptions to their sensible observations and premises, and how by removing these irrational assumptions they can translate their anger back into annoyance, their anxiety back into appropriate fear.

More specifically, I try to show my clients what specific irrational hypotheses and illogical deductions they are making to create their needless anxiety. The main irrational ideas that all humans seem to subscribe to in order to manufacture their own states of panic, self-blame, and self-doubt appear to be:

1. The idea that it is a dire necessity for an adult to be loved or approved by virtually every significant person in his community.

2. The idea that one should be thoroughly competent, adequate, and achieving in all possible respects if one is to consider oneself worthwhile.

3. The idea that human unhappiness is externally caused and that people have little or no ability to control their sorrows and disturbances.

4. The idea that one's past history is an all-important determinant of one's present behavior and that because something once strongly affected one's life, it should indefinitely have a similar effect.

5. The idea that there is invariably a right, precise, and perfect solution to human problems and that it is catastrophic if this perfect solution is not found.

6. The idea that if something is or may be dangerous or fearsome

one should be terribly concerned about it and should keep dwelling on the possibility of its occurring.

The main irrational ideas that men and women seem to endorse in order to create their own states of anger, moralizing, and low frustration tolerance are these:

1. The idea that certain people are bad, wicked, or villainous and that they should be severely blamed and punished for their villainy.

2. The idea that it is awful and catastrophic when things are not the way one would very much like them to be.

3. The idea that it is easier to avoid than to face certain life difficulties and self-responsibilities.

4. The idea that one should become quite upset over other people's problems and disturbances.

It is these fundamentally irrational, unprovable premises that I continually show my clients that they (consciously or unconsciously) believe. These are the premises that literally cause them to feel and behave badly; that they keep endlessly reiterating to themselves without effectively challenging; and that they must persistently, in theory and in practice, work, and work, and work still harder against to disbelieve if they are ever to overcome their basic anxiety and hostility. Exactly how do I induce my clients to look their own irrational assumptions straight in the eye and to question and challenge these self-defeating philosophic premises? In several main ways, including the following:

1. I literally force my clients to look at the simple exclamatory sentences that they are telling themselves to create their emotions of anger and hostility. Whenever a client tells me, for example, "My wife accused me of being unfaithful to her, and that got me terribly angry, because it was so untrue and so unfair of her to accuse me of it," I stop him immediately and ask: "What do you mean *that* got you angry? How could her false accusation do anything whatever to you? You mean, don't you, that your wife accused you unjustly and then *you* got yourself angry by idiotically telling yourself: (1) 'I don't like

her false accusation,' and (2) 'Because I don't like it, she shouldn't make it.' Isn't *that* what got you upset, your own irrational premise, rather than *her* accusation?''

2. I am exceptionally active-directive with most of my clients. The system of rational-emotive psychotherapy that I employ states that not only can clients gain insight into what nonsense they are consciously and unconsciously telling themselves, but that they can also both think and *act* in counterpropagandizing ways. In RET, therefore, actual homework assignments are frequently given to individual and group therapy clients: assignments such as dating a girl whom the patient is afraid to ask for a date; looking for a new job; or experimentally returning to live with a husband with whom one has previously continually quarreled. The therapist quite actively tries to persuade, cajole, and at times even command the client to undertake such assignments as an integral part of the therapeutic process.

On one occasion I very firmly gave a thirty-year-old male, who had never really dated any girls, an assignment to the effect that he make at least two dates a week, whether he wished to do so or not, and come back and report to me on what happened. He immediately started dating, within two weeks had lost his virginity, and quickly began to overcome some of his most deep-seated feelings of inadequacy. With classical psychoanalytic and psychoanalytically oriented psychotherapy, it would have taken many months, and perhaps years, to help this man to the degree that he was helped by a few weeks of highly active-directive rational therapy.

3. I am exceptionally active verbally with my clients, especially during the first few sessions of therapy. I do a great deal of talking rather than passively listening to what the client has to say. I do not hesitate, even during the first session, directly to confront the client with evidences of his irrational thinking and behaving. I most actively interpret many of the things the client says and does, without being too concerned about possible resistances and defenses on his part. I consistently try to persuade and argue the person out of his firmly held irrational and inconsistent beliefs, and unhesitatingly *attack* his neurosis-creating ideas and attitudes after first demonstrating how and why they exist. As I note in *Reason and Emotion in Psy-*

chotherapy, "to the usual psychotherapeutic techniques of exploration, ventilation, excavation, and interpretation, the rational therapist adds the more direct techniques of confrontation, confutation, deindoctrination, and reeducation. He thereby frankly faces and resolutely tackles the most deep-seated and recalcitrant patterns of emotional disturbance."

4. My therapeutic approach is unusually didactic. I continually explain to my clients what the *general* mechanisms of emotional disturbance are, how these usually arise, how they become ingrained, and what can be done to combat them. I freely assign reading material, including my own and other authors' writings on personality and psychotherapy, and discuss any questions the client may have about the material he reads. I firmly believe that people with emotional disturbances do not understand how and why they got disturbed, any more than physics students at first understand how and why the universe got the way it is. I therefore enlighten my clients, as soon as possible, and teach them many things a good psychology professor would teach them—except that the teaching is usually of an individual nature, and is specifically designed to utilize the facts of the client's current life.

5. I make little use of the transference and countertransference relationship in my work with clients. I am deliberately not very warm or personal with most of my clients, even those who crave and ask for such warmth, since, as I quickly explain to them, their main problem is usually that they think they need to be loved, when they actually do not; and I am there to teach them that they can get along very well in this world *without* necessarily being approved or loved by others. I therefore refuse to cater particularly to their sick love demands.

Transference phenomena are also minimized in my form of rational-emotive psychotherapy, because I usually see my clients once a week or less; speak directly to them in a face-to-face situation; directly answer any personal questions that they may ask about me; and do not go out of my way to interpret transference manifestations that do arise unless I think that they are pertinent and helpful. Moreover, I insist that the clients work out their problems with the significant people in their own lives, rather than with me.

At the same time, one highly important aspect of relationship does enter into my form of therapeutic activity, and that is that I serve as a much different kind of model for my clients than do the other significant figures in their lives. Thus, if they become angry at me, as they frequently do, I do *not* return their feelings with anger of my own; and if they indicate that they do not love or approve of me, I do *not* indicate that that is awful, and that I cannot live successfully without their approval. In many ways, I tend to show them, in the course of the therapy sessions, that it *is* possible for a human being to act sanely and appropriately, with a minimum of anxiety and hostility; and by serving as a more rational model than they normally encounter in the rest of their lives, I help them see that it is possible for *them* to behave in a less self-defeating manner.

6. The approach I take to therapy is more philosophic than traditionally merely psychological. Rather than simply showing my clients the psychodynamics of their disordered behavior, I continually demonstrate to them what might be called the philosophical dynamics of this behavior. That is to say, I insist that the real reasons why they act in a certain self-defeating way do not lie in their early experiences or their past history but in the philosphic attitudes and assumptions they have been making, and still *are* making, about these experiences and history.

If, for example, I find that one of my clients has a full-blown Oedipus complex, I do not merely show him the details of how he lusted after his mother and was afraid that his father would castrate him. Instead, I try to get him to focus on the philosophic underpinnings of his complex; namely, the *beliefs* that if he engaged in a wicked act like desiring his mother, he would be no good as a person, and that, if his father jealously disapproved of him for his incestuous feelings, it would be terrible for him to bear this disapproval. Then, when I clarify to the client what his philosophic, disturbance-creating assumptions are, I annihilate these assumptions, demonstrating that they could not possibly be valid, and that as long as the client falsely maintains them, he *must* get the neurotic or psychotic behavioral results that he is now getting.

Quite didactically, moreover, I present to the client what is usually, for him, a quite new, existentialist-oriented philosophy of life. I teach him that it is possible for him to accept himself as being valuable to himself *just because he exists,* because he is alive, and because as a living person he has some possibility of enjoying himself and some likelihood of combatting his own unhappiness. I vigorously attack the notion that his intrinsic value to himself depends on the usual socially promulgated criteria of success, achievement, popularity, service to others, devotion to God, and the like. Instead, I show him that he had better, if he is really to get over his deep-seated emotional disturbances, come to accept himself *whether or not* he is competent or achieving and *whether or not* he has a high value to others.

7. I endeavor, with all my clients who are capable of working hard at overcoming their underlying disturbances, to give them three kinds of insight, rather than the limited "insight" that is usually given them in psychoanalytic therapies. Insight Number 1 occurs when the client sees that his present neurotic behavior has antecedent causes. This is the kind of insight or understanding that is stressed by most psychoanalytic and other schools of therapy. I endeavor to give the client some degree of this brand of self-understanding, but do not particularly harp on his seeing that all his present behavior is rooted in his past experiences or that he is behaving poorly today because he similarly behaved when he was a child.

I much more importantly stress Insight Number 2. This takes place when the client comes to understand that the reason why the original causes of his disturbance still upset and disorganize him is because he himself still *believes in*, and endlessly keeps repeating to himself, the irrational beliefs that he previously acquired. More precisely, I take a client who, let us say, presently hates his parents, and may first show him that this hatred originally arose from (let us assume) his jealousy over his mother's paying too much attention to his father and too little attention to him when he was a child. This would also be helping him acquire Insight Number 1.

At the same time, however, I would show this client that the real cause of his disturbance, even during his childhood, was not his mother's relative neglect of him for his father, but his early belief that *it was horrible* for her to neglect him in this way and that she and his father *shouldn't* have been the kind of people they were. Without this value system or philosophy of life, the client never would have become upset in the first place, no matter how much his parents tended to neglect him; and it is therefore not their neglect but his beliefs *about* it that originally led him to hate.

More important, if he still hates his parents and is upset about them, this proves that he is still endlessly repeating to himself the original philosophy that he had about their behavior toward him: that is to say, he still continually tells himself that it *is* horrible for parents to be neglectful and that they *shouldn't* be the way they are. If I enable this client to see, very clearly and precisely, that *he* has continued to upset himself by continuing, most actively and vociferously, to subscribe to his childish philosophies about the horror of being neglected, and that his *own* internalized sentences about parental neglect, rather than that neglect itself, is *now* bothering him, I have thereby helped him to acquire Insight Number 2.

Still more to the therapeutic point, I then go on to help the client attain Insight Number 3. This is the acknowledgement by the client that there is no other way for him to overcome his emotional disturbance but by *his* continually observing, questioning, and challenging his own belief systems, and *his* working and practicing to change his own irrational philosophic assumptions by verbal and by motor counterpropagandizing activity. Thus, I would show the client who hates his parents that if he is to overcome this irrational hatred (and a host of psychosomatic and other symptoms that may well accompany it), he'd better keep looking at his *own* idiotic assumptions about the horror of being neglected by them when he was a child and work tirelessly against these superstitions until he rids himself of them. Unless he acquires this kind of Insight Number 3, all possible degrees of Insights Number 1 and 2 are not likely to help him overcome his emotional disturbances.

These are some of the main methods used in my rational-emotive therapy. In addition, some of the more conventional methods of psychotherapy, such as dream analysis, reflection of feeling, reassurance, and abreaction are also at times employed, but to a much lesser extent than they are used in most other forms of treatment. The main emphasis is ordinarily active-directive, confrontational, didactic, and philosophic. And the results are significantly better, both in terms of improvements in clients and amount of therapeutic time required to achieve these improvements, than when I previously practiced classical analysis and psychoanalytically oriented psychotherapy. It is also interesting to note that the unusual effectiveness of rational-emotive psychotherapy is duplicated by several other recent modes of therapy, particularly those reported by the late Eric Berne, E. Lakin Phillips, John Nathaniel Rosen, Frederick C. Thorne, and Joseph Wolpe, all of which seem to have in common the element of an active-directive approach to the client's problems.

Although the main emphasis in this type of psychotherapy is on analyzing and challenging the negative thinking of the client, rather than on accentuating the positive aspects of his philosophy of life—as advocated by Emile Coué, E. S. Cowles, Viktor Frankl, Hornell Hart, Maxwell Maltz, Norman Vincent Peale, and others—there are very specific, positive implications of what I do in the therapeutic relationship. I distinctly teach the client that he can fully accept and enjoy himself, just because he is alive, and can *choose* special meanings for his existence. Several other positive goals of mental health are implicit or explicit in the teachings of rational-emotive psychotherapy:

1. *Self-interest.* The emotionally healthy individual is primarily true to himself and does not masochistically sacrifice himself for others. His kindness and consideration for others are largely derived from the idea that he himself wants to enjoy freedom from unnecessary pain and restriction, and that he is only likely to do so by helping create a world in which the rights of others, as well as his own rights, are not needlessly curtailed.

2. *Self-direction.* The healthy individual assumes responsibility for his own life, is able independently to work out most of his problems, and while at times wanting or preferring the cooperation and help of others, he does not *need* their support for his effectiveness or well-being.

3. *Tolerance.* He fully gives other human beings *the right to be wrong* and while disliking or abhorring some of their behavior, does not blame *them*, as persons, for displaying this displeasing behavior.

He accepts the fact that all humans are remarkably fallible, never unrealistically expects them to be perfect, and refrains from despising or punishing them when they make inevitable mistakes and errors (although he may at times objectively penalize them, in order to help them correct their mistakes).

4. *Acceptance of uncertainty.* The emotionally mature individual accepts the fact that we all live in a world of probability and chance, where there are not nor probably ever will be any absolute certainties; and he realizes that it is not at all horrible—indeed, in many ways it is fascinating and exciting—to live in such a probabilistic, uncertain world.

5. *Flexibility.* He remains intellectually flexible, is open to change at all times, and unbigotedly views the infinitely varied people, ideas, and things in the world around him.

6. *Scientific thinking.* He is sufficiently objective, rational, and scientific; and he is able to apply the laws of logic and of scientific method not only to external people and events, but to himself and his interpersonal relationships.

7. *Commitment.* He is vitally absorbed in something outside of himself, whether it be in people, things, or ideas; and should preferably have at least one major creative interest, as well as some outstanding human involvement, which are highly important to him, and around which he structures a good part of his life.

8. *Risk taking.* The emotionally sound person is able to take risks: to ask himself what he would really like to do in life, and then try to do this, even though he has to chance defeat or failure. He is adventurous (though not necessarily foolhardy); is willing to try almost anything once, just to see how he likes it; and looks forward to some breaks in his usual life routines.

9. *Self-acceptance.* He is glad to be alive and to accept himself just *because* he is alive, *because* he exists, and because he, as a living being, invariably has some capacity to enjoy himself, to create happiness and pleasure, and to ward off unnecessary pain. He does not equate his worth or value to himself on his extrinsic achievements, or on what *others* think of him, and preferably does not rate his *self*, his

totality, or being, at all, but accepts his existence and tries to *enjoy* life.

These are the kinds of more concrete positive or constructive goals that I aim to help my clients achieve. As can easily be noted, many of these goals overlap significantly with those posited by such ancient and modern rational-minded philosophers and psychologists, as Epictetus, Epicurus, and Marcus Aurelius, Spinoza, Sigmund Freud, Bertrand Russell, B. F. Skinner, Ayn Rand, Nathaniel Branden, to name a few. Many of the psychotherapeutic goals that I keep in mind in regard to my clients also overlap significantly with the goals of mental health that are endorsed by an increasing number of existentialist and humanistic thinkers, including Andras Angyal, Leif J. Braaten, Kurt Goldstein, Robert Hartman, Abraham Maslow, Rollo May, and Carl Rogers.

The concrete constructive goals of psychotherapy are derivatives of the two primary goals: the minimization of the client's anxiety and hostility. For as long as a human being is needlessly anxious or hostile, he simply is not going to achieve self-interest, self-direction, tolerance, acceptance of uncertainty, flexibility, scientific thinking, commitment, risk taking, self-acceptance, or virtually any other road to positive mental health—for the simple reason that he will be ceaselessly consuming his time and energy in his anxious and hostile behavior, and will be sidetracked from doing almost anything else *but* being self-blaming and angry at others.

It is unfortunately all too easy for a person to cover up his underlying negative views about himself and others with some kind of "positive thinking" that will temporarily divert him from his negative evaluations and make him "happy" despite his still holding such views. But sooner or later, if he mainly uses the technique of diversion, his negative thinking will out, and will rise to smite him down. A permanent solution to his basic neurosis or psychosis, therefore, is for him constantly to observe, challenge, question, and counterattack his self-defeating philosophies of life until they really go away, and he no longer is basically influenced by them.

This, therefore, remains my main goal as a psychotherapist: to induce the client, as often as the results of his underlying disturbance (that is, his negative emotions and the dysfunctional behavior to which they lead) arise, to *examine* fearlessly his fundamental philosophic premises, to *think* about them consciously and concertedly, to *understand* that they are based on illogical and inconsistent assumptions or deductions, and to *attack* them, by consistent verbal and motor activity, until they truly disappear or at least are reduced to minimal proportions. This method of persuading, cajoling, and at times almost forcing the client to observe and to reappraise his *own* conscious and unconscious philosophies of life is the essence of rational-emotive psychotherapy. It is a most effective means for permanently reducing and eliminating the anxiety and the hostility that seem to be the primary sources of almost all neurotic and psychotic symptoms, and that in their turn are created from the false and irrational philosophic assumptions that lie behind much of human behavior.

11
RATIONALITY AND IRRATIONALITY
IN THE GROUP THERAPY PROCESS

The group therapy process obviously aids both rationality and irrationality; but practitioners and theorists rarely explicitly delineate exactly how it is instrumental in both these respects.

There is some degree of rationality in all psychotherapeutic procedures. All therapists appear to have basically rational goals for themselves and their clients; and it may well be impossible for them to remain alive and to be therapists without their consciously or unconsciously working for such goals. For *rational*, as the dictionary defines the term, simply means "1. of, based on, or derived from reasoning: as, *rational powers*; 2. able to reason; reasoning: as an infant is not yet *rational*; 3. showing reason; not foolish or silly; sensible: as a *rational* argument." Applied to human life and health, a rational procedure is one that enables the individual to stay alive, to avoid getting into needless difficulties with others and with the inanimate world around him, to achieve sufficient satisfactions to make his existence worth the effort of continuing it, and preferably to maximize his pleasures, gains, and gratifications, and to minimize his pains, losses, and discomforts.

Rational, of course, does not mean unemotional. For in the last analysis the goal of reasonable and sensible procedures is some form of hedonism or pleasure seeking; and pleasure without emotion is almost unthinkable. What we call emotional*ism*, or *over*reacting to external and internal stimuli in an exceptionally emotional way, is often irrational: it easily leads to short- rather than long-term hedonism (that is, striving only for the pleasure of the moment rather than of now *and* the future); to a dysfunctional narrowing of experience; to considerable amounts of needlss pain; and to various other self-defeating (and antisocial) results. Reason, when it is properly employed, does not necessarily constrict but enhances emotion. On the one hand, it abets such feelings as joy, love, creative involvement, and sensory pleasure; and on the other hand, it minimizes or eliminates such feelings as overweening anxiety, depression, guilt, and hostility, and leaves the individual much more available time and energy to devote to enjoyable emoting.

To think and behave rationally, therefore, means to stop defeating yourself (and by extension, the members of your social group), to plan your life so that you have more intense and growth-enhancing experiences, and to have a maximum of pleasure in spite of the many noxious stimuli and life conditions that inevitably tend to impinge on you.

More specifically, psychotherapy tends to combat irrational thinking, inappropriate emoting, and dysfunctional behavior. When such self-defeating conduct becomes habitual, it is usually labeled emotional disturbance. The rational-emotive therapist sees this kind of disturbance as stemming largely from, and concomitant with, the individual's disordered or inefficient value system. For, along with such cognitive-oriented therapists as George Kelly, Eric Berne, A. T. Beck, E. Lakin Phillips, and Abraham Low, I hold that human beings are primarily evaluating creatures and that they woefully sabotage themselves emotionally by dogmatically and devoutly holding to several central irrational beliefs or philosophies.

Still more concretely, the major forms of human disturbance can be summarized under the heading of childish demandingness. *Demandingness* or *dictating* seems to be, in fact, the essence of virtually all of what we normally call emotional upsettedness. While the less disturbed individual strongly *desires* what he wants and makes himself appropriately sorry or annoyed if his desires are unfulfilled, the more disturbed person dogmatically *demands, insists, commands,* or *dictates* that his desires be granted and makes himself inappropriately anxious, depressed, or hostile when they are not. The emotionally malfunctioning individual foolishly and unrealistically makes three significant demands: (1) that he do consistently well and receive the approval of virtually all the people he considers important in his life; (2) that others treat him with fairness, consideration, and sometimes love; and (3) that the world be an easy and gratifying place in which to live.

Since all three of these demands are irrational, and simply do not accord with reality, it is largely the therapist's task to show his clients exactly how they display, and are rigidly adhering to, their demandingness; how they can give up their childishly dictating that they, others, and the world be quite perfect; and how they can finally acquire a thoroughly reality-centered, rational philosophy of life so that after therapy has ended they will only rarely sink back to their old self-defeating, disturbed ways. Effective psychotherapy, in other words, teaches the individual that he is insisting, in something of the manner of a two-year-old, that he be almost perfect and that the universe revolve around him, when, in actual fact, he is incredibly fallible and the universe is completely impartial to him, has no concern whatsoever for him, and in all probability never will. Even the relatively few individuals in the world who truly seem to love him—such as his family and his close friends—do so with unabashed intermittency. By far most of the time, they are hung up with their own problems and desires, and are amazingly indifferent to or inconsiderate of him; only occasionally do they actively concentrate on abetting his wants and pleasures; and some of the time they are literally unkind, nasty, hostile, and cruel. As for the vast majority of the people in the world, they hardly know he exists—and care exceptionally little whether he does or not.

Psychotherapy, then, would better largely be some form of helping the individual grow up, accept reality, and become more tolerant of himself and others. It may accomplish these rational goals in a great variety of ways, virtually all of which may be subsumed under three major headings. It can proceed on the understanding that man is a cognitive, emotive, and behaving creature; and he almost invariably learns, unlearns, and relearns through these major interacting modalities. Consequently, psychotherapeutic processes—whether or not the therapist is conscious of this fact—normally include perceptual-cognitive, emotive-evocative, and behavioral-motorial techniques. Thus, even old-style nondirective Rogerian methods employ behavioristic reinforcement by putting their "Uh-huh's" in the proper places when their clients do what they think is the right thing; and even orthodox behavior therapists, such as Joseph Wolpe, direct their clients into highly cognitive-imaginative byways and relate to them emotionally, as Arnold Lazarus has shown in his book, *Behavior Therapy and Beyond*.

Rational therapeutic goals, consequently, can be achieved by many methods which at first glance seem to be either nonrational or antirational. Rational-emotive therapy, as I practice it, begins with a premise that for the individual to achieve a fundamental change in his personality structure, he must significantly modify some of his deep-seated and long-standing cognitions and beliefs. Although such philosophic restructuring is most efficiently brought about by philosophic discourse and didactic dialogue or group discussion, at times it is instituted or abetted by several kinds of emotive-evocative methods (such as direct confrontation, the use of dramatic language, role playing, directive risk taking, personal encountering, and supportiveness) and by many varieties of behavioristic-motorial methods (such as desensitization, self-reinforcement schedules, graduated *in vivo* active homework assignments, behavioral rehearsal, modeling, assertion training, and operant conditioning).

In terms of group therapeutic processes, what, then, are some of the most rational and irrational goals and procedures?

Irrational group therapy goals generally have two major aspects. Either (1) the group leader or facilitator believes that rationality is undesirable, and he deliberately strives for nonrational or irrational goals; or (2) the group leader believes that rationality is desirable but that it can be best achieved, at least at times, in nonrational ways.

The first type is seldom clear cut. Although many group leaders talk against rationality and are exceptionally anti-intellectual in their approaches (as shown by Jane Howard), most of the time they are actually pursuing rational goals, albeit in somewhat "irrational ways." Thus, the premise of anti-intellectualism is that human beings are too intellectual for their own good—that is, to live "humanly" and undefeatingly. And the premise of those therapists (and non-therapist group facilitators) who stoutly fight cognitive or rational kinds of problem solving is that these methods dehumanize, inhibit, or deemotionalize people. Such group leaders implicitly if not explicitly seem to believe in the minimizing of severe disturbance and the maximizing of self-actualization; hence they are, at least in my sense of the term, positing and working for highly rational goals.

Occasionally, this does not seem to be true. To encourage a person, for example, to become more self-disciplined is usually to be efficient and rational, since discipline will normally help him, ultimately if not immediately, to function well and to enjoy himself more. But to encourage him, as several religious sects do, to become disciplined for the sake of discipline itself, or to control himself now in order that he may be happier in some hypothetical kind of heaven, does not appear to be sane or rational—in fact, it seems to be taking a reasonable view to unreasonable extremes, and hence to be essentially irrational. Similarly, to encourage a person to be emotional for the sake of emoting, or mystical for the sake of merely being mystical, or experiencing just because it is presumably good for him to experience, is to present him with a dubiously worthwhile goal. I, for one, do not want to live *merely* for the sake of living; and I do not want to experience or to emote *only* because I define experiencing and emoting as good or worthwhile occurrences.

Some therapeutic goals, consequently, seem to be at least partly irrational—or life and joy defeating. When an encounter therapist tries to induce his group member to become permanently more hostile to others, when a Zen Buddhist-oriented therapist endeavors to help his client reach nirvana—the state of perfect blessedness achieved by the extinction of individual existence and by the absorption of the soul into the supreme spirit, or by the extinction of all desires and passions—when an orthodox Christian therapist strives to help an individual deliberately suffer earthly woes and deprivations so that he will presumably enter and be happier in a heavenly afterlife—in these situations, group facilitators are pursuing irrational rather than rational goals. Fortunately, few therapists follow this extreme orientation; but they do exist.

On the other hand, there are a great number of modern therapists who have quite rational goals, but who utilize exceptionally illogical or irrational ways of trying to achieve these goals. This is not a matter of nonrational or irrational therapeutic techniques. Many therapeutic methods tend to bring about irrational, self-defeating results, or at the very least to be quite inefficient (considering the amount of time and effort that goes into utilizing them) in bringing about effective results. Examples of these include:

1. Pure sensitivity training or ultra nondirective procedures encourage group members to mull around endlessly in their own emotional problems, to become unduly upset (partly about the inefficiency of the procedures themselves), and to emote rather than to motivate themselves to behavioral change.

2. Encounter facilitators are often hung up on the compulsive experiencing and expression of *all* feelings, indiscriminately, including some that are violently hostile and disruptive, and abet rather than discourage needless hating of themselves and others by group members.

3. Overly physical measures, such as gouging massage, kicking, biting, pummeling, wrestling, and headstanding often lead (*a*) to injury to oneself or others and (*b*) to the fostering of cruel and inhuman, one-upmanship attitudes.

4. Many group leaders, partly because they are not trained as psychotherapists, stick almost exclusively to physical and nonverbal

methods and compulsively avoid any kinds of problem solving that would much more directly and effectively help most of their group members.

5. Overemphasis on relating procedures, which are again common in many traditional encounter groups, foolishly diverts the participants into believing (*a*) that they can solve their deep emotional problems very easily, (*b*) that temporarily feeling better is equivalent to truly getting better, (*c*) that they do *direly need* (rather than merely *strongly desire*) others to love or approve them and that they are worthless without such human support, and (*d*) that they are now worthwhile *because* the group leader or some group members seem to love them.

6. Some achievement-oriented groups (such as those commonly held for business executives) instil or abet the tragically superficial and often pernicious philosophy that the group member is worthless, and *cannot* possibly accept himself if he does not outstandingly succeed in the world.

7. Many problem-solving groups mainly emphasize practical, one-level solutions to personal and other problems and fail to touch, evaluate, or try to change the group member's basic disturbance-creating philosophy of life.

8. Some groups overemphasize sexual blocks and difficulties and spend so much time and energy, on the part of the leader and the members, presumably working on these blockings, that they ignore the fact that (*a*) they are usually a small part of the individual's basic disturbances, and that (*b*) they tend to stem more from rather than to create deep-seated emotional difficulties.

9. Many encounter-type groups are so replete with clever games, exercises, diversions, pleasure-giving pastimes, and other gimmicks, that the personality of the group members, and their fundamental value systems which underlie this personality, get lost in the shuffle.

10. An increasing number of groups emphasize magical, mystical, religious-oriented experiences that strongly imply that reason and science cannot help the individual, and that there is some supernatural and easily achievable solution to his serious problems.

11. Some group leaders overemphasize positive thinking, pollyannish imagining, and other forms of autosuggestion that have palliative value but that give very inefficient solutions to serious issues.

12. There are a good many groups which condemn the members severely for their acts, particularly when they do not follow the group procedures. Not a few members are actually harmed by this kind of group censure.

13. Some groups unrealistically arrange situations where the individual finds it almost impossible to fail, instead of examining and attacking his perfectionistic attitudes toward failing; and consequently they poorly prepare him to live in the real world where a considerable amount of failure is virtually inevitable.

14. Many analytically oriented groups are so preoccupied with the member's presumably unconscious thoughts and feelings that they sadly neglect his easily available, and often more important, conscious and preconscious thinking and emoting.

15. Some group leaders are so consistently and vehemently anti-intellectual that they help subvert normal reasoning processes and encourage the individual to surrender his most unique and important human powers, namely the power to think deeply and to think about his thinking. Consequently, his problem-solving abilities are sabotaged rather than enhanced, and his emotions tend to become more inappropriate and uncontrollable.

16. Many group processes are so woefully inefficient that the members needlessly suffer for long periods of time before they improve, they become disenchanted with the entire therapeutic process, and they are thereafter given a good excuse to avoid effective therapy.

When a group process is highly rational, it first selects sane and disturbance-undoing goals, and then it goes about trying to achieve these in logical, empirical, efficient ways. In rational-emotive therapy and similar cognitive-behavioral types of group therapy, the leader encourages rational processes in many ways, including the following:

1. The leader and several of the more sophisticated group members collaborate to teach the individual who brings up an emotional problem how to accept grim reality, and how to try to change it by con-

certed, determined effort instead of magically expecting it to evaporate by whining demands.

2. The group shows the troubled member (*a*) what he is specifically thinking to create his inappropriate feelings and behavior, (*b*) how his muddled thoughts are causing his destructive feelings, and (*c*) how logically to parse these thoughts, how empirically to challenge and attack them, and how to persist at trying to modify them. Where less rationally oriented groups emphasize feelings and insight, rationally centered ones stress disputing irrational beliefs until they are surrendered.

3. The group, under the leader's clear-cut direction, is philosophically and cognitively centered, but it tends to use a wide variety of evocative-emotive and motorial-behavioral techniques in order to foster and abet cognitive change. It is rational in the sense that a business enterprise is rational: that is, ready to employ almost any method that truly works to encourage core attitudinal change.

4. The group leader—such as the RET group leader—is unusually active, probing, and challenging. He utilizes the group process partly to foster suggestions, comments, and hypotheses by other group members, which in turn spark him to focus on important issues that he might otherwise neglect, to present premises which he may check on and add to, to reinforce some of his main points, and to allow him at times to stand on the emotive and intellectual shoulders of other group members and thereby augment his therapeutic effectiveness.

5. The group rationally utilizes action within the group session and preferably gives group members activity-oriented homework assignments to be performed outside the session. Thus, it may assign a group member to look for a new job, date a girl he is afraid to date, or deliberately visit his mother-in-law, whom he may detest. Such homework assignments are often more effectively directed and followed up when given by a group than an individual therapist.

6. The group, in using evocative-emotive and motorial-behavioral techniques, does not naïvely accept the members' expressions but specifically probes for and emphasizes their cognitive correlates. Thus, it looks for the actual behaviors that substantiate the indivi-

dual's verbal expressions; and if, for example, he is denying that he has hostile feelings, it provides a laboratory where the emotional, gestural, and behavioral aspects of these feelings may directly be observed and questioned. Moreover, when such feelings are revealed and authentically expressed, the rationally-oriented group shows the member exactly what he is telling himself in order to create them, how he is cognitively sustaining them, and what he can do to minimize or eliminate them if they are self-defeating. In this manner, it goes much deeper into the expression and understanding of feelings than the group that does not emphasize rational analysis and change.

7. The rationally oriented group provides each member with several important kinds of feedback from other group members: (*a*) it shows him that he is similarly troubled and has the same kind of irrational ideas as many or most other group members; (*b*) it gives him honest observations and feelings from other group members in regard to how he comes across to them, how he relates, and what they think he can do to improve his human relationships; (*c*) it provides a forum in which the group member may engage in psychodramatic, role-playing exercises with other members, and hence learn assertion training, social practice, and other kinds of social skills; (*d*) it sometimes offers the individual social participation, and valuable feedback, outside the immediate group situation, and thereby helps him relate and learn significant things about himself; (*e*) it particularly offers him other individuals who, both inside and outside the immediate group therapy situation, show him what his irrational thinking is, indicate how he can dispute and challenge it, give him practice in disputing, and encourage him to keep thinking in a more rational manner about himself and the world; (*f*) by teaching him how to be something of a therapist to the other group members, the rationally oriented group gives him conscious and unconscious practice in seeing some of his own irrationalities and talking himself out of these self-defeating ideas (for in actively confronting others' crooked thinking, he is practically forced, by a unique feedback method, to confront and challenge his own); (*g*) when he questions and disputes other group members' irrationalities, the individual is observed and

corrected by the leader and the remaining members of the group, and he is shown what his *wrong* challenges are, how he can correct them, and how he can think his way through to more appropriate challenges that would be good for the group members and also good for himself.

8. In a rationally oriented group, the member is able to observe the progress, and especially the philosophic progress, of other group members, and thereby to see (a) that treatment can be effective, (b) that he can similarly change, (c) that there are specific things he can learn by which to help himself, and (d) that therapy is hardly magic but almost always consists of persistent, hard, and active work.

9. In a group, the individual is offered a wider range of possible solutions than he would normally be offered in individual therapy. Out of ten or twelve people present at a given group session, one person may finally zero in on his central problem (after several others, including the leader, have failed) and another person may offer an excellent solution to it (after several lower-level solutions have hitherto been offered). Where a single individual, including a single therapist, may well give up on a difficult issue (or person), several group members may collectively persist and may finally prove to be quite helpful.

10. In almost every group process, the individual's revealing intimate problems to a group of people may in itself be therapeutic. In RET group sessions, the client is encouraged and sometimes practically forced to disclose many ordinarily hidden feelings and ideas and thereby to see that nothing is really so shameful as he previously thought it was. The therapist and other group members specifically try to show an inhibited person that nothing awful will happen if he does honestly speak up; that once he has spoken up he usually feels better; and that even if he were excoriated and laughed at, that would be unfortunate and frustrating but would not truly be ego downing or catastrophic—unless he *defined* this experience as being so.

11. A rationally oriented group therapy process includes considerable educational and didactic material, such as explanations, information giving, and the discussion of various problem-solving techniques. Teaching, as John Dewey and Jean Piaget have shown, is

more effective when the individual actively enters the teaching-discussing-doing process than when he is mainly a passive recipient. Group therapy, consequently, is an excellent means for the teaching of emotional education; and it is so effective in this respect that at the Living School, operated by the Institute for Advanced Study in Rational Psychotherapy in New York City, normal children are taught the elements of emotional education in the course of group counseling sessions and during regular classroom group work.

12. Severely disturbed individuals hold on to their irrational ideas and inappropriate feelings so rigidly and determinedly that they usually require persistent and consistent intervention. In RET group procedures, sessions of two and a quarter hours are usually followed by an aftergroup session of an hour or so; massive efforts can be made to intrude on the negative thinking and acting of the group members at regular twelve-hour minithons and twenty-four-hour marathon weekends of rational encounter.

Group processes can include a great many rationally oriented and rationally executed procedures. These procedures incisively and intensively reveal and assail the troubled group member's irrational premises and illogical deductions and help him reconsider and reconstruct his basic self-destructive philosophies. Groups are so effective in this respect that they are frequently employed by leading cognitive therapists.[1]

To conclude: people are unusually prone to self-defeating thinking and inappropriate emoting and behaving. But they can significantly change their cognitions, emotions, and behavior if they clearly understand exactly what they think and do to create so-called emotional upsets. They can do this by exerting the choice to think and act differently; and they can be appreciably helped to do so in the course of active-directive, rationally oriented group psychotherapy.

NOTES

¹ As Berne (1964); Corsini (1966); Dreikurs and Grey (1968); Lazarus (1971); Low (1952); and Phillips and Wiener (1966).

12
THEORY VERSUS OUTCOME IN PSYCHOTHERAPY

The field of psychotherapy is fragmented and splinterized, with schools and approaches so numerous they can hardly be counted, and then with individual variations and subschools within each. Each differs from all others not only in the theoretical underpinnings concerning human behavior, but in the manner in which the problems of clients are to be tackled. Successes are claimed by many, perhaps all, leaving a reader bewildered and skeptical, if not entirely confused.

Nevertheless, there is much that is written by therapists of different persuasions with which most of their colleagues (one might say competitors) can easily agree. After all, there has been *some* uniformity in their training, even though many were indoctrinated with a basically Freudian psychoanalytic view, and others trained to give reasonably strict allegiance to Alfred Adler, Carl Jung, Carl Rogers, or some other theoretician. Clients, moreover, are human beings who must to a degree conform to *some* regularities; and it is only to be expected that experienced and experimenting therapists, no matter what their orientation, will chance upon the same behaviors and treatment methods.

It is not the similarity, but the difference, that can give us pause to wonder: particularly the difference between the techniques of the various schools. Believing strongly as I do in my own method of therapy, and particularly in the need for active-directive aid for clients, I nevertheless note that approaches of a very different nature are used by others. These others furthermore report successes, but even putting aside the matter of their self-reported findings, they are surely dependent upon referrals, which could not be maintained without some degree of success with the clients. Even if these clients may not become completely cured (a matter of dispute about all kinds of therapies), it seems obvious that they must gain a considerable amount of help from the therapy, for otherwise they would not continue to pay for it, nor to report back favorably to the individuals who referred them, nor to recommend (as they frequently do) their friends and relatives to the same therapist.

One can only assume, then, that some of the most wrong-headed therapeutic techniques imaginable (wrong-headed in the view of those practicing RET, for example) actually do some good with many clients. At the same time, RET practitioners have good reason to believe that our own methods would be considered just as wrong by competing schools as we consider their methods to be, and yet we can judge that RET is effective, efficient, and efficacious, not only because of what the clients report to us, but judged also by the large number of referrals.

Now, how is this possible? Can it really be that effective therapy can be done by practitioners using diametrically opposite and apparently mutually exclusive methods? Perhaps, actually, the approaches are not as different as some of us seem to think they are. This, however, seems highly improbable. Let me, for example, give some comments on psychotherapy taken from a journal, *Psychotherapy: Theory, Research and Practice*, along with disimilar remarks which I have made to several of my own clients.

Hans H. Strupp:

I am placing major emphasis upon the therapy situation as a miniature life situation, and I am stressing the alignment of psychic forces rather than specific behavioral acts in the outside world. This view is predicated on the (testable) assumption that there is a close association between the quality of the patient's relationship to the therapist and the quality of his relationships with others, including his adaptation to reality . . . The transference situation, as defined by Freud, is the richest source for observing and studying interpersonal data, and . . . has a unique validity of its own.

Ellis: (To a client who is not eager to enter group therapy, and whom the therapist is practically forcing to do so).

Yes, I know that you feel perfectly comfortable talking to me now and that you can tell me all those horrible things about yourself, which at first you were afraid even to tell me. And I know that you feel comfortable during our sessions. And that's exactly *why* you'd better join a therapeutic group: because you *won't* feel comfortable there, at least at the beginning, and until you do, until you do feel relaxed in a situation like that, which is much more like your situation in the real world, you just are not going to get better. Sure you can make it easily with me now; almost all my clients can. Because it's easy. You now know that I'll accept you, listen to you carefully and not blame you for the mistakes you keep making, including your lack of getting along well with girls. But others, such as these girls, are *not* like me. They're more like you. They *will* not accept you and will blame you for your errors. And it's *them* you have to adjust to in life, not the exceptional, unusually accepting people like me. You can see me and get along fine with me from now till doomsday—and you *still* will probably tend to remain afraid of others, and to goof on your relations with them.

In the group, however, you will learn to live with these others, to let them criticize you severely (as I *won't* do), and to realize that you don't *have* to upset yourself about their criticism. In the group you'll have to take risks—which you can nicely avoid taking as long as you just see me alone. The members of the group are fairly typical of the people in the outside world, and just as kooky as they are. I'm presumably not—or you wouldn't be coming to see me for help. So forget your fears of talking up in the group. We, the group and I, will make you talk up, whether you like it or not. And by our forcing you to open your mouth, and take social risks, in *this* kind of a situation, we'll give you much better practice in adjusting to the real world around you. With me, this kind of practice is minimal. With the group, it will be much better.

Carl R. Rogers:

The basic nature of the human being, when functioning freely, is constructive and trustworthy. For me this is an inescapable conclusion from a quarter century of experience in psychotherapy. When we are able to free the individual from defensiveness, so that he is open to the wide range of environmental and social demands, his reactions may be trusted to be positive, forward moving, constructive. We do not need to ask who will socialize him, for one of his own deepest needs is for affiliation with and communication with others. When he is fully himself, he cannot help but be realistically socialized. We do not need to ask who will control his aggressive impulses, for when he is open to all of his impulses, his need to be liked by others and his tendency to give affection are as strong as his impulses to strike out or to seize for himself. He will be aggressive in situations in which aggression is realistically appropriate, but there will be no runaway need for aggression. His total behavior, in these and other areas, when he is open to all his experience, is balanced and realistic, behavior which is appropriate to the survival and enhancement of a highly social animal.

I have little sympathy with the rather prevalent concept that man is basically irrational, and that his impulses, if not controlled, would lead to destruction of others and self. Man's behavior is exquisitely rational, moving with subtle and ordered complexity toward the goals his organism is endeavoring to achieve.

Ellis: (To a female client who has asked, "If I really keep looking at what you call the *nonsense* that I keep telling myself about eating, will I then be able automatically to stop my compulsive stuffing myself in between meals?")

No, looking at, or getting insight into, your nonsensical internalized sentences is not enough. You seem to be telling yourself "Since I can't get what I really want in life, a fine man to love me, I might just as well get some immediate pleasure by eating, which I enjoy." And also: "Because I obviously haven't been able to keep on any of the diets I've put myself on in the past, I just must be the kind of a slob who *can't* diet. So what's the use?" These beliefs, of course, are nonsensical, since they are not related to objective reality, and can only result in actions which will be self-defeating. So, in order to overcome your compulsive eating, you had better *see* and honestly *admit* that you have these idiotic beliefs. But that's not enough. More importantly, after seeing that these are your beliefs, and that such beliefs *will* lead to self-defeating behavior, you'd better most actively and consistently *challenge* and *tackle* these ideologies: powerfully contradict them, as you would do any other superstition, until they finally go away, and you no longer truly believe them. But even *that* is not quite enough. For you are, you were born and raised, a human; and humans are *always*, for all their days, fallible, irrational, and to some degree self-defeating. Thus, you were born with the tendency to like food, and other immediate gratifications; and because of your biological inheritance and your early upbringing—which itself tends usually to be over-indulging—you now find it exceptionally *easy* to overeat and to tell yourself that you *deserve* to do so, or that you cannot *stop* doing so, or that there is some other "good" reason for doing so. And even though you now come, through the help of this psychotherapy, to see exactly what you are doing and why you are doing it, you will *still* have the inborn and early acquired tendency to indulge yourself, to be a short-range hedonist, and to fall back into undisciplined paths of living even after you have spent several weeks or months being more disciplined.

"Human" means "fallible"; and "fallible" means biologically as well as sociologically handicapped. Just as you will always, because of your fallible humanity, have to force yourself, to some degree, to get up early in the morning every day, to brush your teeth, to wear uncomfortable clothes to dressy affairs, and to do hundreds of other things which you do not particularly like doing but which you realize you just have to do if you are not to destroy yourself, so you will always, long after you have attained the weight you want to attain, force yourself to diet, and to diet, and to diet. Or, in psychotherapeutic terms, you will have to force yourself to *remember*, consistently, that overeating *is* self-defeating, and that you'd damned well *better* keep this in mind.

You are not, nor will ever be, an automatically self-preserving animal just because you *see* what is wrong with you or how defensive you have been against admitting your wrongdoing. To get any goodly degree of healthful automaticity—and even a relatively small degree at that—you had better work and work and work all your life—yes, *all your life*—and keep preaching sanity to

yourself and practicing, and I really mean *forcing* yourself
to keep practicing, what you preach. And even then, as
long as you are still human and not superhuman or angelic,
you will constantly find yourself backsliding to undisciplined, self-sabotaging ways. Tough! That's what
humans are: self-defeaters and backsliders. When are you
going to admit *that* reality—and then spend the rest of
your life working to minimize, though never entirely to
change, it?

Bertram P. Karon: (To a male client who became very angry at his
two-timing girl friend and had the strong urge to kill her with an
icepick).

"And maybe you were angry at her [a previous fiancée
who jilted him] for leaving you for another man, and when
your new girl did the same thing, it was like living it over."
He agreed and said that it might have been the first girl
whom he wanted to kill. He was then asked to go back even
further.
"But I think that's still not the whole story. I think
there's somebody earlier. Somebody who also left you for
another man. And it was easier to kill your girl than to face
the idea that you wanted to kill her."
"That's all there was. There ain't any girl before the first
one. Just two of them, that's all."
"But the girl you really want to kill is your mother.
Didn't you ever feel that she left you?"
"When the old man came back."
"Came back?"
"He used to take off and just leave her and the kids. He'd
take up with some woman or just go off and leave her. And
when he was gone, she'd tell me I was the man in the
house."
"And you'd feel like you were married to her."

"Yeah. And then he'd come back. And she'd always take him back."

"And you were a kid again."

"Yeah, I was nothing when he was around."

"Then you must have wanted to kill her for that. That's reasonable enough. When first one girl and then the other left you, it was like your mother all over again. And it was your mother you wanted to kill."

We went on to discuss the idea that it was all right for him to want to kill somebody, how one always wants to kill someone, when they hurt you.

Ellis: (To a male client who asked, "Do you think I keep punishing my wife the way I do because I still am angry at my mother for treating me the way she did, and that I'm really getting back at her through my wife?")

"No. I'm sure that that's how the Freudians and many of the other analysts would interpret your current cruelty toward your wife; but it largely misses the whole point of why you (or anyone else, for that matter) are disturbed. In the first place, there seems to be no evidence that you really *are* very angry at your mother any more, although you once were. If anything, you're on the best terms you ever were with her, and seem to have forgiven her all the stuff she leveled against you when you were a child. Isn't that so?"

"Yes, we've never got along so well as we now do. She's still got her problems, of course, but I tell myself, just the way you've taught me to do, 'Well, that's the way she is. Too bad! But I can easily take it.' And I do take it very well, and practically never get upset, any more, about her."

"All right. So there's no evidence that you still do hate your mother. We could, of course, insist that you still do so *unconsciously*, even though you consciously seem to get along very well with her these days. But again: there's no evidence for such an hypothesis. We do know, however, that you definitely act badly toward your wife. And, for that matter, toward your boss, when he doesn't appreciate you, and toward just about everyone who, as you say, 'hurts' you. Is that correct?''

"Yes. Even if my wife or my boss does ten things that are nice, and that are helpful to me, just as soon as they say something nasty, and unfairly hurt me, I get upset and strike right back.''

"O.K., then: *that* seems to be the problem. That when you feel hurt, you strike back. With your mother, these days, you no longer seem to take what she says or does seriously, so you don't feel hurt in that area any more. But you definitely *do* take your boss and your wife, and other people like them, seriously; do hurt yourself with their negative words, gestures and attitudes; and *then* lash back at them, presumably to hurt them back and to salve your own feelings of being vulnerable.''

"What do you mean I hurt myself with their words and gestures?''

"Well, *don't* you? Can, really, anything they say or in dicate about you, as long as they don't literally follow up their words with physical actions, such as refusing to feed you or firing you from your job, can any such words or gestures of theirs hurt you?''

"They certainly seem to!''

"Yes—because you let them; or more accurately, *make* them hurt. You say to yourself, ''I don't like the way they're treating me, and especially the fact that they're unfairly accusing me,' and that's a perfectly sane sentence that causes you little trouble. But then you add, to yourself, the perfectly insane sentence, ''And because I don't like what they're doing, they *shouldn't* be doing it to me; and I can't *stand* the fact that they're doing what they are.' It's this sentence that really does the damage—that directly causes your hurt and your anger.''

"You mean I don't even have to be angry at people when they act badly to me, even though they have no right to do so?''

"I mean that people who act badly toward you always *do* have a right to do so—have a right to be wrong. For that's what human beings are: fallible, wrong, mistaken. And whenever you get angry at them, and wish to kill them for being the way they are, you're irrationally demanding that they *not* be wrong or infallible—that they be angels. And it's this unreasonable demand of yours, rather than their wrongheadedness, that truly causes your anger and makes you want to kill them. If we can get you to look at, and then question and challenge, your own unreasonable demands here, we can get you to stop hating people like your wife, when they say something nasty to you—just as you have already stopped hating your mother.''

"Does this mean that I'll get to a point, with someone like my wife, where I'll never get angry at her, no matter how much she hurts me—or, as you say, no matter how much I hurt myself by taking her words and gestures too seriously?''

"No, that would be utopian to expect. You, too, are a fallible human being. So you'll always, from time to time, make the mistake of hurting yourself when your wife treats you nastily, and you'll always tend to make yourself angry at her for her nastiness. But if you get yourself into the habit of seeing and admitting that it is really you, yourself, who are hurting and angering yourself, and that she really has very little to do with the whole process, then you will become much less hurt and angry than you now do; and when you do have a bad emotional outbreak, which then should only be every once in a while, you will be able to get on to it quickly, challenge and question your own nonsense that is creating this outburst, and soon get over it. But the *tendency* to think crookedly, and hence hurt and anger yourself, will always be there, though in reduced degree, and you will have to keep coping with this tendency for the rest of your life."

From the foregoing excerpts, it appears that my therapeutic methods are quite different from, and in some ways almost diametrically opposed to, those used by many other therapists. Yet it would also appear that all of the therapists get good results. Several hypotheses arise as possible answers to this dilemma. For example:

Hypothesis No. 1. One or all of us are lying. Either we are not doing what we actually say we are doing in therapy; or we are truthful about what we are doing, but we are not truly getting the good results we say that we are. Although this hypothesis may be partially supported by the available evidence (since I am reasonably sure that at least *some* therapists often do not do what they say they do in therapy), it is also contradicted by other evidence. Thus, I have many tape recordings that conclusively show that I do exactly what I say I do; and a good number of these recordings also show that my clients are clearly improving. Recordings and verbatim typescripts that I have examined also indicate that some other therapists do pretty much what they say they do; and some of their clients, too, seem to improve.

Hypothesis No. 2. Our criteria of improvement are faulty. Thus, it may be hypothesized that the clients of most therapists (including, perhaps, myself) begin to *feel* better rather than to *get* better. That is to say, these clients may convince themselves that because the therapist (in one way or another) accepts them, they are no longer the worthless individuals they previously thought they were, and may therefore temporarily feel better about themselves. Actually, however, they may still believe that if someone (including the therapist) finds them unacceptable again, they must then go back to hating themselves: in which case they have *not* effected a true personality change. These kinds of "transference cures" are probably quite common in therapy, and explain much of the so-called improvement that occurs. The question is: Do they explain *all* such improvement? My own personal hypothesis is that while my clients truly tend to *get* better, many other therapists' clients merely *feel* better, and are not basically changed. But how valid is this hypothesis?

Hypothesis No. 3. There is a common factor in all kinds of effective therapy that the adherents of the "different" schools simply fail to recognize. Thus, Carl Rogers stresses unconditional positive regard, or the therapist's accepting the client fully in his own right, as the basic requisite for effective therapy. Paul Stark holds that the therapist's giving the client the freedom to experience himself unfettered by irrational demands from the significant other is the essence of good psychological treatment. In *Reason and Emotion in Psychotherapy*, I have shown that the therapist's indirectly or (preferably) directly teaching the client not to blame himself, no matter what his errors are, is the core of what leads to basic personality change. It is therefore possible that, no matter what the therapist does, in accordance with the dictates of the school he overtly follows, he is *also* (consciously or unconsciously) doing something else, and something that practically all efficient therapists do, and that it is this something else which *really* helps his clients.

Hypothesis No. 4. It is not *what* system the therapist uses that helps the client, but the fact that he *has* a pretty well integrated approach to personality formation, even if his approach is largely wrong. For the client's system of thinking and behaving, and especially of evaluating himself as a human being, is so palpably *dis*organized and *un*integrated, or else is so rigidly aligned so that it can only produce self-defeating results, that virtually *any* other systematic approach to personality will bring better results if he starts to follow it. If this is a correct hypothesis, it explains why all sorts of irrational systems of thought, from witch doctoring and Christian Science to Dianetics and orthodox Freudianism, report thousands of cures which are remarkably like those obtained by more rational systems of therapy.

The foregoing hypotheses are hardly exhaustive; any psychotherapist can add a few more of his own to the list. The fact still remains that many therapists continue to be just as effective with their clients as are just as many supposedly radically different therapists with *theirs*.

Is this really true? This extremely important question could well be explored as fully as possible. At the very minimum, some researcher could select a few seemingly successful cases from members of one pronounced school of psychotherapy and an equal number of successful cases from members of what appears to be a radically opposed school. Full recordings (or preferably films) of all sessions of all these cases could then be examined. Such a study, well executed, would provide some fascinating information on how patients really do improve in therapy, and why.

13

A COGNITIVE APPROACH TO BEHAVIOR THERAPY

Many forms of cognitive-behavior therapy have existed for years. Thus, Alfred Adler was one of the first educational therapists; and of course, he was very cognitively oriented, as was Paul Dubois. Knight Dunlap, in the early 1930's, expounded cognitive-behaviorist (and incidentally, anti-Freudian and anti-psychodynamic) theories of making and unbreaking dysfunctional habits; and more recently, many cognitive learning therapists have worked and written in this area. To mention but a few: Aaron T. Beck, Rogelio Diaz-Guerrera, John Dollard and Neal E. Miller, Viktor Frankl, Alexander Herzberg, Glenn A. Holland, Lloyd E. Homme, George Kelly, Arnold A. Lazarus, Perry London, David B. Lynn, Adolph Meyer, E. Lakin Phillips, Julian B. Rotter, W. S. Sahakian, Andrew Salter, Frederick C. Thorne, and Daniel N. Wiener and Donald R. Stieper.

My own use of a cognitive behavior therapy began in 1955, when I became disillusioned with both classical Freudian and psychoanalytically-oriented methods of therapy, which I had previously practiced for half a decade. Conventional psychodynamics, I found, were misleading and ineffective, and stimulus-response therapy—modeled after Mary Cover Jones and B. F. Skinner— seemed to be too atomistic and limited. So I devised rational-emotive psychotherapy, a combination of rational analysis of the client's basic value system and a mechanism for teaching him how to use the scientific method of challenging and annihilating his irrational philosophic premises, integrally tied up with giving him specific *in vivo* desensitizing exercises and assignments by which he could more effectively question his disturbance-creating premises and train himself to stop catastrophizing and to accept reality. I soon found that rational-emotive therapy was far more effective than psychodynamic analysis and that it took considerably less therapeutic time and energy. It is based on a fundamental principle that human beings are not passively trained or conditioned to become disturbed by their early childhood experiences, as the Freudians claim, but that they actively accept or reject environmental teaching, that they continually reindoctrinate or recondition themselves with these self-defeating ideas, and that they can deindoctrinate, reeducate and retrain themselves so that their thinking, emotions, and overt behavior all significantly change. A few years after I stated these principles and began clinically working with this hypothesis, considerable experimental evidence in support of this view began to appear, including studies by T. X. Barber, William A. Carlson, C. W. Eriksen, Maxie C. Maultsby, Jr., Neal E. Miller, Milton Rokeach, and Emmett C. Velten.

Rational-emotive therapy is not only a cognitive-emotive-behavioristic method of treating behavior disorders, but it has been specifically designated as one of the behavior therapies by Hans Eysenck, Lloyd E. Homme, R.R. Pottash and J. E. Taylor, Joseph Wolpe, and Arnold A. Lazarus, among others. It is practiced by scores of American and foreign therapists, has a training center and a special grade school. It is representative of a number of other cognitive-behavior therapies that seem to be assuming an important place in contemporary life, that are quite different from the old-time psychodynamic treatment methods, and that are more practical for psychiatrists and psychologists to use with regular office clients than are most of the stimulus-response (S-R) therapeutic techniques.

An increasing number of conventional behavior therapists have recently added cognitive elements to their previous S-R formulations and practices. Lazarus found Wolpe's desensitization procedures so sterile and boring that he now calls his treatment method "broad spectrum behavior therapy," and adds role playing, rational-emotive discussion, and other philosophic techniques to his therapeutic armamentarium. Although Wolpe squirms at the thought of this "self-disclosure" methodology, some of the leading behavior therapy practitioners, such as Gerald Davison and Joseph Cautela, are much closer to Arnold Lazarus than to Joseph Wolpe in their clinical work.

Many or most of the "orthodox" behavior therapists are, whether they are aware of the fact or not, using cognitive (and emotive) techniques with their "counterconditioning" procedures. F. H. Kanfer and J. S. Philips note that of three main types of behavior therapy commonly employed—instigational, replication, and intervention therapy—only the last type is truly of the S-R variety and it alone resembles the methods used in the animal learning laboratory. The first type includes "reinforcement of change in the patient's attitudes and modes of thinking," and the second type "provides the patient with the opportunity to evaluate his problematic behaviors and to try out new responses without fear of traumatic consequences." Note the serious cognitive implications!

B. M. Brown observed Joseph Wolpe treating clients for a period of two years. He reports that this presumably S-R behavior therapist repeatedly advised clients to "speak up for their rights," that his assertion training method "often involves Dr. Wolpe's telling the patient what to say and how to say it," and that Wolpe's remarks "definitely indicate that cognition occurs during the desensitization procedure, that the patient frequently has thoughts revealing basic attitudes about the phobic items, and that by becoming aware of the thoughts and seeing that they are exaggerations or distortions, he can adopt thinking that is more in accord with the reality of the situation."

A number of other writers have indicated the cognitive and relationship elements in supposedly S-R behavior therapy. These include

L. Breger and J. L. McGaugh, Cecil H. Patterson, M. H. Klein, A. T. Dittman, M. B. Parloff, and Merton M. Gill. Albert Bandura and R. B. Sloane point out that in all kinds of therapy, including behavior therapy, reinforcement may work because it encourages the client to imitate the behavior of the therapist and to adopt his values. Even the most cautious and "nondirective" therapists, as R. Rosenthal has shown, help their clients improve by inducing them to become more like their therapists in their value systems.

S-R behavior therapy may work partly or largely because it creates positive expectancy or "hope" in the client. Because of cognitive belief that desensitization is "scientific" and will work, the client may use "positive thinking" on himself and may, by a process of autosuggestion, make it work.

More and more therapists are discovering that the use of S-R therapy is not incompatible with psychodynamic procedures but actually supplements cognitive methods. RET practitioners have found that clients can be shown how to use reinforcement principles on themselves, so that behavior therapy comes to be cognitively self-directed. David Premack has theorized that although lower animals are largely reinforced by primary rewards, such as food and water, humans are quite reinforceable by any action or process that they find or *construe* as more satisfying than another. Thus, Lloyd E. Homme and his associates have found that even young children will train themselves to perform a relatively unpleasant task, such as quietly paying attention to their teacher, if they are told that they will soon be rewarded with a relatively pleasant activity, such as having a recess period during which they can wildly run around the room.

In RET, we frequently get clients to do "unpleasant" tasks, such as finishing a term paper or going to the dentist, by scheduling for themselves a much more "pleasant" activity, such as talking to their friends or looking at TV, and making the performance of the latter activity contingent upon the execution of the former task. In this manner, reinforcement theory and practice is directly employed but is specifically associated with cognitive therapy.

Behavior therapy, although rooted in the early experimental work of Ivan Pavlov and John B. Watson, has only recently become a widely used tool of psychotherapy, largely owing to the enthusiastic writings of B. F. Skinner, Hans Eysenck, and Joseph Wolpe. It has much to offer to the psychotherapist, and there is every reason to believe that its practice will significantly increase in the future. However, even Pavlov, its main originator, stressed the importance of cognitive factors, or what he called the secondary signal system, in human conditioning. It is important to keep in mind, especially if a comprehensive theory and practice of psychological treatment is to be developed, that man is the kind of animal who becomes cognitively as well as reflexively conditioned, who not only is capable of high-level thinking but who frequently thinks about his thinking, and who has the unique ability to condition or train (and to recondition and retrain) himself. An understanding and application of S-R behavior therapy is therefore a valuable but not a sufficient part of the well-rounded therapist's methodology. He had better, as well, employ cognitive behavior therapy, in its own right and in conjunction with whatever other techniques—such as emotive, experiential, and relationship techniques—that are found useful.

14

A PSYCHOTHERAPY SESSION WITH
AN ALCOHOLIC MALE

What goes on during a session of a rational-emotive psychothera-apist and a client? Many such sessions have been tape re-corded. A verbatim report is reproduced here. John S. was married, white, thirty-five years of age. He originally came for seven sessions of marriage counseling with his wife in the summer of 1968. At that time, he was not having very frequent sex relations with her, largely because of his heavy drinking; also had colitis, presumably connected with his anxiety. He made some progress during the original contacts, particularly in becoming less anxious, but his alcoholism did not decrease nor his sex relations with his wife increase. She benefited considerably from therapy and continued to come sporadically after he quit. She consequently became much less anxious, was more ef-fective as a mother, lost most of her feelings of worthlessness, and began to go to graduate school. As she felt more adequate, she became more determined to leave John if he did not do something about his alcoholism, their infrequent sex relations, and their poor social life. He returned to therapy in 1970, and had two sessions before this present one. His return was largely motivated by his wife's progress and her determination to leave him if he did not change.

Therapist-1: Well, what's doing?

Client-1: Well, it's been a very busy, and, I think, a very successful two weeks.

T-2: Yeah? Are you still a reformed crook on the alcohol?

C-2: Oh, yeah. I've had a few drinks.

T-3: What'ya mean by a few drinks?

C-3: Well, we. . . . Like last night, we went in swimming. . . .

T-4: Yeah?

C-4: (*Inaudible*) . . . We had a pleasant time. Buying sodas. Rested before dinner. Yeah, I mean, just that sort of thing. . . .

T-5: Yeah. Just social drinking. And you haven't been bringing home alcohol and drinking it after supper or anything like that?

C-5: No.

T-6: So you've done sort of well, but you're still able to drink?

C-6: Oh, yeah.

T-7: Which A.A. says you can't do—but they're wrong.

C-7: [*Laughs heartily.*]

[I remember noting his particularly hearty laugh at this point, and feeling it was genuine and feeling relieved about its genuineness. I had been wondering, when the session began, whether he was going to keep up his seeming miracle cure of two weeks before, when I had last seen him. He had been drinking steadily for many years, and fooling himself about the amount of his drinking. Seeing him, together with his wife, for seven sessions two years previously had helped him gain some insight into his perfectionism and consequent anxiety, which he habitually drowned in alcohol; but had not helped him allay his symptoms in any way. After a resumption of therapy and a single session three weeks prior to the present session, and after reading some of the books by my colleagues and myself, he suddenly began to face his perfectionism, especially at his job. As he stopped demanding that he do marvelously well, and as he stopped blaming himself for not performing outstandingly, his anxiety disappeared and he was able to do without alcohol entirely for a week, with no strain whatever. I strongly wondered, to myself, whether he was going to keep this up, and suspected that he was not. But his hearty laugh reassured me that he was not merely putting me on and that he really *did* believe, against the rules of Alcoholics Anonymous, that he could not only stop drinking to drown his anxiety, but could at the same time continue to be a social drinker. Maybe I was *too* willing to be convinced in this respect; but for the moment, I was convinced.]

T-8: You see, they say that once a person has this—is described as alcoholic—and you would have been described as alcoholic—then he cannot touch another drink for the rest of his life. And I have several people whom I've seen, whom I've got to give up drinking, and they *do* drink socially from time to time. But I usually give them the rule of thumb: "Never more than *two* drinks a day." And they stick to that, and do it once in a while; and they don't go back to drinking. So A.A. is wrong.

C-8: Oh, I think they are too. I—I think that A.A. doesn't provide the basis for a solution. . . .

T-9: Yeah. What they probably mean is that while a person remains a screwball, it's very dangerous for him to drink at all. Cause one drink may make him feel good, and two drinks better, and then he deludes himself that his problems are solved. And there may be some people who can't drink at *all*; but I don't see that most alcoholics are in that category. Anyway, you certainly were not drinking in the last two weeks. Right?

C-9: Oh, no. Not at all. Socially, yes. And on certain occasions. It's no problem. And—I don't have any difficulty really at all any more. Having a drink at a business meeting, a brief business meeting, after work. . . . And going off from there to, uh, other things. What's happened a couple of times in the last two weeks. It's no big deal!

T-10: Right! And how have you been getting along with your wife?

[With his giving these additional details of how he could drink at a business meeting and then simply stop, I was more relieved than ever. It seemed that he certainly was licking the alcoholism. To make sure that he was making real progress in other ways as well, and was not developing some kind of substitute symptom, I picked the one other major area in which he had been doing poorly: his relations with his wife. She had been seeing me from time to time, recently, and bitterly complaining that he was no companion to her and that she was very seriously thinking of leaving him. I wanted to see whether he was facing this important problem, too.]

C-10: Uh . . . splendidly. And, under . . . She has been marvelous, too. Uh, the last two weeks she's had some physical problems. She had a coil put in and started bleeding. And then she lost the coil, and so . . .

T-11: Yeah. . . .

C-11: A week ago, she was off her feet . . . I insisted she get the hell off her feet a couple of days. And something of the normal routine was driving her up the wall—taking care of all four children, uh, full time. . . . I'm just able to *be* there now. And, uh, it's O.K. . . . And we're gonna get [inaudible] backup; and we're gonna take care of school, too. . . . Anyway, it's no problem. But there are other things. And, uh, on the positive, on the positive side, that's a positive thing, and the drinking business is a positive thing. . . . But also, uh, I'm terribly productive at work. And I'm, uh [Laughs] this is not grandiose! I think a reasonable thing, in fact, I've been finding out that I've been *extremely* competent. I *am*, in fact, very competent in my field. . . . And I think quite possibly, in some ways, I really don't think I have any peers. Or if I have, I haven't found them yet, in my particular field. And, uh . . . On the other side of the, the coin, also, I've been finding that I'm a rather interesting person myself. . . . And also, happily, a rather interesting person to, uh, other people. And, uh . . . Well, on the other side of the coin, I'm finding that an awful lot of people, uh, with whom I've been associated with, are really very dull and boring. . . . And I've been to business things, and going-away parties. . . . And, uh, it's just dull, dull, dull!

T-12: Yeah?

C-12: [Laughs heartily.] I—I know I'm developing a greater appreciation all the time for your emphasis on the notion of becoming creatively absorbed, and becoming involved in *some* kind of creative projects or, or in dealing with, uh, other peoples' problems. Or *something*. Because, uh, so much of what I do all along is so artificial, and a byproduct of the system itself, rather than having any meaning—any creative meaning or any problem-solving meaning. It's just a *process* of a corporate life and, uh, the related social life, and this sort of thing. And I—I find my energies. I, just—there just wasn't enough there to absorb, uh, [Inaudible] energies. It used to be the damned work, because of the way I approached it, absorbed *all* of my energies. Uh, and, uh. . . . But, anyway, on the uh, and I think it's part of the same problem I've had, and what I'm telling myself, is perfectionism and concern about one thing or another. . . . In thinking about things, uh, Susan and I will be thinking about, uh, what we, what we wanted to do. We want to get a summer place, or where we want to live, or this sort of thing. . . . And we say, okay, a farm. Now, what if we were living on a farm. And the first thing that comes to my mind is, uh, horses and horses' hooves kicking, kicking one of the children, you see. Or all these very negative things—always the worst possible things that happen in any particular situation. Now, I'm going to Memphis, Tennessee, to handle a, well, doing some work for the antipollution commission. It's a very ill-advised project, which is neither here nor there, but I'll be flying to Memphis on Monday, and I'll be there for a few days. And I know; when I go to that airport and climb on that plane, I'm going to feel a great sense of foreboding. . . . And I'm going to be thinking the worst of *all* possible things that could happen—whether it be the plane just dropping out of the sky or, or being hijacked to Cuba!

[I remember wondering, first, where he got the idea of becoming creatively absorbed in something other than his work and the somewhat meaningless social life that often went with it. Did I go over this with him at the last session? I couldn't remember doing so. Then I remembered that he had been reading *A Guide to Rational Living* and that one of its chapters is entitled, "Overcoming Inertia and Becoming Creatively Absorbed." I assumed that he had mainly got the idea from this chapter that he'd better develop a vitally absorbing interest; and I felt very pleased that I was again receiving evidence in favor of the effectiveness of bibliotherapy. As soon, however, as the client came back to his anxieties and his tendency to think of the worst of all possible things that could happen to him, I said to myself something like, "Ah! I knew he could not have yet conquered his basic problem in so short a period of time. I'm glad that he is facing the fact that he is still terribly anxious at times; because if he doesn't, he'll run right back to his defensiveness, and probably to his compulsive drinking again. Let me see, now, if I can't quickly zero in on his anxiety-producing philosophies, to show him how to tackle and change them."]

T-13: All right. But let's suppose you *do* think of the worst possible things—the plane falling, and your children starving, and all kinds of things like that. Let's suppose that—which is not that abnormal. Because innumerable people, probably most people, think of that at some time. They wouldn't be obsessed with it; but they would say, "Suppose the goddamned plane falls—."
C-13: It doesn't prevent me from doing things, but . . .
T-14: But you still get anxious?
C-14: Yes.
T-15: All right. So we'll call C, the Consequence, anxiety. And we'll call A, the Activating Event, the fact that you're going to take this plane trip—or your taking it. Let's assume that—to Memphis. Now, the question is: "What really causes C? Is it A, the trip, or is it some-

thing else?'' And we know it can't be A, because sometimes you might *not* think of these worst things; and other times you might think of them really, continually, etc. It isn't any *event* that causes the Consequence. So it must be B—your Belief System. Now, first let's get you to see the *rational* Belief that causes, that is implicated, in C. It doesn't exactly cause C, the anxiety, but it causes *another* emotion. Now that *rational* Belief—it's a negative belief, prediction of something negative, but still pretty rational. Now, what do you think *that* is?

C-15: [Ten second pause.] Well, it's [Pause], it's prediction of something that's possible, and something that has happened, and uh [Pause].

> [I thought, at this point, "Watch it! Don't tell him too quickly! You know perfectly well what rational and irrational beliefs are causing his reactions, especially his anxiety. But if you tell him too quickly, he may merely accept your view and parrot it back to you, but not really see it or believe it. Better let him figure it out for himself, if possible. He probably can do this, and it would be better to let him figure it out and see it in his own words."]

T-16: Right. "I could—If I go on this plane, if I go on this trip, something quite bad *could* happen. . . . ''

C-16: Yes, and I could. . . .

T-17: And, and . . .

C-17: I could get killed. . . .

T-18: "I might be killed . . . '' Right. "And that would be. . . '' What? What was the *rational* conclusion? Because that's an *observation*: that something bad—you could be killed, you could be hurt, etc.— could definitely happen. And we know that's possible. That's perfectly sane. Now, what . . .

C-18: And I don't want to get killed, and it would be very, uh, an unfortunate thing, uh. . . .

T-19: Right! That's exactly right. Now, let's suppose you just put a *period* there. "I could get killed. And I don't want to. And it would be very unfortuante, not only for me, because I couldn't live; and now that I'm becoming happy that certainly would be very unfortunate that my life would be snuffed out. And it would be quite unfortunate for my wife, children, etc." Now if you just stuck to that, you put a period instead of a comma or a semicolon there, what *feeling* would you feel at C, the Consequence? You'd have a *feeling* if you said that. Now what do you think that feeling would be?

C-19: [Pause.] Let's see. I suppose now I'd get these mildly depressed results or . . .

T-20: Probably. But mild depression is what we usually call—I think what you're calling mild depression—is sorrow, regret. . . .

C-20: Regret . . .

T-21: Concern, caution. Something like that. Right?

C-21: Um-huh.

T-22: Because you say, "Well, *since* that could occur, and since I wouldn't want it, maybe I shouldn't take the trip, maybe I should go by train instead of by airplane. You certainly wouldn't feel *happy* about that thought. So you would feel sad or regretful or frustrated or annoyed or cautious or concerned. But that's all, you see, if you really stuck to that. And then, being cautious or concerned, you'd go back to, "Now what are the *chances* of this dreadful thing happening?" Then you'd probably conclude, very few.

C-22: They'd be low.

T-23: Yeah; right. "It could happen. And I could *more likely* get hit by a car, or something like that."

C-23: I'm more likely to get killed in a taxicab on the way.

T-24: Right. But you wouldn't feel *good*. You'd feel *sad* or sorry or cautious. O.K. Now, you know, however, you feel *anxious*—which is a lot different. It's not even a greater degree of depression, as it were, or sorrow. It's real anxiety—it's *catastrophizing* about it. And your exaggerating of the plane's really crashing at all. And this is your tendency. Now, what's the *catastrophizing* thought, the thought that leads to the real anxiety or *real* depression?

C-24: Well, I think I'm saying something like, uh, probably it's grandiose. This would be *awful*, uh, this just shouldn't happen to *me*. And what if, uh, if, uh, something happened to Susan and the children, this would be my fault. I wouldn't—it would prove that I wasn't, uh, perfect and that I can't handle every situation, uh. . . .

T-25: Which I *should* be able to. . . .

C-25: Which I *should* be able to do! [Laughs.]

T-26: You see, that *is* grandiose. You're—you're also saying a magical thing, I believe, because most people do under these circumstances.

C-26: That's a very interesting word that you've got: *magical*. For that's the magical thing.

T-27: Yeah.

C-27: For that's been encouraging me this last week. I had, uh, Susan and I [Laughs], Susan started playing yossling. You know what yossling is?

T-28: No.

C-28: It's just rolling, just rolling five dice, you see. . . .

T-29: Yeah.

C-29: You roll five at a time.

T-30: Yeah.

C-30: You can roll five of a kind, or a full house, or a large straight.

T-31: Right.

C-31: You sort of fill out these things, and they all have so many points.

T-32: Yeah?

C-32: And, uh, I, uh, I would start predicting when Susan or I would get a certain thing. And it happened that, that it worked out that way on certain occasions. Of course, neither one of us remembered the times when it didn't work out [Laughs.]

T-33: Yeah, naturally!

C-33: Yeah, and, uh, you know, uh, and it had a sort of mystical, magical, fatalistic, uh, fear. And I think that I have this about a lot of things.

T-34: Yes. That's right. The dice feeling, as if "I can control those dice. Look what *I* did that somebody else couldn't do!"

C-34: [Laughs.] Yeah. Right!

T-35: And that's what gamblers really think: "If I win the race, then *I've* done this."

C-35: Somehow forced that horse to move faster!

T-36: Yeah: right. Which is magic!

C-36: By the power of my, uh, will.

T-37: Yeah. So that it's good that you see that. But there's another magical element in this catastrophizing about airplanes. Not only are you saying, sort of, that "I might have some power over the airplane, etc. to let it fall or not." But you're really saying, "If I were dead,"—let's suppose that this really occurred—"it would be awful for *me*."

C-37: Yeah.

T-38: Not only for *them*. And, of course, it *wouldn't* be awful for you.

C-38: Uh, that is ridiculous.

T-39: Yeah, you, you, it would be, uh, the end of your life. But you wouldn't *know* it. And you're seeing yourself as both dead and alive, at the same time.

C-39: Mm-huh.

T-40: You really think, magically, "I wouldn't *quite* be dead. I'd *know* I were dead. And I'd see and hear my wife and children suffering."

C-40: Uh-huh.

T-41: Which is not true! They might suffer.

C-41: Right.

T-42: But you wouldn't be around. So. . . .

C-42: There's a probability they wouldn't very much anyway.

T-43: Right, and . . . That's right, she'd probably get a job and get remarried or something like that. *But* the other thing of course is the real magic, is the *should*. "I *should* be able to do perfectly well and control that airplane and control their happiness, etc. I should be Jesus Christ or Jehovah."

C-43: (Inaudible.)

T-44: What?

C-44: "He who walks on water," senior, or something like that.

T-45: Right. Right, you see. So that's real nonsense! Now, how would you *challenge* those irrational ideas: "I *should* be able to control my destiny! It would be horrible, awful, and catastrophic if I died! Etc." Now how could you *challenge* that, *dispute* that at D? C is the Consequence of iB—your *irrational* Belief. Now how could you Dispute those irrational Beliefs?

[I remember feeling all right, though perhaps a little let-down about my raising the issue of his magically seeing himself, at one and the same time, as dead and alive. I have recently pointed this out to several of my clients who have been greatly afraid of dying, and most of them have quickly, and sometimes dramatically, seen that they are thinking of themselves as "dead" but *also* thinking of themselves as "alive" and *realizing* and *emoting about* their own death. I wanted to see if he could get this point, too. He seems to have understood it, but passed a little too blithely over it for my tastes. So I felt both pleased and disappointed. I mainly decided, however, to get back to the irrational, magical ideas about dying in an airplane crash which he himself had raised, and to show him how they specifically fitted into my A-B-C-D model of rational-emotive therapy; and how, by using this model, he quickly could zero in on his self-defeating ideas, change them, and thereby stop feeling anxious. I felt pleased, so far, that he seemed to be getting the model and that he might therefore make some good use of it to help himself.]

C-45: Well I did, uh, I think I have disputed it successfully on certain occasions last week.
T-46: How?
C-46: I, uh, we go down to our neighborhood park. There's a small playground at Sixty-third Street. And, uh, there's a big swing. They've installed a big swing in the small toddler's park, really, and. . . .
T-47: Right.
C-47: And there're older children on the swings. And I, uh, a couple of years ago saw one of the kids racked up on the swings, and so on. And, uh, interestingly, this week I saw that it was finished. Anyway, so I'm always concerned about the children when I'm down there. They want to swing on the big swings. And so I can't just sit down on

the bench to read or something. I'm always concerned that they're going to get hit with the swing or this or that. And it is possible. And that caring, that far, is really reasonable and rational.

T-48: Oh, yeah. It could occur.

C-48: It could occur.

T-49: But how did you stop that catastrophizing, this week?

C-49: Well, I said. . . . First of all, I, uh, brought things to read. And I said, "Look, uh, uh, first of all, uh, you can't, you can't be everywhere. It's ridiculous to think you could. You don't have this power, in the first place, to prevent anything happening to anyone else." And . . .

T-50: Right.

C-50: And, secondly, these children come to the park every day with their mother, and they play quite competently and seem quite able to take care of themselves. And if they weren't able to take care of themselves and they got bumped, they'd get bumped. And I'd go pick them up and comfort them or, uh, do whatever was necessary.

T-51: Right.

C-51: If something happens, uh, I . . . And I just found myself deeply involved, and fully concentrated on my reading and I . . .

T-52: Right.

C-52: And I woke up when Susan indicated that, uh, why don't we get an ice cream or something.

T-53: Right. But there were two other things you could have done which would have added to this—and what you did was good—and, thirdly, you could have said, "Look, if I protect them, really, by stopping them from swinging, etc., then it's a dubious aid to their lives."

C-53: Right. Well, I, I, I've gone over this with myself many times, and you know, I know the ridiculousness of frustrating their lives or preventing their, their development and their own happiness, by restricting their freedom.

T-54: Right. They might survive, but they wouldn't be very happy surviving if you rendered them, aided them in being supercautious, noninvolved in swinging, etc. You see, and then there's a final thing which we're loathe to do. The elegant solution to the problem is "If the worst comes to the worst, and they really got killed on the swing (which is highly, highly unlikely, but anything could happen) *would that be* HORRIBLE! Could I *stand* it?''

[I remember fleetingly asking myself whether it was necessary, at this point, to bring out to the client the most effective solution: to show him that he could always, no matter what, accept the worst and not catastrophize about it. I wondered whether he could accept this elegant solution; and very quickly decided that he probably could; so that it would be best to bring it up. I knew that if he couldn't, I would merely retreat for the present, and leave him with a less effective solution.]

C-54: [Pause.] That's interesting. Because I've discussed this with my wife. I've gone through that and, uh, I don't . . . Well, frankly, if I'm honest with myself, I, I don't think it would. I mean it wouldn't, it would be something that you would, uh, mourn about, something that you couldn't *do* anything about, and, uh . . .
T-55: Right.
C-55: Uh, unless you spent your time catastrophizing to yourself, uh, you, you'd, unless you made an effort to sustain the thing by telling yourself how awful and horrible it was, and being, uh, grandiose, I, uh, it would pass. It would pass rather, as a matter of fact, I think. But I posed this dilemma. Because I said, ''Now, in thinking about all these things, and Ellis and his book, face the fact that there's nothing in life that with the possible exception, up to a point, of dying of very painful cancer of the kind that can't be, uh, subdued by or relieved, pain relieved, by medication. But, even there, you have the option of suicide, and eliminating that pain. So there's really literally, virtually literally, *no* circumstance in life that, if you're *rational* about it, uh, that should cause you more than fairly brief discomfort.'' Or, and, uh, but, uh, Susan said well, she couldn't quite go along with that. She said that I have *known* people—and of course in her own family, when her older sister, Gretchen, committed suicide, and so on, she, I think she tends to attribute qualities and things about her mother, that

she tends to romanticize things a great deal. But she says she's never known anyone who's lost a child who hasn't been seriously and permanently and adversely affected by it.

T-56: Well, they'd better be seriously and permanently adversely affected by it, if by adversely we mean that from time to time, at least, for the rest of their lives, they'll think, in a very sorrowful, mournful way, about it.

C-56: That's what she's talking about.

T-57: But she means really, depressed.

C-57: Becoming embittered, rigid, uh, any number of things—uh, their whole personalities becoming frozen.

T-58: And she's probably right.

C-58: She is right.

T-59: But, the point is: Isn't there magic in what these people are doing?

C-59: Yes, uh . . .

T-60: What do you think the magic is that they're doing, to make themselves embittered and depressed and rigid?

C-60: Well, they, they, they are are either living both lives simultaneously, or they think or, it's clear, they think the person is not really dead, or they're living all the things, they're living all of the things they think that person is *not* doing but is experiencing—"death" or something.

T-61: Right. And also—that's one element of magic—the other one is that the universe *should* be such that it *should* not have done this to them; and the awful, awful universe *did* what it should not have done to them; and they'll *never* accept that horrible cruelty from the universe.

C-61: Yeah.

T-62: In other words, they won't accept the fact that the universe doesn't give a *shit* about them.

C-62: [Laughs.] We all know it, even though we won't accept it. I think, well, I've accepted this *intellectually*, and I think an awful lot of people have intellectually, but . . .

T-63: Meaning, *once in a while*!

C-63: That's right.

T-64: That's what *intellectually* means. Once in a while, I think about it and I say, "Well, the universe *doesn't* have to give a shit about it. So it doesn't." But then I go back to, most of the time, "But it *should!*"
C-64: Yeah. [Laughs.] You're absolutely right.
T-65: Intellectual insight means, "Once in a while I believe it, and I *wish* I always believed it, but I really *don't.*" I go back to the magic—the horseshit.

[I felt good, at this point, about the client's being able to see that his wife and her relatives were wrong—because they could not see that a woman could *sorrow* strongly about a lost child but that she did not have to make herself *depressed* or *embittered* about this loss. I felt somewhat disappointed that his wife, with whom I had worked for about a dozen sessions during the last two years, was still somewhat hung up about this important distinction, and was not making it clearly. I could see her keenly in my mind—since she is a highly attractive, very bright young girl. I could just see her pouting, charmingly, that she could *never* accept the loss of one of her own children, and that she would *have* to be embittered by it; and I tried to think of some way in which I might possibly get her to see that these were irrational conclusions. I mentally made a note of trying to work on this with her, the next time she came in to see me.]

C-65: Well, I, uh . . . I have, uh, well, that's precisely it. Because I have these periods of time when I'm really in gear with it, with the intellectual concept.
T-66: Yeah.
C-66: And, uh, my God, the fear in life goes and everything that happens is just exhilarating, uh, during those periods. [Laughs.] I'm not suggesting now that life can *always* be exhilarating, but uh, you're right, it's a brief period. And then I get all, uh, get in process, uh, things start accumulating. Something that, uh, I have a gross lack of self-discipline.

[I remember feeling pleased that the client seemed to be able to realize that intellectual insight, so called, is not really full insight, but only momentary or occasional belief of a rational nature, while the individual who holds it still intensely and devoutly believes, at the same time, arrant irrationalities—which he then acts upon. At the same time, when he raised the problem of his lacking self-discipline, which meant that he still had hardly heeded all the things we had been talking about and which were mentioned in *A Guide to Rational Living,* I was kind of glad that he was still seriously beset with disturbed behavior. For I felt that, so far, this session had largely been a reporting of progress on his part, and that he had not brought up anything too much that I could help him with. Since I knew that this half-hour session was going to end soon, I was happy to see him raise a real-life issue, which we might be able to get our teeth into somewhat, so that he would leave the session feeling that he had received some distinct therapeutic benefit. I prefer to have a client receive such specific benefit from each session, so that he will have an incentive to finish therapy, and so that he will have something to work on during the time that elapses in between sessions.]

T-67: Yeah?

C-67: And, uh, I suppose it's just something. I suppose I know what I can do.

T-68: But that means—let's just explore that—that lots of times "I know what I'd better do and I don't *do* it. I goof. I'm lazy; I'm procrastinating."

C-68: For the last couple of weeks, I've been much, much improved in that respect. I'm just going from one thing to another, and nothing is, nothing really in the last two weeks—I've not allowed anything to intimidate me to the point that I couldn't just go ahead and do it. I might have a twinge of doubt and concern . . .

T-69: "But usually, I put things off . . ."

C-69: Right. Now the area that I'm most into now is, is physical. Now I, I know, or I feel strongly. And, again, it's probably something magical in this. Trying to make myself special. But I really feel as if I'm killing myself off with these goddamned cigarettes!

T-70: Yes: right.

C-70: Respiratory problems are part of my whole family. And my father died of lung cancer, and he would have died a few months later of heart failure if he hadn't died of that. And, you know, things like that . . .

T-71: All right. "So I know it's wise of me to go through the pain of giving up the cigarettes, and having the pleasure of living longer and healthier. But I don't do it. I go for the short-range goal of the pleasure of the cigarette."

C-71: Yeah. I quit for seven months, at one time. But I . . .

T-72: "Because *if* I were right *now* to give up the cigarettes . . . " Let's suppose, right now, next week you gave up the cigarettes. Which, incidentally, one of my clients, at the age of thirty-eight, after thirty *years* of three packs a day (he started at the age of eight!) gave up. "If I were to give that up right now, next week, the cigarettes, what would happen that I construe as awful?"

C-72: I'd, well, it'd . . . I would know plenty of times in which I would prefer to have a cigarette.

T-73: And? And I would sanely tell myself, first—what? rB, the *rational* Belief. "When I was in pain about not having the cigarette, I would sanely tell myself, what, first?"

C-73: [Pause.] Well, it . . . I'd tell myself that it, uh, that I would be better off not having the cigarette.

T-74: "And it's too goddamned *bad* that I'm in pain."

C-74: Yes.

T-75: "So I'd be sorrowful, regretful, frustrated. But I would *insanely* tell myself, to create the lack of discipline, and the going *back* to the cigarettes . . . ?" What would I *insanely* tell myself at the irrational Belief, iB?

C-75: Oh, I'd be saying that "I *must* have a cigarette," or "I can't get along without one," or "I shouldn't be *deprived!*"

T-76: That's right. "Now, how could I, in *pain*, deprive—combat

those insane, irrational Beliefs? How could I Dispute them, at D?''
C-76: Well, I could say that ''I'm in pain *now*, but that, uh, that if I want to get rid of the pain I'd damned well better not have the cigarette. That I want to feel better and become healthier in the *long* run, more able to do things . . . And that although I'd prefer to have cigarettes, and it might be giving me some momentary relief, that I know the relief wouldn't last more than a few moments, and that I'd be back in this pique repeatedly and having . . .''
T-77: Cancer, etc. But also, you'd better Dispute, at D, ''Why *should* the world be such that I *ought* to get away with smoking and not get the respiratory disorders, etc. Why is it *awful* that I have to give them up?'' You see, you're not disputing the magic: ''that the world shouldn't *be* this way; and it's *horrible* that I have to deprive myself, in order to get gain in the future. But right now, I really would have to deprive myself.'' And this other client went through about two or three weeks of *real* pain. And he went through the motions, in his head, of reaching for the cigarette, etc. He was habituated for thirty years.
C-77: Actually, I don't have that, anything like that kind of discomfort. In fact, when I quit, when I quit in the past, successfully for a matter of months, it was simply that I just quit. And I, I just simply said No, if it occurred to me. I did, but I didn't see the irrational ideas.
T-78: You did the behavioral work, what we call the homework assignments—you gave yourself the active homework assignment, ''No more cigarettes! Screw it! I'm not going to have any more cigarettes!'' But you didn't get rid of, or attack very much, the magical thinking: ''But I *ought* to be able to get away with this! It's *horrible* that the world is this way! Etcetera.'' Now if we can get you to do the homework assignment again, the activity—not smoke—beginning next week—*and* quit the magic; fight it; dispute it, actively, vigorously—challenge it, question it, then not only could you stay off the cigarettes but do yourself a great deal of philosophic and general good, and get rid of it.
C-78: How do you do it, besides simply . . . My inclination, and this—? I haven't been doing very well at precisely parsing the, uh . . .

T-79: By looking for the *should*. Because when you feel great discomfort . . .

C-79: Well, my answer is usually, say, well, "You're being grandiose." Or "Bullshit!"

T-80: No, you see, that's, that's shorthand.

C-80: I know. I know. This . . .

T-81: You see, that's true. But that's like saying, "Well, you're being neurotic. Don't be neurotic!" And that will temporarily work. But you'd better zero in on the *exact belief*. Which is something like—and you have to find it for yourself—"The world shouldn't *be* this way." The same thing those mothers are saying about their children.

C-81: Yes.

T-82: O.K. You go work on that. And I'll give you the homework assignment of not smoking *and* challenging the magic.

C-82: Yeah.

T-83: O.K. See you.

C-83: Right on! I was wondering about the thing in Miami [the meetings of the Association of Humanistic Psychologists and American Psychological Association]. How did it go?

T-84: Oh, fine!

C-84: Lots of confrontations?

T-85: Yeah. Right. Goodbye!

[I felt distinctly rushed at the end of the session. I now have half-hour sessions and usually, with rational-emotive therapy, they are sufficiently long, since little time is spent on the client's history or even on lengthy elucidations of his feelings, and a good portion of time is spent—as in this session—on teaching him how to think more scientifically about himself and the world. But I realize that I began the discussion of his lack of self-discipline and his smoking habits a little too late in the session, and that there would not be ample time to explore it for the few more minutes that would have been desirable. Since another client was waiting, I therefore chose to end this session by giving the client a specific homework assignment, so that he could carry on during the week some of the points we had been talking about, and report in more detail on them during the next session. At that time, I knew that I would check on his homework assignment and, especially if he had not done it well, use it as a method of getting him to see exactly what rational and irrational Beliefs he was employing—at point B—to result in his lack of self-discipline (or the Consequences, at point C.) I would then be able to get him to Dispute his irrational Beliefs, at point D, and presumably wind up with two Effects, at point E; first, the cognitive Effect, or change in philosophy: "There is no reason why I *should* be able to smoke and keep my good health. It is not *horrible*, but merely *inconvenient*, to give up smoking; and in the long run, it is more inconvenient to continue it." Second, I would hope that the client would wind up with the behavioral or emotional Effect: a considerable increase in his frustration tolerance and a feeling of relative ease when he resorted to desirable self-discipline. Although, therefore, I was not entirely satisfied with the abrupt ending of this session, I felt that it did set the stage for a logical continuation of the therapeutic work during the subsequent session].

15

PHOBIA TREATED WITH RATIONAL-EMOTIVE THERAPY

In a comprehensive view of the literature on the psychotherapy of phobias, J. D. W. Andrews points out that "the phobic disturbance appears to consist of two main elements: avoidance and dependence." To combat these tendencies he recommends a double-barreled therapeutic approach:

> The first element in therapeutic strategy is the support which the therapist must provide for the phobic patient; this is the role-complement of the dependency which characterizes such patients. Within the context of this supportive relationship, however, the therapist introduces a very new element: he begins to use his guiding, directing, helpful role to urge the patient to become more self-assertive and to deal with his fears directly. This strategy of encouragement is thus a frontal attack on the avoidance which has been the phobic's major strategy previous to entering therapy.

It is not difficult for an experienced therapist to agree with Andrews's formulation. Anyone who has seen large numbers of individuals with severe phobias is impressed that the vast majority of them are not neurotic but are basically psychotic. They rigidly and pervasively cling to two main irrational beliefs: (a) the world is much too difficult and dangerous a place for them to live in and it *should* be made much easier, and (b) they cannot single-handedly cope with it and therefore they desperately and absolutely *need* the acceptance, love, and support of others in order to accept themselves and to perform even minimally well. Practically all serious phobiacs have many anxieties rather than the one crippling form that drives them to treatment. They demand certainty in a world where there are no absolutes or certainties for any of us. In addition to blaming the universe for being as rough as it is, they also condemn themselves for not being able to cope with it better. They are just as unrealistic, in their own way, as are hallucinators, catatonics, and others who refuse to tolerate frustrations, take risks, and find some happiness for themselves in life's difficult ball game.

Can much be done to help phobiacs? Yes, a great deal, as far as their presenting symptoms are concerned; but much less, in most cases, in regard to their general attitudes and disturbances. Most of them, in fact, seem to get over some of their specific phobias without any treatment whatever. They are afraid, for example, of riding in cars; find that they must do so in order to get and keep a good job or see a girl with whom they are in love; force themselves, because of this specific incentive, to think against and act against this particular fear; and after a while conquer it so completely that they sometimes forget that they once were crippled by it. A phobia is usually based on what L. Breger and J. L. McGaugh call "a set of central strategies (or a program) which guide the individual's adaptation to his environment," or, in Andrews' words, it "arises not from a single, isolated learning experience that produces an equally isolated habit, but rather as a manifestation of a broader pattern of handling avoidance-learning situations *as a class.*" Hence, the phobiac is often not greatly helped by overcoming a specific symptom, since he easily can, and almost always does, react in an overly fearful manner to literally scores of other undangerous objects and events as well. Real cure consists of his facing the fact that *virtually nothing* is truly terrible, horrible, or catastrophic (though many things in life are distinctly frustrating or inconvenient); and the phobiac has to work so hard and long against biologically predisposed *and* environmentally conditioned conviction that hundreds of things are too rough for him, that he rarely does the necessary amount of challenging (both in theory and in action) of his self-defeating philosophies. Consequently, he almost always becomes *less* fearful rather than *non*phobiac, and his cure remains highly partial.

In rational-emotive psychotherapy, an effort is made to get clients afflicted with phobic reactions to surrender their extremely *basic* catastrophizing outlook rather than merely their presenting symptoms. But it is realistically acknowledged that many phobiacs will not be willing to go this whole way; so they are shown how to overcome their current specific phobias and how to apply the methods they learn in this connection to ridding themselves, now or later, of *any* severe phobic reaction. They are thus given a choice between working only on the present symptoms or also working on their general phobia-creating attitudes. The therapist tries to get them to take the latter, more global approach; but if they won't, they won't, and he philosophically accepts more limited improvement.

To show how rational-emotive therapy works with a phobiac, here is a summary case presentation. The client was a twenty-seven-year-old stenographer, who consistently worked at a job below her educational and intellectual level because she felt "contaminated" by contact with certain places—such as subway trains and various parts of the city. She therefore had to get jobs within short distances of her home. Although quite attractive, and having normal desires for sex, love, and marriage, she rarely dated—because her dates would either insist on going to places that she could not stand or else would have to be told about her "contamination" ideas, of which she was ashamed and which she was loath to talk about. She was entirely dependent on her parents, since she restricted her life so drastically by giving in to her phobia; and although she got along reasonably well with the people in her office, she had no real social life because of these same self-imposed restrictions.

With this client, I employed a number of techniques which are frequently used in rational-emotive therapy. First of all, I was highly active-directive. With direct questioning, the facts of the client's problem were elicited from her; also a brief history, which indicated that she had always been shy and retiring but that her fear of "contamination" had not erupted until she was faced with three main problems:

1. Going out on dates.
2. Masturbation.
3. Doing well at school.

Coming from a strict Methodist family, and believing that she had to be extremely successful as well as sexually "pure," her demands on herself at this time proved to be too onerous; and rather than honestly face failure, she used the excuse that certain people and places were contaminated to withdraw from danger and to punish herself for her masturbatory practices. Then, as the years went by, and her defenses against failing made her fail all the more—because she couldn't go out on dates, was unable to attend college, and could only work at low-level jobs—she castigated herself even more severely and felt like a complete failure. Finally, she condemned herself for her "foolish" symptoms and thought herself more worthless than ever.

This client was shown that her phobias stemmed from and were still being kept alive by her extreme fears of doing poorly and being thought of badly by others. Her basic values in these respects were vigorously counterattacked. I firmly insisted that she did not have to base her estimation of herself on succeeding at dating or at work, and that she could fully accept herself even though she never notably succeeded in these areas, nor ever was very popular with others. I showed her how her old-time religious views about sex were benighted and that, as long as she was not yet dating, she would be highly unwise not to masturbate frequently. I repeatedly indicated how she kept berating herself for being phobiac; and I forcefully contended that no matter how crippling her symptoms were, she was not to be condemned for maintaining them, and that she had better stop blaming herself for being disturbed if she wanted to have any chance whatever of overcoming her disturbances.

There was no close relationship between this woman and myself. On the whole, I was very didactic with her, seeing her about once every three weeks (since she had financial problems and did not want to go into debt to pay for her therapy). But I was very authoritative with her, and unequivocally let her know that if she accepted my authority and followed the directions I would give her, she could get over her phobic reactions. In this sense, I allowed her to be dependent on me, at least temporarily, although I informed her, from the very start, that the purpose of rational-emotive therapy was to get her *not* to need me or anyone else, but to be able soon to think for herself and follow her own bent. As is usually the case with rational-emotive therapy, she was shown that no matter what she thought of herself, I accepted her unconditionally, with her silly thinking and her foolish behavior, and that I was not going to condemn her no matter what she did, including no matter how badly she reacted to therapy. So although the "transference" relationship between me and the client was by no means what it should have been according to most schools of psychotherapy, she did come to look upon me as an authority on whom she could depend and as an individual who would unconditionally accept her with her past and present handicaps and failings.

This phobic client was given clear-cut homework assignments that were aimed at depropagandizing her and getting her to break her habit patterns. Thus, she was made to take trips to certain parts of the city that she might consider contaminated, to talk to various people of whom she was afraid; to move from one place of residence to another, and to attend functions where "contaminated" people would appear. When she did not follow up on these assignments—which at first was quite frequent—I calmly and unirritably got her to look at the sentences and meanings she was telling herself to block her doing so. For example, when she did not immediately move from her parental home, as I had urged her to do, our dialogue went as follows:

T: Did you move yesterday, as we had agreed you would do?

C: No. I'm still where I was.

T: Why? What did you tell yourself to stop yourself from moving?

C: I was too tired.

T: You mean, you said to yourself, "I'm too tired to do anything about moving today"?

C: Yes.

T: But that's obviously false. You told me, just a minute ago, that you woke feeling well yesterday morning, and you went for a long walk.

C: I did; but I just didn't feel like moving.

T: Because?

C: Because I've made some friends where I'm at.

T: And it would be difficult making friends again, where you're moving to?

C: Yes.

T: But you could make new friends, couldn't you, where you are moving? And you could still keep the old ones, too, could you not?

C: Yes, I could.

T: Then . . .?

C: I guess I told myself what we discussed the other day.

T: Which was?

C: That I might do poorly if I tried to make new friends. And I already know these people and they seem to like me. So why risk, uh, you know . . .

T: Why risk what?

C: Why, uh, risk, uh, failing with the new ones.

T: Ah, yes! There you go again. "If I try a new place and new people, I may fail with them. And that would be . . ."

C: That would be, uh, awful.

T: Right! That's what you told yourself. But *would* it be? If you *did* try for new friends, and they didn't accept you at the new place, would it *really* be awful?

C: Uh, no. I guess it wouldn't be so awful. But that's how I felt it would be yesterday.

T: All right, then. And that's the way you'll practically always keep feeling, unless you look at that drivel you're telling yourself, and question yourself: "*Why* would it be awful? Suppose I *can't* make friends easily at the new place. *Why* would I be a slob?"

In conjunction with the homework assignments, I kept pounding away with the theme that it was not terrible if she failed; she did not have to hate herself as a person if she was inept; she was not an awful individual because she had a bad symptom; and she did not deserve to be punished because she was so silly. I kept forcing her to question and challenge her own negative self-evaluations and showed her, over and over, how to think scientifically, assess her behavior objectively, and stop rating her entire being when her performances were poor.

Through these means, I first got her to accept herself even when she was reacting in a highly phobic manner. As she stopped condemning herself, she was more and more able to carry out her antiphobic homework assignments. Then she was able to do them with more ease and less pain. Finally, she began to enjoy doing some of them and to make them habitual. She became adept, for instance, at meeting men and having dates with them, an entirely new experience for her; and then she began to enjoy these dates, to become more selective about making them, and to feel a little restless and unoccupied when she had a free evening and was not engaging in some kind of heterosexual encounters. When, however, she settled on a steady boyfriend, she gave up this kind of activity, and was content to see him a few times a week and to occupy herself nonsexually the rest of the time.

At first, it was a terrible chore for this woman to reoccupy any "contaminated" territory in the city, and she frequently reverted to almost complete withdrawal to "safe" places. After a while, she went about her "decontamination" activities with almost scheduled regularity, reoccupying one territory one week, another the next week, and so on. After about two months of this regular kind of decontamination, her antiphobic activity accelerated greatly. She started to realize that no territory itself was really contaminated, but only the ideas in her own head were. She rapidly went everywhere she could, and in about ten days visited scores of places that she had previously prohibited to herself. Several weeks after this, she considered herself cured of territorial contamination and began to work on various of her less dramatic anxieties, including her sex fears. After forty-five psychotherapy sessions (spread out over a period of thirty months), she was virtually nonphobic, was engaged to be married, and considered herself cured. I saw her a few times during the next several years, in regard to crisis situations about her husband and her in-laws, and she still appeared to be basically nonphobic and to be making a better than average general adjustment to life. She still had a decided tendency to catastrophize about many events, but she quickly went to work at challenging most of her own catastrophizing and was able to do so successfully. Her husband (whom I also saw a few times) thought she was a very well adjusted individual; but I felt that she was more underlyingly troubled than most people, still gave herself a needlessly hard time on many occasions, but was doing remarkably well for an individual who had previously been so globally disturbed.

Not all extremely phobic individuals can or do react this well to rational-emotive psychotherapy; some are simply not convinced at all to take significant risks and to prove to themselves that the whole world will not crash around their heads. But this kind of a direct, philosophically based homework-assigning attack on the phobiac's basic perfectionism works beautifully with some patients and reasonably well with many who are not reached at all by more passive and historically centered approaches.

16

THERAPY WITH PSYCHOTICS AND BORDERLINE PSYCHOTICS

Rational-emotive psychotherapy was originally devised largely for use in the treatment of so-called "neurotics." However, most of these clients, it appears, can be more accurately labeled borderline psychotics or outright psychotics, and the classification of them as neurotics may have been a gross underestimation of the gravity of their condition.

It will be recalled that several years ago an article appeared in the *American Journal of Psychiatry* that pointed out that Freud had misdiagnosed most of his early analysands, since he referred to them as "hysterics" or "neurotics" when actually, in the light of our modern diagnostic methods, they would be labeled as schizophrenic. This Freudian type of misdiagnosis may still be prevalent. Particularly if a psychotherapist is in private practice, he will soon find that because he charges a rather high fee per session, and because his clients (partly because of their severe sickness) tend not to be wealthy individuals, he is largely seeing people who are practically *driven* to seek help, rather than those who would merely benefit if they did receive it. These clients, who think they *need* steady and often prolonged support from a therapist, are the ones most likely to be overt or borderline psychotics.

A great many regular psychotherapy clients, in the experience of numerous therapists, including myself, have had histories of prior institutionalization. Some of them are seen when they are temporarily on leave from a mental hospital; and many more after they have been discharged. Many of those who have never been hospitalized come for treatment because they feel they are on the verge of cracking up or because they are suicidal. Obviously, these are very "sick" people.

It was once widely believed that almost all highly disturbed individuals, including those who are basically psychotic, are made the way they are by their early environment—especially by traumatic occurrences during their first few years of life. There is increasing, and in fact overwhelming, evidence for abandonment of this view, and for the belief that probably all human beings are born with rather distinct "holes in their head." Psychotics, then, are born with a much bigger hole than the rest of us inherit.

By this is meant that the human animal is biologically predisposed to think crookedly on many occasions, to defeat his own ends, to be oversuggestible and overgeneralizing, to become both anxious and hostile with very little or no objective provocation, and to continue to reinfect himself with anxiety and hostility no matter what kind of upbringing he has, nor in what kind of society he has been reared. The belief that men and women are *first* genetically predisposed to emotional disturbance, and that they then *later* are the victims of environmental traumata that help actualize these predispositions, and that induce them to become perhaps four or five times as disturbed as they might biologically tend to be, has been forced on a growing body of psychotherapists, including myself, by clinical observation during recent years.

The resistance of seriously disturbed clients to treatment can often be traced to the innate inherited tendencies of these people. In some cases, it has become clear that they resist because they are telling themselves, that they *cannot* help themselves; or because they resent having to *work* at therapy; or because they want to spite the therapist; or for some other ideological reason. In many other instances, however, it eventually becomes evident that the clients very much *do* want to improve and *are* working hard at doing so; but they just have great *difficulty* helping themselves, and it is highly probable that this difficulty is inborn, has plagued them all their lives, and is an essential component of their disturbance. In other words, whereas many neurotic individuals, for various perverse reasons, simply *will* not think clearly and logically about themselves, it appears that these particular clients who resist getting better on non-ideological grounds are usually psychotic or borderline psychotic individuals who *cannot* think straight, or who can do so only with great difficulty.

Observation of these clients over a long period of time has convinced me that they seemed to have severe focusing difficulties. Either they did not focus adequately on solving their life difficulties, and instead were unusually diffuse, discursive, and disorganized in their thinking; or else, in many instances, they overfocused, in a highly rigid manner, on some specific aspect of their life, usually some negativistic or catastrophic aspect, and therefore were unable to focus adequately on other aspects of any problem-solving situation. The more of this behavior one observes, the more apparent it becomes that these clients are not in the neurotic range, even though their behavior is often typical of that of so-called neurotics, but that they are basically psychotic. They have a true thinking disorder—as Eugen Bleuler insisted is fundamentally true of schizophrenics. It is also interesting to note that Shakow has summed up his thirty years of studying schizophrenics with this observation: "If we were to try to epitomize the schizophrenic person's system in the most simple language, we might say that he has two major difficulties: first, he reacts to old situations as if they were new ones (he fails to habituate), and to new situations as if they were recently past ones (he perseverates); and second, he overresponds when the stimulus is relatively small, and he does not respond enough when the stimulus is great.'' In both these two major difficulties that Shakow notes, it is obvious that the schizophrenic is, at one time or another, under- *and* over-focusing.

Clinical observations by Aaron T. Beck confirm that seriously disturbed people have a fundamental, and probably innate focusing or thinking disorder. Beck notes that ''the present study indicates that, even in mild phases of depression, systematic deviations from realistic and logical thinking occur. . . . The thinking-disorder typology outlined in this paper is similar to that described in studies of schizophrenia. . . . These findings suggest that a thinking disorder may be common to all types of psychopathology.''

Beck also notes that ''*magnification* and *minimization* refer to errors in evaluation which are so gross as to constitute distortions. These processes were manifested by underestimation of the individual's performance, achievement or ability, and inflation of the magnitude of his problems and tasks. Other examples were the exaggeration of the intensity or significance of a traumatic event. It was frequently observed that the patients' initial reaction to an unpleasant event was to regard it as a catastrophe. It was generally found on further inquiry that the perceived disaster was often a relatively minor problem.''

Beck's statement has two most important implications. It implies, first, that the Freudian theory of the great importance of childhood trauma is untenable, since individuals who are thus ''traumatized'' may very well *invent* their ''traumas'' by exaggerating the significance of the usual life difficulties that occur to them. And it implies, second, that these patients have a basic thinking disorder, probably with innate as well as socially determined roots, that causes them to be qualitatively different from other so-called neurotics, who are unduly upset about life's problems, but who can fairly easily be taught to cope with and live with such problems.

There is considerable other evidence that indicates many cavalierly diagnosed ''neurotics'' are really fundamentally psychotic, that they *can*not (and not just *will* not) easily think straight about themselves and others, and that they are therefore most difficult to help when they come for psychotherapy. A few illustrations will show that even the most normal human beings are born with serious thinking deficiencies, and that in consequence they usually tend to have some kind of emotional disturbances and to act in self-defeating ways.

Take, for example, scientists, who in their own fields of endeavor are supposed to think scientifically, which means that they are supposed to be among the most objective and dispassionate observers and experimentalists. Actually, as a writer showed in an article in *Science*, some of the greatest scientists, such as Charles Darwin, had great difficulty in changing their ideas, and frequently refused to do so when clear-cut factual evidence indicated that it would be wise if they did. When data presented to them showed that something they believed in wholeheartedly was untrue, they by no means enthusiastically changed their views. Men of science are known to cavil with the evidence, ignore it, sometimes refuse to accept it; and it may be only ten or twenty years later that they finally reluctantly accept it and give up their original fallacious hypotheses. And these, remember, are often great minds, and great scientific minds at that, who are thinking in this irrational manner.

It is a human failing to resist accepting new information, even when it would be to our best interests to do so. Moreover, we humans tend, because of the principle of inertia, to fail to make use of much valuable information and insight that we theoretically accept. Because we are in a well-oiled groove of behavior, riding in reasonable comfort in what can be called Groove A, we find it exceptionally difficult, on many occasions, to pull ourselves out of that Groove, and to start swinging in Groove B—even though we know that it would be much wiser if we got ourselves to do so. When, for example, we are dully watching television, and know that it would be much better if we got up and started to work on some task that we have to do, we resist getting up, and stubbornly keep giving ourselves silly rationalizations why we should still watch the television screen. Then, when we finally manage to get to the required task, and we somehow start swinging easily and pleasantly in *that* Groove, which we may call Groove B, we refuse, with surprising frequency, to get out of it, when it comes time for us to go on, sensibly, to Groove C—which may consist of going to bed, playing with our children, eating, or even returning to Groove A again (because, perhaps, there is then a special show on television which it really would be wise for us to see).

Human beings—and in fact, in my belief *all* human beings—are perversely like this. They don't merely occasionally but *continually* behave stupidly and sabotage their own best interests, no matter how bright or educated they may be. How serious this self-defeating, utterly irrational tendency of the human animal can be struck me with great force when I picked up a medical magazine and saw a photo of a very brilliant young female physician who had won a prize for her valuable researches. Lo and behold!—it was obvious from her picture that she weighed at least two hundred pounds.

Now this set me to thinking. For I know at least fifty or sixty physicians intimately. All of them, of course, have four years' training at medical school, one year of internship, and years of medical experience. In addition, some of them have three or more years of residency in some medical specialty and a good deal of unusual clinical or research experience. Most of them are internists and general practitioners who spend a good deal of their time advising their patients to stop overeating, give up smoking, refrain from drinking too much, and get enough sleep.

Suppose we ask, now: What percentage of these physicians follow to a reasonable degree the simple laws of physical hygiene which are taught to practically all school children? Probably no more than 5 percent; for practically all these physicians whom I personally know are overeating, smoking, drinking too heavily, or sleeping too little, and some of them are doing all these self-defeating things. Which means that 95 percent of a highly intelligent, well-educated population is clearly destroying itself!

One of my own clients, a highly competent physician, came in to see me a while ago and said: "Doctor Ellis, you may think that I'm disturbed, but you really should be seeing everybody on the staff of my hospital, because they're all at least as crazy as I am! Especially one man, who has his M.D. and is also a Ph.D. in physiology. He's under thirty-five years of age, and is undoubtedly one of the outstanding authorities on obesity in the country. Well, you wouldn't believe it. He weighs at least three hundred pounds!"

Don't take my word for any of this, but open-mindedly look around you. Observe the scores of really self-destructive people whom you personally know—including (naturally!) most of the psychiatrists, psychologists, and psychiatric social workers with whom you are intimately acquainted. And look also, if you will, at the scores of other individuals you know who have had years of psychoanalysis and other forms of therapy, and who may possibly be getting along better now than they were when they first entered treatment, but who mentally are still far from well balanced. Does not the ubiquity and the incidence of neurosis and psychosis among your closest relatives and associates indicate something highly significant about the human, all-too-human, *tendency* of modern men and women, not to mention adolescents, to be severely disturbed?

If one honestly looks at the facts of moderate and serious emotional disturbance in this nation (as well as in virtually all other parts of the contemporary world), one will soberly ask: How come that 95 to 99 percent of the population is acting in such a childish, irrational, self-destructive manner? Is this kind of behavior *truly* the result of early childhood rearing?

The evidence would appear to enlist a negative answer to this last question. My own clients, for example, come from many different parts of the world, and have been reared in a hundred different ways by radically different kinds of parents. Some of them were brought up most permissively, some with exceptionally rigid, moralistic codes of behavior. Some of them were adored and pampered by their parents; others were constantly hated and punished. Some were members of large families; some were only children; and still others were raised in orphanages. It is almost impossible to describe the large variety of different kinds of upbringings that these clients had. Yet, particularly when they are schizophrenic, it is amazing how similar are their ways of thinking in many instances, and how incredibly alike their symptoms often are.

An alcoholic schizophrenic male, forty years of age, was having much trouble in his marriage but was afraid to leave his highly dominating (and also schizophrenic) wife because she took all the main responsibilities in their relationship and let him avoid making any major life decisions. I was then doing psychoanalytically oriented psychotherapy and largely showed this client how his passivity and avoidance of decision making was related to the passive role that he had been raised to play with his highly dominating and negativistic mother, and that he was perpetuating, in his relations with his wife (and with others), the same kind of "safe" symbiotic relationship he had engaged in with his mother. The client clearly saw this lifetime pattern of passivity and agreed that he was behaving as if his wife were his mother, and as if he still had to be dependent on the former as he had previously been (and still to some extent was) on the latter. In consequence, he was presumably able to acquire some additional ego strength and to get a divorce from his wife. He seemed to be significantly improved, was very grateful for the help he had presumably received in therapy, and quit treatment about eight months after he had first entered it.

Unfortunately, however, the client still kept drinking heavily; got into trouble on a succession of jobs because of his drinking; and within the next few years made two more poor marriages, in both of which he played a somewhat less passive role than before, but both of which were to exceptionally weak, gutless women whom he continually had to support and father. These marriages ended in divorces; and the client was unable to make and maintain any solid heterosexual relationships. He returned for occasional sessions of therapy during this time, but only to agree verbally that he was still messing himself up and that he needed much more self-discipline and less of a dire love need if he truly was to get better and become nonalcoholic.

Several years later, this client returned for regular psychotherapy, and was seen for twenty-seven individual sessions and forty-five group sessions during the year. This time, he was systematically treated with rational-emotive psychotherapy. His past history with his mother, and his other passive-dependent relationships, were hardly mentioned; instead, a concerted effort was made to get him to define, most precisely and concretely, his present philosophic assumptions that lay behind his self-destructive behavior.

It was quickly ascertained that he was strongly saying several self-defeating assumptions to himself, namely: (1) "It would be absolutely terrible if I made all my decisions and frequently made the ones that later turned out to be wrong. For then I would be utterly incompetent and could not possibly respect myself." (2) "Since it is awful if I make mistakes on major decisions, I had better maintain intimate relations with a woman (such as my mother or my first wife) who dominates me and is glad to make all the decisions herself; then, at least, I can't be blamed for making any serious blunders. Or, if I find it inconvenient living with such a woman, I then would better become intimately associated with one who is weaker than I and who will therefore accept me and still love me *even* if I make such errors. For if I am loved in spite of my mistake making, then I am not totally worthless." (3) "Because, one way or the other, I am bound to wind up with a dominating woman or one who is quite weak, and because I really would *like* to be intimately related to one who is strong in her own right and who would *still* accept me without dominating me, I am really utterly inadequate for remaining the weak way I have always been. My alcoholism and my poor relationships with women over the years clearly prove that I am a jellyfish in spite of my years of psychotherapy and my attempts at joining Alcoholics Anonymous groups; so how can a jellyfish like me *ever* expect to get any better?" (4) "Other people, such as my mother and first wife, on the one hand, and my second and third wives, on the other hand, really don't appreciate me, and *want* me to remain weak and unmanly; so they are no damned good, too, and I hate their guts!"

In the course of his year of rational-emotive psychotherapy, this schizophrenic client was clearly shown that he had had these negative evaluations of himself and others for many years, and that he still kept reindoctrinating himself with them on many occasions. He was then shown *why* these were irrational philosophies:

1. How, he was asked, would making wrong decisions for himself make him *utterly* incompetent? How could he possibly expect *always*, or even *usually*, to make correct decisions when he, like all the rest of us, was definitely a fallible human? Suppose, in fact, he were truly

incompetent at decision making. That would certainly be inconvenient and unpleasant; but how would his incompetence in that respect make him a thoroughly worthless individual, who could not possibly respect himself? Could not a truly incompetent person—such as a mentally deficient individual—*still* accept himself as incompetent, refrain from belaboring himself, and thereby manage to find *some* life enjoyments? Why, then, could not the client—if he *were* quite inadequate?

2. Why, in his relations with women, would it be awful if he kept making mistakes in regard to major life decisions? It is true that if he had a dominating wife who made his decisions for him, he would then make fewer grave errors. But then *she* might very well make the same kind of errors that he was avoiding making—and what good would *that* do him or her? Even, indeed, if she made fewer errors than he would make, would giving up his independence to her truly be worth it? Then, again, if he married a weaker wife, made more than his share of errors, but was forgiven by her for making them just because she *was* a weakling, would that really make his errors any the less inconvenient? *Why* did he need the love of such a weaker woman? And *how* would his getting her approval make him only a kind of half-shit? Would not his opinion of himself, both when he related to a stronger woman who took over decision making for him and when he related to a weaker woman who would not blame him for his errors, actually be purely definitional?

3. Assuming that he did wind up with either a dominating woman or a very weak one, how did *that* prove that he was thoroughly inadequate and that he could *never* gain any true measure of self-sufficiency? Similarly, assuming that he was still alcoholic after years of A.A. meetings and of psychotherapy, how did *this* behavior show that he was a *hopelessly* disturbed person? Obviously, it was undesirable for him to be still dependent and alcoholic after many years of suffering—but why was it *horrible* for him to have such symptoms? Why was he thoroughly worthless for still remaining sick? Would, moreover, severely castigating himself for his disturbance be likely to help him, in any way, *rid* himself of this disturbance? Or would it not be much more likely, this self-blaming, to help him re-

main disturbed indefinitely? Could he not manage first to accept and forgive himself for having serious behavioral symptoms—and then work concertedly at ridding himself of these symptoms by comprehending and reevaluating the philosophic assumptions that were causing them?

4. Assuming that other people, such as his dominating mother and first wife and his weak second and third wives, didn't really appreciate him and did want him to remain weak and unmanly, why was *that* terrible? Wasn't it only to be *expected* that these individuals would behave toward him in the way that they had behaved? And even if their behavior was unhelpful, why did *he* have to take it seriously and go along with it? Why, especially, did he have to *give in* to the domination of his first wife or to *father*, in his turn, his second and third wives? They had no real control over him; so why should he blame *them* for being the way they were?

During the original sessions of psychotherapy, he had mainly concentrated on learning how to live comfortably with his basic self-destroying philosophies, rather than to root them out and destroy them. He had consequently divorced his first wife—who really was *so* dominating and irritating that it was hardly worth staying with her, in spite of her taking over his decision making—and then managed to find other women who were even weaker emotionally than he and with whom he could *afford* to assume responsibilities and make mistakes, since they would hardly ever criticize him for doing so. Thus, he had never really questioned, challenged, and surrendered his fundamental view that "It is terrible for me to make mistakes, especially when some significant figure in my life is around to criticize me for making them." He had merely arranged to be intimately related to significant figures who did not berate him when he erred.

In his second major round of psychotherapy, this client was induced to admit that he *must* change this basic self-defeating philosophy if he was to get better, and he was pushed by me and his therapy group to work determinedly against this world view. Whenever he failed to speak up adequately and take the risk of being wrong in individual or group sessions, he was forced to keep doing so, and was continually asked what *was* so terrible about his failing, if he did fail to do remarkably well, in that respect. He was given specific homework assignments—which are usually an integral part of rational-emotive psychotherapy—to look for female companions who were neither overly dominating or terribly weak and to keep going with them even when they were critical of his behavior. He was shown, time and again, by the therapist and the group, that he still *did* have a notable fear of failing, even when he sometimes claimed that he had pretty well gotten over it; and that he simply *had* to keep working and practicing, and especially working at taking significant risks, before he could expect to minimize this fear.

An interesting aspect of this case is that whereas during the first round of therapy, the therapist emphasized the transference relationship between him and the client, made sure that a highly positive transference was obtained, and often showed the client that he was trying to use the therapist as a father-figure who would make his decisions for him, during the second round of therapy there was a minimal utilization or interpretation of the transference relationship. The therapist was much firmer than he had previously been; kept indicating that he would definitely *not* give him reassurance or love; and instead kept prodding and pushing him to stand on his *own* feet, and to examine his *own* internalized attitudes. And the therapy group was, if anything, even firmer and harsher with the client, and would not let him get away with almost anything, especially when he endeavored to give rationalizations for his lack of risk taking. On one occasion, when he complained to the group that he could not easily look for a new job, since he had such a bad employment record in the past and could hardly expect to get a decent position now, the group vigorously tore apart his rationalizations, and gave him the homework assignment of writing up a brand new resumé, made to order for the kind of job he said he wanted. As a result of their taking this no-nonsense attitude, he immediately wrote up the kind of resumé they insisted that he write, and within two weeks he had obtained a much better job than he had held in years.

In the second round of therapy, again, no attention whatever was given to the client's dreams (which had been intensively analyzed on several occasions during the first series of sessions). Only current rather than past material from his life was dealt with; and he was directly taught, on many occasions, many principles of rational living. The client was also induced to read books and other material on sane living and on several occasions reported that he had benefitted more from this kind of reading than he had from some of the therapy sessions.

As a result of this highly active-directive treatment, the client began to improve in a much more significant manner than he had previously done. For the first time in his life, he began going with the kind of females who were really on his educational and social level. He started to talk out at public meetings, such as at Alcoholics Anonymous, where he had previously kept quite silent; and with personal friends, he began to express feelings and attitudes he had been previously afraid to express, for fear of being criticized. After he had been in the second series of therapy sessions for two weeks, he stopped drinking entirely.

The client's exceptionally low estimation of himself notably began to improve as the weeks went by; and even when he tried to do something and clearly failed, he was able to accept his failure philosophically and refrain from excoriating himself. He still retained some underlying perfectionistic tendencies, but he was able to reduce them to a level far below that which he had previously demanded of himself and to live fairly successfully with those tendencies that remained. At times, he reverted to the negativistic kind of thinking about himself and others that is so characteristic of schizophrenics; but he did so far less frequently than before. Finally, it appeared that his hostility to others almost entirely disappeared, even though his self-denigrating tendencies were by no means as significantly reduced.

This, incidentally, is a common finding among schizophrenic clients treated with rational therapy. At first, they tend to like themselves better—but at the expense of becoming more hostile to others. Then, when the philosophic sources of this hostility are attacked, they often are able to accept others remarkably well, even when these others are behaving in a frustrating, unjust fashion. At the close of therapy, they may well be considerably less hostile than self-hating, although their self-depreciative propensities have also significantly decreased. The reason for this greater improvement in hostility than in self-criticism may stem from the human propensity—which many not too severely disturbed persons show as well—for an individual to find it easier to forgive others than himself, and to hold these others up to less rigid standards of behavior than he insists on holding himself up to.

In any event, this client ended the second round of therapy with a remarkable lack of hostility to others; and at the same time he also became much less self-deprecatory and more self-expressive and risk taking. He had not been completely cured, and one may wonder whether true schizophrenics are *ever* shriven of their basic tendency to think in an imprecise, out-of-focus manner. But he is now getting along unusually well in his vocational, amative, and social life, and it appears as if he will continue to do so indefinitely. For all practical purposes, he is behaving, at worst, in a moderately neurotic way, and is not acting psychotically.

The basic incurability of severe emotional disturbance is awesome to behold. Although I know many significantly improved and ostensibly cured schizophrenics walking the streets today (former and present clients of mine and other therapists), I have never seen a former schizophrenic who has been truly cured. Many of my own ex-clients, diagnosed as pyschotics and borderline psychotics, are getting along rather well in life, keep their heads above water, refrain from getting into any serious difficulties, and manage to make their way in the world without being dependent on others. But whether they are my own clients or those treated by others, one cannot conclude that they are mentally well, that they are in good mental-emotional health. Among other problems, they still have a significant degree of what Paul Meehl calls "cognitive slippage," and they never exactly think in the same well-focused, clear-headed way about themselves and others as do nonschizophrenics. They are doing wonderfully well, in many instances, with their underlying psychological deficits; but they are still basically psychotic, and can fairly easily be detected as such by an experienced clinician.

Nonetheless, rational-emotive psychotherapy with schizophrenics does not depend for its efficacy on the acceptance of the fact that psychosis is largely inborn and that it is by no means entirely the result of early upbringing. In fact, practitioners of this therapy would find it most convenient to hold that all emotional disturbance is the result of social conditioning, since it has a more precise explanation of just how negative conditioning comes about than do virtually all other therapeutic systems. The Freudians, for example, vaguely talk of the child's superego being constructed by his listening to the moralistic views of his parents; while the rational therapist talks in terms of the precise philosophies which the parents are teaching the child and the exact sentences into which the child translates these philosophies, and then uses to reindoctrinate himself continually in a neurotic or psychotic manner.

It would be very convenient to acknowledge the all-important influence of early childhood conditioning on the child—if it actually *were* that important. The hard facts seem to show, however, that the child becomes emotionally aberrated not *merely* because his parents blame him for his mistakes and shortcomings (which they all too often quite harmfully do), but because he *is born* the kind of individual who is *easily* harmed by such blaming.

To be more specific: parents or other early teachers usually help a child plummet down the toboggan slide toward disturbed feelings and behavior by doing two things when he does something that displeases them: (*a*) they tell him that he is wrong for acting in this displeasing manner, and (*b*) they strongly indicate to him that he is a worthless individual for being wrong, and that he therefore deserves to be severely punished for his wrongdoing. Now, the fact that parents in just about every part of the world tend to behave in this same manner, and at one and the same time to show the child that (*a*) he is wrong, and (*b*) he is a good-for-nothing when he is wrong, indicates that there is something essentially *biologically* based about their own slippery thinking and silly behavior in this connection. For if they were really sensible about bringing up their children, they would obviously show the child that: (*a*) he is wrong when he engages in activities that displease them and other members of their social group; and that (*b*) he is still a highly worthwhile individual who will merely, if he wants to get along well in his community, eventually have to discipline himself and learn to do less wrong in the future.

Perfectly sane and intelligent parents, in other words, would be much more concerned about the child's *future* rather than with his *present* behavior when he makes mistakes, and would calmly and persistently educate him so that he stopped focusing on his *past* mistakes, and concentrated instead on the possibility of his not making them again in the *future*. Consequently, they would practically never blame or vindictively punish the child for his misdeeds, and thereby induce him to devalue himself *as a person*; but instead they would objectively evaluate his wrongdoings, at times penalize him *without* blame (just as we objectively penalize rats in mazes when they go into the wrong passageways), and slowly teach him to be less error-prone while still letting him know that, just *because* he is human, he will always be distinctly fallible and imperfect. Stated once again, then: if parents were truly straight thinkers themselves, they would unperfectionistically correct but never moralistically castigate a child when he was patently wrong or annoying or antisocial. The fact that practically no group of parents in any part of the world has ever raised children in this manner is another bit of evidence that leads me to believe that man is born to be a blaming, emotionally disturbed, and hence self-defeating animal.

A human child is not easily able objectively to assess himself and his surroundings. Instead, he almost invariably accepts the castigating attitudes of his parents, internalizes them, and makes them his own for the rest of his life. Even, in fact, where his parents do not happen to be exceptionally critical individuals, he usually manages to pick up negative, perfectionistic attitudes toward himself from his teachers, peers, reading material, TV dramas, motion pictures, and other sources and media, and almost invariably begins to become guilty, or to hate himself, for his blunders, instead of thinking about them in a reasonable manner, calmly accepting the fact that he is and will always be fallible, and concentrating on how he is going to make fewer errors in the future instead of on how he should severely punish himself for his present mistakes. Once again, therefore, it would appear that the human child is programmed, at birth, so that he *easily* accepts a philosophy of perfectionism and self-blame, and so that it is quite difficult for him to live with a minimum of guilt, even though he is often able to rationalize away some of his conscious self-blaming. Underneath, he almost invariably still *feels* worthless, because he remains unable to distinguish clearly between wrongdoing and blaming—or between his doing a misdeed and his being a valueless *person* for committing this misdeed.

Once humans are born the way they are, and once they are raised in a society—such as our own—where they are encouraged to keep blaming themselves for their wrongs, they not only easily acquire negative philosophies early in their lives, but thereafter keep reindoctrinating themselves with these same self-sabotaging philosophies; and it is their continual reindoctrinations, rather than the early views themselves, that keep their disturbances going. More concretely, they take others' disapproval of their behavior, and instead of saying to themselves (*a*) "I don't like this disapproval," and (*b*) "Now, how do I get them to approve of me in the future, or else how do I get myself to live happily *in spite of* their disapproval," they say (*a*) "I don't like this disapproval," and (*b*) "Because others disapprove of me, I can't *stand* it. It is absolutely terrible that they disapprove of me; and this proves that I am worthless!"

Emotional illness is, at bottom, metaphysically founded: since the disturbed person unempirically and unvalidatably is convinced that because he *now* may be little valued by *others*, he is forever doomed to be worthless to himself *and* to all significant others. Or else, in the case of exceptionally hostile rather than self-hating sick people, the disturbed individual bigotedly and antiscientifically assumes that be-

241

cause *he* does not like others' behavior *they* must be absolutely valueless to themselves and everyone else and that they deserve to be everlastingly punished or killed. This is particularly true of the schizophrenic individual, who more than most other disturbed persons rigidly and ruthlessly believes in his own utter worthlessness and/or that of other significant people in his life.

By the same token, emotional disturbance is *definitional* in nature. The seriously disturbed person takes an annoyance, an irritant, or a frustration and he *defines* it as a horror or a terror. Or he takes a mistake, or an inefficiency, or a human handicap and he *defines* it as an unforgivable atrocity or sin. He mightily *exaggerates the significance* of his own fallible behavior and that of others; he perfectionistically *demands* instead of sanely *preferring* minimal errors from himself and others. He unrealistically translates his *wants* into *dire needs*, thereby expects the impractical or impossible, and concretely *creates* his own continual misery and hostility.

More specifically, disturbed humans, and schizophrenics in particular, invariably dogmatically believe in several highly irrational philosophic assumptions, which they never or rarely question or challenge, and which they keep insisting, unconsciously or consciously, are absolutely true. These irrational ideas are briefly mentioned below:

Irrational Idea No. 1: The idea that it is a dire necessity for an adult human being to be loved or approved by virtually every significant other person in his community.

Irrational Idea No. 2: The idea that one should be thoroughly competent, adequate, and achieving in all possible respects if one is to consider oneself worthwhile.

Irrational Idea No. 3: The idea that certain people are bad, wicked, or villainous and that they should be severely blamed and punished for their villainy.

Irrational Idea No. 4: The idea that it is awful and catastrophic when things are not the way one would very much like them to be.

Irrational Idea No. 5: The idea that human unhappiness is externally caused and that people have little or no ability to control their sorrows and disturbances.

Irrational Idea No. 6: The idea that if something is or may be dangerous or fearsome one should be terribly concerned about it and should keep dwelling on the possibility of its occurring.

Irrational Idea No. 7: The idea that it is easier to avoid than to face certain life difficulties and self-responsibilities.

Irrational Idea No. 8: The idea that one should be dependent on others and need someone stronger than oneself on whom to rely.

Irrational Idea No. 9: The idea that one's past history is an all-important determiner of one's present behavior and that because something once strongly affected one's life, it should indefinitely have a similar effect.

Irrational Idea No. 10: The idea that there is invariably a right, precise, and perfect solution to human problems and that it is catastrophic if this perfect solution is not found.

These basic unreasonable premises, and innumerable variations on them, underlie, I contend, just about all so-called emotional disturbance. Moreover, these ideas are not subscribed to in mystical, symbolic, or pictorial form by the vast majority of human beings; but are thought of in simple declarative or exclamatory sentences for the most part. Thus, when a disturbed person believes Irrational Idea No. 2, that he should be thoroughly competent, adequate, and achieving in all possible respects if he is to consider himself worthwhile, he tells himself, when he is not or may not be competent in some area that he defines as being important (*a*) "I am not very good at this job (or sport, or game, or artistic field)" and (*b*) "Therefore, I am a thoroughly inadequate person, who cannot possibly live a happy existence, and who might just as well kill myself unless I somehow manage to be much better at this performance."

The disturbed individual, of course, may not *consciously* realize that he devalues himself as a person because he demands that he be thoroughly competent in some area or areas; but, at the very least, he *un*consciously believes this nonsense in innumerable instances when he feels worthless. Moreover, his unconscious, irrational beliefs and value systems are *not,* as the Freudians erroneously contend, so deeply buried in the individual's unconscious mind that it necessarily takes years of psychoanalysis to dig them up and make them conscious. On the contrary, almost all of them are just below the top level of consciousness, and can quite easily and quickly be revealed by an active rational therapist (and often by the individual himself).

The schizophrenic or other emotionally disturbed person is sick not only because something happened to traumatize him and help him think distortedly about himself and others in the past, but also because—*being* human—he is still, in the present, reindoctrinating himself with all kinds of false beliefs about himself and the world; and that therefore his present-day value system, or set of philosophic assumptions, not only is to be shown to him very clearly, but is to be systematically and vigorously attacked, by the therapist and then by the client himself, before he can be expected to change his world view and to make himself better. This is exactly what is done in rational-emotive psychotherapy.

In rational psychotherapy the schizophrenic, as well as the nonschizophrenic, client is consistently shown that it is practically never the stimulus that upsets him and makes him respond in an abnormal manner; rather, it is what he tells himself or interpretatively and evaluatively signals to himself about the stimulus. This exceptionally important aspect of human behavior was first clearly and fully expounded by the Roman Stoic philosopher, Epictetus, some two thousand years ago, and was later reformulated by his disciple Marcus Aurelius. It has been repeated over the centuries by a great many other philosophers and psychologists, notably by Robert S. Woodworth, who insisted that the stimulus-response, or S-R, formula did not sufficiently explain human behavior, but that it had to be replaced by a stimulus-organism-response (S-O-R) formula, which was truer to the facts of human existence.

It is the Epictetus-Woodworth explanation of behavior that I teach my schizophrenic clients. That is to say, I show them precisely how, in every instance that they become anxious, guilty, depressed, angry, or otherwise self-defeatingly overemotional, they have consciously or unconsciously, immediately preceding their negative emotion, told themselves a declarative or exclamatory sentence (or signaled themselves in some other communicative manner in a few instances), and how this sentence *caused* their dysfunctional emoting. Then I show them how to parse their own disturbance-creating phrases and sentences, logically rather than grammatically, to see exactly why they *are* irrational or illogical. Finally, I teach them to contradict and challenge their own irrationalities, until they replace them with sane, nondisturbing philosophies of life.

Stated a little differently: schizophrenic individuals usually have absolute needs for certainty and order (as well as perfection); and a good many of their paranoid and other delusions represent a desperate attempt to create certainty where none, in fact, exists. If I can rationally get them to admit that there isn't, as far as we know, any absolute order in the universe, and that they can live happily in this world of probability and chance, they frequently surrender their delusionary symptoms, conquer their overweening anxiety, and live much more fulfillingly.

BIBLIOGRAPHY

Adler, Alfred. *Understanding human nature*. New York: Garden City Publishing Co., 1927.
————. *The science of living*. New York: Greenberg, 1929.
————. *What life should mean to you*. New York: Basic Books, 1932; New York: Capricorn, 1958.
————. *Social interest: a challenge to mankind*. New York: Capricorn, 1964*a*.
————. *Superiority and social interest*. Evanston, Ill.: Northwestern University Press, 1964*b*.
Andrews, J. D. W. Psychotherapy of phobias. *Psychological Bulletin*, 1966, 66: 455-480.
Angyal, A. *Foundations for a science of personality*. New York: Commonwealth Fund, 1941.
Ansbacher, H. L., and Ansbacher, Rowena R. (Eds.). *The individual psychology of Alfred Adler*. New York: Basic Books, 1956.
Ard, B. Bruising the libido. *Rational Living*, 1966, 1 (No. 2): 19-25.

————. The A-B-C of marriage counseling. *Rational Living*, 1967, 2 (No. 2): 10-12.

————. Rational therapy in rehabilitation counseling. *Rehabilitation Counseling Bulletin*, 1968, 12: 84-88.

————. A rational approach to marriage counseling. In Ben N. Ard, Jr., and Constance C. Ard (Eds.). *Handbook of marriage counseling*. Palo Alto: Science and Behavior Books, 1969.

Argabite, A. H., and Nidorf, L. J. Fifteen questions for rating reason. *Rational Living*, 1968, 3 (No. 1): 9-11.

Arnheim, Rudolf. *Visual thinking*. London: Faber and Faber, 1969.

Arnold, Magda. *Emotion and personality*. New York: Columbia University Press, 1960.

Bach, G. R., and Wyden, P. *The intimate enemy*. New York: Morrow, 1969.

Baker, Juanita N. Reason versus reinforcement in behavior modification. Ph.D. Thesis, University of Illinois, 1966.

Bandura, A. Psychotherapy as a learning process. *Psychological Bulletin*, 1961, 58: 143-159.

Barber, T. X. *Hypnosis: a scientific approach*. Cincinnati: Van Nostrand Reinhold, 1969.

Beck, Aaron T. *Depression: clinical, experimental and theoretical aspects*. New York: Hoeber-Harper, 1967.

————. Cognitive therapy: nature and relation to behavior therapy. *Behavior Therapy*, 1970, 1: 184-200.

Beck, Aaron T., and Hurvich, M. S. Psychological correlates of depression. *Psychosomatic Medicine*, 1959, 21: 50-55.

Beck, Aaron T., and Stein, D. The self-concept in depression. Unpublished study, summarized in Aaron T. Beck: *Depression: clinical, experimental and theoretical aspects*, *q.v.*

Becker, J. Achievement-related characteristics of manic-depressives. *Journal of Abnormal and Social Psychology*, 1960, 60: 334-339.

Becker, J.; Spielberger, C. D.; and Parker, J. B. Value achievement and authoritarian attitudes in psychiatric patients. *Journal of Clinical Psychology*, 1963, 19: 57-61.

Berkowitz, L., Lepinsky, J. P., and Angulo, E. J. Awareness of own anger level and subsequent aggression. *Journal of Personality and Social Psychology*, 1969, 11: 293-300.

Berne, E. Ego states in psychotherapy. *American Journal of Psychotherapy*, 1957, 11: 293-309.

———. *Games people play*. New York: Grove Press, 1964.

Bleuler, E. *Dementia praecox or the group of schizophrenias*. New York: International Universities Press, 1950.

Bourland, D. D. The un-isness of is. *Time*, May 23, 1969, 69.

Braaten, L. J. The main theories of existentialism from the viewpoint of a psychotherapist. *Mental Hygiene*, 1961, 45: 10-17.

Branden, N. *The psychology of self-esteem*. Los Angeles: Nash, 1970.

Breger, L., and McGaugh, J. L. Critique and reformulation of learning theory approaches to psychotherapy and neurosis. *Psychological Bulletin*, 1965, 63. 338-358.

Breznitz, S. Incubation of threat: duration of anticipation and false alarm as determinants of the fear reaction to an unavoidable frightening event. *Journal of Experimental Research in Personality*, 1967, 2: 173-179.

Brown, B. M. Cognitive aspects of Wolpe's behavior therapy. *American Journal of Psychiatry*, 1967, 124: 854-859.

Buhler, Charlotte. *Values in psychotherapy*. New York: Free Press of Glencoe, 1962.

———. Basic theoretical concepts of humanistic psychology. *American Psychologist*, 1971, 26: 378-386.

Buhler, Charlotte, Allen, and Melanie. *Introduction to humanistic psychology*. Monterey, Calif.: Brooks/Cole.

Burkhead, D. E. The reduction of negative affect in human subjects: a laboratory test of rational-emotive psychotherapy. Ph.D. Thesis, Western Michigan University, 1970.

Burton, A. (Ed.). *Encounter*. San Francisco: Jossey-Bass, 1969.

Callahan, R. Overcoming religious faith. *Rational Living*, 1967, 2 (No. 1): 16, 21.

Carlson, W. A., Travers, R. M. W., and Schwab, E. A. A laboratory approach to the cognitive control of anxiety. Paper presented at the American Personnel and Guidance Association meeting, Las Vegas, March 31, 1969.

Cautela, J. Treatment of compulsive behavior by covert sensitization. *Psychological Record*, 1966, 16: 33-41.

Conklin, R. C. A psychometric instrument for the early identification of the underachievers. Master's Thesis, University of Alberta, 1965.

Cook, S. W., and Harris, R. E. The verbal conditioning of the galvanic skin reflex. *Journal of Experimental Psychology*, 1937, 21: 201-210.

Coons, W. H., and McEachern, D. L. Verbal conditioning acceptance of self and acceptance of others. *Psychological Reports*, 1967, 20: 715-722.

Corsini, R. J., with Cardono, S. *Role playing in psychotherapy: a manual*. Chicago: Aldine, 1966.

Coué, E. *My method*. New York: Doubleday, 1923.

Cowles, E. S. *Conquest of fatigue and fear*. New York: Holt, Rinehart and Winston, 1954.

Davies, R. L. Relationship of irrational ideas to emotional disturbance. M. Ed. Thesis, University of Alberta, 1970.

Davison, G. C. Anxiety under total curarization: implications for the role of muscular relaxation in the desensitization of neurotic fears. *Journal of Nervous and Mental Disease*, 1967, 143: 443-448.

————. Systematic desensitization as a counterconditioning process. *Journal of Abnormal Psychology*, 1968, 73: 91-99.

Deane, G. E. Human heart rate responses during experimentally induced anxiety: effects of instruction on acquisition. *Journal of Experimental Psychology*, 1966, 67: 193-195.

Diamond, L. Destroying self-defeat: two case histories. *Rational Living*, 1967a, 2 (No. 1): 13-14.

————. Restoring amputated ego. *Rational Living*, 1967b, 2 (No. 2): 15.

Diaz-Guerrera, R. Socratic therapy. In S. W. Standal and R. J. Corsini (Eds.). *Critical incidents in psychotherapy*. Englewood Cliffs, N.J.: Prentice-Hall, 1959.

Di Loreto, A. A comparison of the relative effectiveness of systematic desensitization, rational-emotive and client-centered group psychotherapy in the reduction of interpersonal anxiety in introverts and extroverts. Ph.D. Dissertation, Michigan State University, 1969.

―――. *Comparative psychotherapy*. Chicago: Aldine, 1971.

Dilthey, Wilhelm. *Pattern and meaning in history*. New York: Harper, 1961.

Dollard, J., and Miller, N. W. *Personality and psychotherapy*. New York: McGraw-Hill, 1950.

Dollard, J., *et al. Frustration and aggression*. New Haven: Yale University Press, 1965.

Dorsey, J. M. *Illness or allness*. Detroit: Wayne State University, 1965.

Dreikurs, R., and Grey, L. *Logical consequences: a handbook of discipline*. New York: Meredith, 1968.

Dubin, R., *et al. Leadership and productivity*. St. Louis: Concordia Publishing, 1965.

Dubois, P. *The psychic treatment of nervous disorders*. New York: Funk and Wagnalls, 1907.

Dunlap, K. *Personal adjustment*. New York: McGraw-Hill, 1946.

Ellis, A. See pages 265-268.

Epictetus. *The works of Epictetus*. Boston: Little Brown, 1899.

Eriksen, C. W. (Ed.). *Behavior and awareness*. Durham, N. C.: Duke University Press, 1962.

Erikson, Erik H. *Identity and the life cycle*. New York: International Universities Press, 1959.

―――. *Identity: youth and crisis*. New York: Norton, 1968.

Eysenck, H. J. *Experiments in behavior therapy*. Elmsford, N. Y.: Pergamon Press, 1964.

Fenichel, O. *Psychoanalytic theory of neurosis*. New York: Norton, 1945.

Ford, Donald, and Urban, Hugh. *Systems of psychotherapy*. New York: Wiley, 1964.

Frankl, V. E. *The doctor of the soul: an introduction to logotherapy*. New York: Knopf, 1955.

Freud, A. *The ego and the mechanisms of defense*. London: Hogarth Publishing, 1937.

Freud, A. *Collected papers*. New York: Collier, 1962.

Freud, S. *Basic writings*. New York: Modern Library, 1938.

———. *Collected papers*. London: Imago Publishers, 1924-1950.

Fritz, C. E., and Marks, E. S. The NORC studies of human behavior in disaster. *Journal of Social Issues,* 1954, 10: 26-41.

Garfield, S. L., *et al*. Chemically induced anxiety. *International Journal of Neuropsychiatry*, 1967a, 3: 426-433.

———. Effect of "in vivo" training on experimental desensitization of phobia. *Psychological Reports,* 1967a, 20: 215-219.

Geer, J. H., *et al*. Reduction of stress in humans through nonveridical perceived control of aversion stimulation. *Journal of Personality and Social Psychology*, 1971.

Geis, H. J. Toward a comprehensive framework of unifying all systems of counseling. *Educational Technology*, 1969, 9 (No. 3): 19-28.

Gellerman, S. W. *The management of human relations*. New York: Holt, Rinehart and Winston, 1965.

Gendlin, E. *Experiencing the creation of meaning*. New York: Free Press of Glencoe, 1962.

———. A theory of personality change. In P. Worchel and D. Byrne (Eds.). *Personality change*. New York: Wiley, 1964.

Gewirtz, J. L., and Baer, D. M. Deprivation and situation of social reinforcers as drive conditions. *Journal of Abnormal and Social Psychology*, 1958, 57: 165-172.

Ginott, H. G. *Between parent and child*. New York: Macmillan, 1965.

———. *Between parent and teenager*. New York: Macmillan, 1969.

Glass, D. D., *et al*. Psychic cost of adaptation to an environment stressor. *Journal of Personality and Social Psychology*, 1969, 12: 200-210.

Glasser, W. *Reality therapy*. New York: Harper and Row, 1965.

Glicken, M. D. Counseling children. *Rational Living*, 1966, 1 (No. 2): 27, 30.

————. Rational counseling: a new approach to children. *Journal of Elementary Guidance and Counseling*, 1968, 2 (No. 4): 261-267.

Gliedman, L. H., *et al*. Reduction of symptoms by pharmacologically inert substances and by short-term psychotherapy. *Archives of Neurology and Psychiatry*, 1958, 79: 345-351.

Goldstein, Kurt. The concept of health, disease, and therapy. *American Journal of Psychotherapy*, 1954, 8: 745-764.

Greenberg, I. Psychotherapy: learning and relearning. *Canada's Mental Health*, Supplement No. 53, 1966.

Grossack, M. Why rational-emotive therapy works. *Psychological Reports*, 1965a, 16: 464.

————. *You are not alone*. Boston: Christopher Publishing, 1965b.

Grossack, M; Armstrong, T.; and Lussiev, G. Correlates of self-actualization. *Journal of Humanistic Psychology*, 1966, 6: 87.

Gullo, J. M. Useful variations on rational-emotive therapy. *Rational Living*, 1966a, 1 (No. 1): 44-45.

————. Counseling hospital patients. *Rational Living*, 1966b, 1 (No. 2): 11-15.

Gustav, Alice. "Success is—" Locating composite sanity. *Rational Living*, 1968, 3 (No. 1): 1-6.

Hadas, Moses (Ed.). *The stoic philosophers*. New York: Bantam Books, 1961.

Haley, J. *Strategies of psychotherapy*. New York: Grune & Stratton, 1963.

Harper, Robert A. *Psychoanalysis and psychotherapy: 36 systems*. Englewood Cliffs, N.J.: Prentice-Hall, 1959.

————. Marriage counseling as rational process-oriented psychotherapy. *Journal of Individual Psychology*, 1960, 16: 192-207.

Hart, H. *Autoconditioning*. Englewood Cliffs, N.J.: Prentice-Hall, 1956.

Hartman, B. J. Sixty revealing questions for 20 minutes. *Rational Living*, 1968, 3 (No. 1): 7-8.

Hartman, R. S. *The measurement of value*. Crotonville, N.Y.: General Electric Co., 1959; Carbondale: Southern Illinois Press, 1967.

————. *The individual in management*. Chicago: Nationwide Insurance Co., 1962.

Hauck, P. The neurotic agreement in psychotherapy. *Rational Living*, 1966, 1 (No. 1): 31-34.

————. Challenge authority—for thy health's sake. *Rational Living*, 1967a, 2 (No. 1): 1-4.

————. *The rational management of children*. New York: Libra Publishers, 1967b.

————. An open letter to us. *Rational Living*, 1968, 3 (No. 1): 29-30.

Herzberg, A. *Active psychotherapy*. New York: Grune & Stratton, 1945.

Holland, Glenn A. *Fundamentals of psychotherapy*. New York: Holt, Rinehart and Winston, 1965.

Homme, L. E. Control of coverants: the operants of the mind. *Psychological Record*, 1965, 18: 501-511.

————. Contingency management. *Newsletter*, Section on Clinical Child Psychology, Division of Clinical Psychology, American Psychological Association, 1966, 5 (No. 4).

Horney, Karen. *Neurosis and human growth*. New York: Norton, 1950.

Howard, J. *Please touch*. New York: Dell, 1971.

Jones, Mary Cover. The elimination of children's fears. *Pedagogical Seminar*, 1924, 31: 308-315.

Jones, R. G. A factored measure of Ellis' irrational belief system, with personality and maladjustment correlates. Ph.D. Thesis, Texas Technological College, 1968.

Jordan, B. T., and Kempler, B. Hysterical personality: an experimental investigation of sex-role conflict. *Journal of Abnormal Psychology*, 1970, 75: 172-176.

Jung, Carl G. *The practice of psychotherapy*. New York: Pantheon, 1954.

Kamiya, J. Conscious control of brain waves. *Psychology Today*, 1968, 1 (No. 11): 57-61.

Kanfer, F. H., and Philips, J. S. Behavior therapy, panacea or passing fancy. *Archives of General Psychiatry*, 1966, 15: 114-128.

Karon, B. P. The resolution of acute schizophrenic reactions: a contribution to the development of nonclassical psychotherapeutic techniques. *Psychotherapy*, 1963, 1: 27-43.

Karst, T. O., and Trexler, L. D. Initial study using fixed-role and rational-emotive therapy in treating public-speaking anxiety. *Journal of Consulting and Clinical Psychology*, 1970, 34: 360-366.

Kelly, G. *The psychology of personal constructs*. New York: Norton, 1955.

Klein, M. H., *et al.* Behavior therapy: observations and reflections. *Journal of Consulting and Clinical Psychology*, 1969, 33: 259-266.

Korzybski, A. *Science and sanity*. Lancaster, Pa.: Lancaster Press, 1933.

Krippner, S. Relationship between reading improvement and ten selected variables. *Perceptual and Motor Skills*, 1964, 19: 15-20.

Lafferty, J. C. Values that defeat learning. *Proceedings of the Eighth Inter-Institutional Seminar in Child Development*. Dearborn, Mich.: Edison Institute, 1962.

————. *Proceedings of the Blue Cross Association Seminars in Leadership and Management*. Detroit: Adams, Lafferty, Madden and Moody, 1965.

Lafferty, J. C., *et al.* A creative school mental health program. *National Elementary Principal*, 1964, 43 (No. 5): 28-35.

Lang, P. J., *et al.* Effects of feedback and instructional set on the control of cardiac variability. *Journal of Experimental Psychology*, 1967, 75: 425-431.

Lazarus, A. A. *Behavior therapy and beyond*. New York: McGraw-Hill, 1971.

Lazarus, R. S. *Psychological stress and the coping process*. New York: McGraw-Hill, 1966.

Lecky, P. *Self-consistency*. New York: Island Press, 1943.

Lewis, B. T., and Pearson, W. W. *Management guide to human relations in industry*. New York: John F. Rider Publishing Co., 1966.

Litvak, S. B. Attitude change by stimulus exposure. *Psychological Reports*, 1969*a*, 25: 391-396.

————. A comparison of two brief group behavior therapy techniques on the reduction of avoidance behavior. *Psychological Record*, 1969*b*, 19: 329-334.

London, P. *The modes and morals of psychotherapy*. New York: Holt, Rinehart and Winston, 1964.

Lorenz, K. *On aggression*. New York: Harcourt, Brace and World, 1968.

Low, Abraham A. *Mental health through will-training*. Boston: Christopher Publishing Co., 1952.

Lynn, David B. The organism as a manufacturer of theories. *Psychological Reports*, 1957, 3: 353-359.

————. Personal philosophies in psychotherapy. *Journal of Individual Psychology*, 1961, 17: 49-55.

Maes, Wayne R., and Heimann, Robert A. *The comparison of three approaches to the reduction of test anxiety in high school students*. Washington: U. S. Dept. of Health, Education, and Welfare, 1970.

Maltz, M. *Psychocybernetics*. Englewood Cliffs, N.J.: Prentice-Hall, 1960.

Maslow, Abraham. *Motivation and personality*. New York: Harper, 1954.

————. *Toward a psychology of being*. Princeton: Van Nostrand, 1962.

————. Further notes on the psychology of being. *Journal of Humanistic Psychology*, 1964, 4: 45-58.

————. *The psychology of science*. New York: Harper and Row, 1966.

————. A conversation with Mary Harrington Hall. *Psychology Today*, 1968, 2 (No. 2): 34-37, 54-57.

Maultsby, Maxic C., Jr. The pamphlet as a therapeutic aid. *Rational Living*, 1968, 3 (No. 2): 31-35.

————. Psychological and biochemical test change in patients who were paid to engage in psychotherapy. Mimeographed. Department of Medicine, University of Wisconsin, 1970*a*.

————. Systematic, written homework in psychotherapy: a clinical study of 87 unselected OPD patients. *Rational Living*, 1970*b*, 5 (No. 1); 8-23.

May, Rollo. *Psychology and the human dilemmu*. Princeton: Van Nostrand, 1967.

————. *Love and will*. New York: Norton, 1969.

McGill, V. J. *Emotions and reason*. Springfield, Ill.: Charles C Thomas, 1954.

McGrory, J. E. Teaching introspection in the classroom. *Rational Living*, 1967, 2 (No. 2): 25.

Meehl, Paul E. Schizotaxia, schizotype, schizophrenia. *American Psychologist*, 1962, 17: 27-37.

Meyer, Adolph. *The commonsense psychiatry of Dr. Adolph Meyer*. New York: McGraw-Hill, 1948.

Miller, N. E. Learning of visceral and glandular responses. *Science*, 1969, 163: 434-445.

Morris, Desmond. *The naked ape*. New York: McGraw-Hill, 1967.

Mowrer, O. H. "Sin," the lesser of two evils. *American Psychologist*, 1960, 15: 301-304.

————. *The new group therapy*. Princeton: Van Nostrand, 1964.

Nisbett, R. E., and Schacter, S. Cognitive manipulation of pain. *Journal of Experimental Social Psychology*, 1966, 2: 227-236.

Nuthmann, Anne M. Conditioning of a response class on a personality test. *Journal of Abnormal and Social Psychology*, 1957, 54: 19-23.

O'Connell, W. E., and Hanson, P. G. Patients' cognitive changes in human relations training. *Journal of Individual Psychology*, 1970, 26: 57-63.

Otto, H. *Group methods designed to actualize human potential: a handbook*. Chicago: Achievement Motivation Systems, 1968.

Overall, J. E., and Gorham, D. Basic dimensions of change in the symptomatology of chronic schizophrenics. *Journal of Abnormal and Social Psychology*, 1961, 63: 597-602.

Patterson, C. H. *Theories of counseling and psychotherapy*. New York: Harper and Row, 1966.

Pavlov, Ivan P. *Conditioned reflexes*. London: Oxford University Press, 1927.

Peale, Norman Vincent. *The power of positive thinking*. Englewood Cliffs, N.J.: Prentice-Hall, 1952.

Perls, Frederick S. *Gestalt therapy verbatim*. Lafayette, Calif.: Real People Press, 1969.

Perls, F.; Hefferline, R.; and Goodman, P. *Gestalt therapy*. New York: Julian Press, 1951.

Phillips, E. Lakin. *Psychotherapy*. Englewood Cliffs, N.J.: Prentice-Hall, 1956.

Phillips, E. Lakin, and Wiener, D. R. *Short-term psychotherapy and structured behavior change*. New York: McGraw-Hill, 1966.

Pottash, R. R., and Taylor, J. E. Discussion of "Phobia treated with rational-emotive psychotherapy" by Albert Ellis. *Voices*, 1967, 3 (3): 39-40.

Premack, David. Reinforcement theory. In D. Levine, (Ed.). *Nebraska symposium on motivation*. Lincoln, Neb.: University of Nebraska Press, 1965.

Rand, Ayn. *For the new intellectual*. New York: Random House, 1961.

————. *The virtue of selfishness*. New York: New American Library, 1964.

Rimm, D. C., and Litvak, S. B. Self-verbalization and emotional arousal. *Journal of Abnormal Psychology*, 1969, 74: 181-187.

Ritter, Brunhilde. The group desensitization of children's snake phobias using vicarious and contact desensitization procedures. *Behavior Research and Therapy*, 1968, 6: 1-6.

Roe, Anne. A psychological study of eminent psychologists and anthropologists and a comparison with biological and physical scientists. *Psychological Monographs*, 1953, 67 (No. 352): 1-55.

Rogers, Carl R. *Client-centered therapy*. Boston: Houghton-Mifflin, 1951.

————. *On becoming a person*. Boston: Houghton-Mifflin, 1961.

————. The concept of the fully functioning person. *Psychotherapy*, 1963a, 1: 17-26.

————. The interpersonal relationship: the core of guidance. *Journal of Client-Centered Counseling*, 1963b, 1: 2-5.

————. A conversation with Mary Harrington Hall. *Psychology Today*, 1967, 1 (No. 7): 19-21, 62-66.

Rokeach, Milton. *Beliefs, attitudes and values: a theory of organization change*. San Francisco: Jossey-Bass, 1968.

Rosen, Joseph N. *Direct analysis*. New York: Grune & Stratton, 1953.

Rosenthal, R. Changes in some moral values following psychotherapy. *Journal of Consulting Psychology*, 1955, 19: 431-436.

Rotter, Julian B. *Social learning and clinical psychology*. New York: McGraw-Hill, 1954.

————. *Clinical psychology*. Englewood Cliffs, N.J.: Prentice-Hall, 1964.

Russell, Bertrand. *The conquest of happiness*. New York: Pocket Books, 1950.

Sahakian, W. S. Stoic philosophical psychotherapy. *Journal of Individual Psychology*, 1969, 25: 32-35.

Salter, Andrew. *Conditioned reflex therapy*. New York: Creative Age, 1949.

Satir, Virginia. *Conjoint family therapy*. Palo Alto, Calif.: Science and Behavior Books, 1967.

Schacter, S. The interaction of cognitive and physiological determinants of emotional states. In L. Berkowitz (Ed.). *Advances in experimental social psychology*. Volume I. New York: Academic Press, 1964.

Schacter, S., and Singer, J. E. Cognitive, social and physiological determinants of emotional state. *Psychological Review*, 1962, 69: 379-399.

Schell, I. H. *Technique of executive control*. New York: McGraw-Hill, 1965.

Schutz, W. *Joy*. New York: Grove Press, 1967.

Shakow, David. Psychological deficit in schizophrenia. *Behavioral Scientist*, 1963, 8: 275-305.

Shapiro, M. B.; Neufield, I.; and Post, T. Experimental study of depressive illness. *Psychological Reports*, 1962, 10: 590.

Shapiro, M. B., and Ravenette, E. T. A. A preliminary experiment on paranoid delusions. *Journal of Mental Science*, 1959, 103: 295-312.

Sharma, K. L. A rational group therapy approach to counseling anxious underachievers. Thesis, University of Alberta, 1970.

Sherman, S. Alcoholism and group therapy. *Rational Living*, 1967, 2 (No. 2): 20-22.

Skinner, B. F. *Science and human behavior*. New York: Macmillan, 1953.

———. *Walden two*. New York: Macmillan, 1962.

Sloane, R. B. The converging paths of behavior therapy and psychotherapy. *American Journal of Psychiatry*, 1969, 125: 7-17.

Spinoza, B. *Improvement of the understanding, ethics, and correspondence*. New York: Dunne, 1901.

Stark, Paul. Success in psychotherapy—a common factor. *American Journal of Psychotherapy*, 1961, 15: 431-434.

Steffy, Richard A.; Meichenbaum, Donald; and Best, J. Allan. Aversive and cognitive factors in the modification of smoking behavior. *Behavior Research and Therapy*, 1970, 8: 115-125.

Stekel, W. *Technique of analytical psychotherapy.* New York: Liveright, 1950.

Stieper, D. R., and Wiener, D. N. *Dimensions of psychotherapy.* Chicago: Aldine, 1965.

Stoller, F. The long weekend. *Psychology Today*, 1967, 1 (No. 7): 28-33.

Storr, Anthony. *Human aggression.* New York: Atheneum, 1968.

Strupp, H. H. The outcome problem in psychotherapy revisited. *Psychotherapy*, 1963, 1: 1-13.

Sullivan, H. S. *The interpersonal theory of psychiatry.* New York: Norton, 1953.

Szasz, Thomas. *The myth of mental illness.* New York: Hoeber, 1961.

————. Mental illness is a myth. *New York Times Magazine,* June 12, 1966, 7-13.

Taft, G. L. A study of the relationship of anxiety and irrational beliefs. Doctoral Dissertation, University of Alberta, 1965.

Tead, Ordway. *Human nature and management.* New York: McGraw-Hill, 1929.

————. *The art of administration.* New York: McGraw-Hill, 1964.

Thorne, Frederick C. *Principles of personality counseling.* Brandon, Vt.: Journal of Clinical Psychology, 1950.

————. An evaluation of eclectically-oriented psychotherapy. *Journal of Consulting Psychology*, 1957, 21: 459-464.

Tillich, Paul. *The courage to be.* New York: Oxford University Press, 1953.

Tinbergen, N. On war and peace in animals and man. *Science*, 1968, 160: 1411-1418.

Valins, S. Cognitive effects of false heart-rate feedback. *Journal of Personality and Social Psychology*, 1966, 4: 400-408.

Valins, S., and Ray, Alice A. Effects of cognitive desensitization on avoidance behavior. *Journal of Personality and Social Psychology*, 1967, 7: 345-350.

Velten, Emmett C., Jr. A laboratory task for the induction of mood states, *Behavior Research and Therapy*, 1968, 6: 473-482.

Von Bertalanffy, Ludwig. *Organismic psychology and the systems theory*. Worcester, Mass.: Clark University and Barre Publications, 1968.

Wagner, E. E. Techniques of rational counseling. *High Spots*, 1963, 3 (No. 6): 2.

————. Counseling children. *Rational Living*, 1966, 1 (No. 2): 26, 28-30.

Watson, J. B. *Behaviorism*. New York: Norton, 1924.

Weston, D. *Guidebook for alcoholics*. New York: Exposition Press, 1964.

————. *Different approaches to alcoholism*. Cleveland: Better Health Center, 1970.

Whitaker, C., and Malone, T. A. *Roots of psychotherapy*. New York: McGraw-Hill, 1953.

White, Alice M.; Fichtenbaum, Leonard; and Dollard, John. Measurement of what the patient learns from psychotherapy. *Journal of Nervous and Mental Disease*, 1969, 149: 281-293.

Wiener, D. N., and Stieper, D. R. *Dimensions of psychotherapy*. Chicago: Aldine, 1965.

Wolberg, Lewis R. The technique of psychotherapy. New York: Grune & Stratton, 1954.

Wolfe, Janet L., *et al*. Emotional education in the classroom: The Living School. *Rational Living*, 1970, 4 (No. 2): 22-25.

Wolpe, Joseph. *Psychotherapy of reciprocal inhibition*. Stanford: Stanford University Press, 1958.

————. The systematic desensitization of neuroses. *Journal of Nervous and Mental Disease*, 1961, 132: 189-203.

Wolpe, Joseph, and Lazarus, A. A. *Behavior therapy techniques: a guide to the treatment of neuroses*. Oxford: Pergamon Press, 1966.

Woodworth, Robert S. *Dynamics of behavior*. New York: Holt, 1958.

Young, Maxim F. Talk on the treatment of schizophrenics with rational-emotive psychotherapy. Workshop of the Institute for Rational Living, Inc., Philadelphia, Sept. 1, 1963.

Zajonc, R. B. Attitudinal effects of mere exposure. *Journal of Personality and Social Psychology*, 1968, 9 (Part 2), Monograph Supplement.
Zingle, H. W. A rational therapy approach to counseling underachievers. Doctoral Dissertation, University of Alberta, 1965.

SELECTED WRITINGS OF
ALBERT ELLIS

1950. *An introduction to the scientific principles of psychoanalysis.* Provincetown, Mass.: Journal Press.

1951. *The folklore of sex.* New York: Albert & Charles Boni. 2nd ed., New York: Grove Press, 1961.

1957a. The effectiveness of psychotherapy with individuals who have severe homosexual problems. *Journal of Consulting Psychology,* 20: 191-195.

1957b. Outcome of employing three techniques of psychotherapy. *Journal of Clinical Psychology.* 13: 344-350.

1957c. Rational psychotherapy and individual psychology. *Journal of Individual Psychology,* 13: 38-44.

1957d. *How to live with a neurotic.* New York: Crown; reprinted, New York: Award Books, 1969.

1958a. Case histories: fact and fiction. *Contemporary Psychology,* 3: 318-319.

1958*b*. Rational psychotherapy. *Journal of General Psychology*, 59: 35-49.

1960. *The art and science of love*. New York: Lyle Stuart; reprinted, New York: Bantam Books, 1969.

1961*a*. With Robert A. Harper. *Creative marriage*. New York: Lyle Stuart; reprinted as *A guide to successful marriage*. Hollywood, Calif.: Wilshire, 1972.

1961*b*. With Robert A. Harper. *A guide to rational living*. Englewood Cliffs, N.J.: Prentice-Hall; reprinted, Hollywood, Calif.; Wilshire, 1972.

1962*a*. The case against religion: a psychotherapist's view. *The Independent*, October, 3-4; revised, *Mensa Bulletin*, September, 1970, No. 28: 5-6.

1962*b*. Rational-emotive psychotherapy. Paper read at annual meeting of American Psychological Association, St. Louis, August 31.

1962*c*. *Reason and emotion in psychotherapy*. New York: Lyle Stuart.

1963*a*. Constitutional factors in homosexuality. In H. Beigel (Ed.). *Advances in sex research*. New York: Hoeber.

1963*b*. Homosexuality: the right of a man to be wrong. Talk to East Coast Homophile Organizations.

1963*c*. *If this be sexual heresy* . . . New York: Lyle Stuart; reprinted, New York: Tower Publications, 1966.

1963*d*. The origins and the development of the incest taboo. Published with Emile Durkheim. *Incest: the nature and origin of the taboo*. New York: Lyle Stuart.

1963*e*. Toward a more precise definition of "emotional" and "intellectual" insight. *Psychological Reports*, 13: 125-126.

1965*a*. *Suppressed: seven key essays publishers dared not print*. Chicago: New Classics House.

1965*b*. *Sex and the single man*. New York: Lyle Stuart; reprinted, New York: Dell.

1965*c*. *Sex without guilt*. New York: Lyle Stuart; reprinted, New York: Grove Press.

1965*d*. *The case for sexual liberty*. Tucson, Ariz.: Seymour Press.

1965*e*. *Homosexuality: its causes and cure*. New York: Lyle Stuart.

1965*f*. *The search for sexual enjoyment*. New York: MacFadden-Bartell.

1965*g*. An answer to some objections to rational-emotive psychotherapy. *Psychotherapy*, 2: 108-111.

1965*h*. The use of printed, written and recorded words in psychotherapy. In L. Pearson (Ed.). *The use of written communications in psychotherapy*. Springfield, Ill.: Charles C Thomas.

1965*i*. *The intelligent woman's guide to man-hunting*. New York: Lyle Stuart; reprinted, New York: Dell.

1966*a*. With J. L. Wolfe and S. Moseley. *How to prevent your child from becoming a neurotic adult*. New York: Crown; reprinted as *How to raise an emotionally healthy, happy child*. Hollywood, Calif.: Wilshire, 1972.

1967*a*. Phobia treated with RET. *Voices* (Fall), 3: 34-40.

1967*b*. Psychotherapy and moral laxity. *Psychiatric Opinion*, 4 (No. 5): 18-21.

1968*a*. *Is objectivism a religion*? New York: Lyle Stuart.

1968*b*. Is psychoanalysis harmful? *Psychiatric Opinion*, 5 (No. 1): 16-24.

1968*c*. What *really* causes psychotherapeutic change? *Voices*, 4: 90-97.

1968*d*. Sexual promiscuity in America. *The Annals of the American Academy of Political and Social Science*, 378: 58-67; reprinted in A. Birenbauam and E. Sagarin (Eds.). *Social Problems: Private Troubles and Public Issues*, New York: Scribner's, 1972.

1968*e*. With Roger O. Conway. The art of erotic seduction. New York: Lyle Stuart.

1969*a*. Rationality and irrationality: their significance in sexual morality. In L. Kirkendall and R. Whitehurst (Eds.). The New Sexual Revolution. New York: D. W. Brown.

1969*b*. A cognitive approach to behavior therapy. *International Journal of Psychiatry*, 8: 896-900.

1969*c*. A weekend of rational encounter. In A. Burton (Ed.). *Encounter*. San Francisco: Jossey-Bass Publishing Co.

1969*d*. Rational-emotive therapy in the private practice. *Journal of Contemporary Psychotherapy*, 1: 82-90.

1969*e*. How to get better instead of merely to feel better. Talk presented to Southern Florida University.

1969*f*. A tape recording of a psychotherapy session. Institute for Advanced Study in Rational Psychotherapy.

1969*g*. Teaching emotional education in the classroom. *School Health Review*, November, 10-14.

1970*a*. The emerging counselor. *Canadian Counselor*, 4: 99-105.

1970*b*. Rational-emotive therapy. In Leonard Hersher (Ed.). *Four psychotherapies*. New York: Appleton-Century-Crofts.

1970*c*. With John Gullo. *Murder and assassination*. New York: Lyle Stuart.

1971. *Growth through reason*. Palo Alto, Calif.: Science and Behavior Books.

1972*a*. Psychotherapy and the value of a human being. In J. W. Davis (Ed.). *Value and valuation: axiological studies in honor of Robert S. Hartman*. Knoxville: University of Tennessee Press.

1972*b*. *Executive leadership: a rational approach*. New York: Citadel Press.

1972*c*. *The sensuous person: critique and corrections*. New York: Lyle Stuart.

1972*d*. *The civilized couple's guide to extramarital adventure*. New York: Peter Wyden.

1973*a*. Rational-emotive therapy. In Ratibor M. Jurjevich (ED.). *Directive psychotherapies*. Coral Gables, Florida: University of Miami Press.

1973*b*. Rational-emotive psychotherapy. In Raymond Corsini (ED.). *Current psychotherapies*. Itasca, Ill.: F. E. Peacock Publishers.

INDEX

Catalog

If you are interested in a list of fine Paperback
books, covering a wide range of subjects
and interests, send your name and address,
requesting your free catalog, to:

McGraw-Hill Paperbacks
1221 Avenue of Americas
New York, N.Y. 10020